CHARLES DICKENS

Critical Issues

Published

George Eliot	Pauline Nestor
Virginia Woolf	Linden Peach
Charles Dickens	Lyn Pykett
Henry James	Jeremy Tambling

In preparation

Geoffrey Chaucer	Ruth Evans
Jane Austen	Darryl Jones
Charlotte Brontë	Carl Plasa
James Joyce	Kiernan Ryan
D. H. Lawrence	Rick Rylance
William Wordsworth	John Williams
Thomas Hardy	Julian Wolfreys

Critical Issues

Charles Dickens

Lyn Pykett

palgrave

First published 2002 by
PALGRAVE
Houndmills, Basingstoke, Hampshire RG21 6XS and
175 Fifth Avenue, New York, NY 10010
Companies and representatives throughout the world

PALGRAVE is the new global academic imprint of
St. Martin's Press LLC Scholarly and Reference Division and
Palgrave Publishers Ltd (formerly Macmillan Press Ltd).

ISBN 0–333–72802–5 hardback
ISBN 0–333–72803–3 paperback

This book is printed on paper suitable for recycling and
made from fully managed and sustained forest sources.

A catalogue record for this book is available
from the British Library.

Library of Congress Cataloging-in-Publication Data

Pykett, Lynn.
Charles Dickens/Lyn Pykett.
    p. cm. – (Critical issues)
Includes bibliographical references and index.
ISBN 0–333–72802–5 – ISBN 0–333–72803–3 (pbk.)
1. Dickens, Charles, 1812–1870 – Criticism and interpretation. I. Title.
II. Critical issues (Palgrave (Firm))

PR4588. P95 2002
823'.8–dc21

                                                      2002020891

10 9 8 7 6 5 4 3 2 1
11 10 09 08 07 06 05 04 03 02

Printed in China

Contents

Acknowledgements

It will be evident on every page of this book that I owe a great debt of thanks to the 'Dickens industry' and to Dickens critics in general. More particular thanks are due to the University of Wales, Aberystwyth, and the R. D. Roberts bequest for the award of a period of study leave which allowed me to complete a number of other projects and begin this one. As ever my greatest debt is to Andrew, and to Ben, Rachel and Jessica, without whom ...

A Note on Editions

Works by Dickens

As readers of this book are likely to be using a range of different editions of Dickens's novels I always cite chapter (or book and chapter) references in the text. Page references are to the editions noted below, and follow the chapter reference in the text.

BH   *Bleak House*, ed. and intro. Stephen Gill (Oxford: Oxford University Presss, World's Classics, 1996).

BR   *Barnaby Rudge*, ed. and intro. Donald Hawes (London: Dent, 1996).

CB   *The Christmas Books*, ed. and intro. Sally Ledger (London: Dent, 1999).

D   *Dombey and Son*, ed. and intro. Valerie Purton (London: Dent, 1997).

DC   *David Copperfield*, ed. Nina Burgis, intro. and notes Andrew Sanders (Oxford: Oxford University Press, World's Classics, 1997).

DJ   *Dickens' Journalism*, ed. and intro. Michael Slater, 4 vols (London: Dent, 1994–8).

ED   *The Mystery of Edwin Drood*, ed. and intro. Margaret Cardwell (Oxford: Oxford University Press, World's Classics, 1982).

GE   *Great Expectations*, ed. and intro. Kate Flint (Oxford: Oxford University Press, World's Classics, 1994).

HT   *Hard Times*, ed. and intro. Kate Flint (Harmondsworth: Penguin, 1995).

LD   *Little Dorrit*, ed. and intro. Stephen Gill, notes by Helen
      Small (Harmondsworth: Penguin, 1998).

MC   *Martin Chuzzlewit*, ed. Margaret Cardwell (Oxford:
      Oxford University Press, World's Classics, 1984).

NN   *Nicholas Nickleby*, ed. and intro. Mark Ford
      (Harmondsworth: Penguin, 1999).

OCS   *The Old Curiosity Shop*, ed. and intro. Paul Schlicke
      (London: Dent, 1995).

OMF   *Our Mutual Friend*, ed. Adrian Poole (Harmondsworth:
      Penguin, 1997).

OT   *Oliver Twist*, ed. Kathleen Tillotson, intro. Stephen Gill
      (Oxford: Oxford University Press, World's Classics,
      1999).

PP   *The Pickwick Papers*, ed. and intro. James Kinsley
      (Oxford: Oxford University Press, World's Classics,
      1988).

S   *Sketches by Boz*, ed. and intro. Dennis Walder
      (Harmondsworth: Penguin, 1995).

SJ   *Selected Journalism, 1850–1870*, ed. and intro. David
      Pascoe (Harmondsworth: Penguin, 1997).

TTC   *A Tale of Two Cities*, ed. and intro. Richard Maxwell
      (Harmondsworth: Penguin, 2000).

UCT   *The Uncommercial Traveller and Other Reprinted Pieces*,
      intro. Leslie Staples (London: Oxford University Press,
      1958).

Other frequently cited texts

Ackroyd Peter Ackroyd, *Dickens* (London: Minerva, 1991).

CH   *Dickens: The Critical Heritage*, ed. Philip Collins
         (London: Routledge and Kegan Paul, 1971).

DL   *The Pilgrim Edition of the Letters of Charles Dickens*, ed.
         Madeline House, Graham Storey and Kathleen Tillotson
         et al., 11 vols (Oxford: Clarendon Press, 1965–).

Ford   George H. Ford and Lauriat Lane Jr (eds), *The Dickens
         Critics* (Ithaca, NY: Cornell University Press, 1961).

Life   John Forster, *The Life of Charles Dickens* (3 vols,
         1872–4), 2 vols (London: Dent, 1966).

1

Introduction: the Dickens Phenomenon and the Dickens Industry

I Everybody's writer

> No words can express the secret agony of my soul as I … felt my early hopes of growing up to be a learned and distinguished man crushed in my breast. The deep remembrance … of the misery it was to my young heart to believe that, day by day, what I had learned and thought, and delighted in, and raised my fancy and emulation up by, was passing away from me … cannot be written.
> (Charles Dickens, on his experience of being put to work in Warren's Blacking Factory at the age of twelve, in 'Autobiographical Fragment', *Life*, I: 22)

> [Dickens's] graphic and eloquent pages have issued to the world more political and social truths than have been uttered by all the professional politicians, publicists, and moralists put together.
> (Karl Marx to Friedrich Engels, quoted in Peter Demetz, *Marx, Engels and the Poets* (Chicago: University of Chicago Press, 1967), p. 45

The compulsively repeated writing out of an inexpressible private trauma, or a sustained, 'graphic and eloquent' engagement with the social, political and moral realities of his day? These are just two of the myriad ways of reading the formidable literary production of Charles Dickens. To many of his contemporaries Dickens was 'emphatically the novelist of his age', in whose novels 'posterity will read, more clearly than in any contemporary records, the character of our nineteenth century life'.[1] At the same time he was also 'the great magician of our time', whose 'wand is a book'.[2] By the early twentieth century, Virginia Woolf, who sought in her own modernist experimentation to escape from what she saw as the yoke of the form of the novel created by Dickens and his contemporaries, could take Dickens for granted, as 'everybody's writer and no one's in particular', an 'institution, a monument, a public thoroughfare trodden dusty by a million feet'.[3] Woolf's contemporary, John Middleton Murry, on the other hand, found Dickens a challengingly 'baffling figure', whose 'chief purpose in writing' sometimes appears to be 'to put a spoke in the wheel of our literary aesthetics', but one whose work has a 'curious trick of immortality' despite the fact that it cannot be contained within accepted canons of value.[4] One of Dickens's most recent re-readers has delighted in the challenge that this author's work poses to our turn-of-the-twenty-first-century aesthetics, and to the ways in which we usually subdivide the cultural field, and understand the human subject and fictional character, and even the processes of history.[5]

The twenty-first-century critic writing about the nineteenth-century novelist Charles Dickens must inevitably engage with that complex historical phenomenon, the Dickens industry. Dickens, who was quick to exploit the possibilities for the work of literary art in an age of mechanical reproduction, was himself a one-man fiction industry, whose organization of his professional life and whose writings exemplify both a Victorian commitment to 'self-sufficiency through work',[6] and the anxieties of modern authorship. From the early 1830s until his death in 1870, he produced fourteen massive novels (plus one unfinished at his death), together with numerous sketches, essays, and stories, many of which appeared in the two magazines that he founded and edited – or, as he put it, 'conducted'. He collaborated with several illustrators, one of whom (Robert Seymour) had the original idea for the 'sporting sketches' which developed into the *Pickwick Papers*, and another (George Cruikshank) who claimed to have had the original idea for *Oliver Twist*. At the beginning of his career he wrote plays, working closely with actors and musicians such as John Pritt Harley and John Hullah. Later on he contributed to the plays of friends such as Mark Lemon, and to the adaptations of novels for the stage (both his own and those of friends). From around 1856 onwards Dickens also collaborated closely with Wilkie Collins in the production of stories and articles, including the annual Christmas stories. This industrious literary production has in its turn generated an international critical industry whose organization and output, in some cases at least, would no doubt have amused and exasperated the man who thought up the Circumlocution Office. This book will address both branches of the Dickens industry. It will look at Charles Dickens as a (perhaps *the*) nineteenth-century man of letters, whose work played a central role in the shaping of the English-language novel and a modern fiction industry, in the construction of the figure of the modern author, and even in the making of the modern subject. It will also focus on 'Charles Dickens' as a cultural and critical site: a site not only for the formation and definition of the novel in the nineteenth century, but also for twentieth-century theorizations (and contestations) of the novel.

The novels of Charles Dickens, and the Dickens phenomenon more generally, were landmarks of literature in English and of English (even British) culture in the nineteenth century. As Peter Ackroyd writes, in his monumental biography of Dickens, 'no novelist, no writer had ever achieved such national acclaim'. Patronized by some contemporaries as 'a little Shakespeare – a Cockney Shakespeare',[7] Dickens has, nevertheless, come to occupy a place in English cultural history as Shakespeare's equal. Dickens was 'the Shakespeare of the novel',[8] the people's Shakespeare, as it were. As his friend and literary collaborator Wilkie Collins put it, Dickens was 'eminently the people's author';[9] an author, moreover, whose work was read by '[p]eople who never read any other novels'.[10]

From the point at which he launched himself fully into the profession of letters in 1836 with the publication of *The Posthumous Papers of the Pickwick Club* and the two series of *Sketches by Boz* (two collections of his fugitive pieces for the *Morning Chronicle*, the *Evening Chronicle* and other journals), Dickens has always been read by – or his work has been mediated in some form to – a very large and diverse audience. His fiction was issued in a wide range of formats: monthly parts (usually in distinctive green paper covers, priced at a shilling each); weekly instalments in magazines; in hard covers in three-volume, and later in the cheaper one-volume form. In Dickens's lifetime, his novels were often adapted for the cheap press and for the stage, in both cases with scant regard for issues of copyright. Further stage adaptations (including musical versions of *Oliver Twist* and *Nicholas Nickleby*) followed in the twentieth century, along with numerous adaptations (including animated cartoon versions) for the cinema and for television. At the same time Dickens's novels have been incorporated into school and college syllabi throughout the English-speaking world, sometimes in the service of conceptions of education that might have offered a bitterly ironic amusement to the creator of Charley Hexam, Bradley Headstone and Mr M'Choakumchild.

As one of the first, and certainly one of the most successful, mass-circulation authors, Dickens's central position in British and Anglophone culture derives in large part from his continuing appeal to the general or 'common' reader.[11] At the same time, Dickens's cultural centrality has ensured that professional critics and academic institutions have not been able to ignore his work, although some English Departments in British universities succeeded in avoiding the issue by failing to include him on their syllabi until after the Second World War.[12] From the 1830s onwards both individual critics and the institutions of criticism have had to find some way of accounting for Dickens's fiction – if only to dismiss it, or deplore or deny its importance. Indeed, a study of the critical reception of Dickens's work could also serve as a case study of the main trends in novel criticism and the study of narrative in the last 170 years. A survey of that massive enterprise known as the Dickens industry would serve – among other things – as a survey of the main trends in academic literary studies in the twentieth century, as well as providing an interesting and sometimes amusing guide to the fluctuations of literary taste.

Although, during the last century and a half, there has been considerable variation in the methodological approaches of Dickens criticism and the language or discourse in which it is mediated, several of the critical issues relating to Dickens's work which have been explored by the highly professionalized disciplines of literary and cultural studies in the twentieth century were first raised in reviews and assessments of his work as it was coming out, and as Dickens was establishing his central position in fiction publishing. These issues include: the aesthetic status of the novel in general and Dickens's novels in particular; Dickens's relationship to high art and to the forms of popular culture; the aesthetics and ideology of Dickens's narrative forms; the complex multiple plot; characterization and caricature; the issue of verisimilitude or 'truth to life' of Dickens's fictions; the significance and shape of Dickens's career and the relative status of his novels; topicality versus typicality (or, as some nineteenth-century critics might have put it, 'universality'); the politics of Dickens's fiction; Dickens's relationship to modernity; the gender of Dickens's writing and its representation of gendered subjects; Dickens's class position and his representation of the various social classes. Several of these issues were addressed in a perspicacious (if not entirely sympathetic) early assessment of his work by Margaret Oliphant:

> It is to the fact of class that he owes his speedy elevation to the top of the wave of popular favour. He is a man of very liberal sentiments, an assailer of constituted wrongs and authorities – one of the advocates in the plea of Poor *versus* Rich. ... But he is a *class* writer, the historian and representative of one circle in the many ranks of our social scale. Despite their descents into the lowest class, and their occasional flights into the less familiar ground of fashion, it is the air and the breath of middle class respectability which fills the books of Mr Dickens. ... Home bred and sensitive, much impressed by feminine influences, swayed by the motives, the regards and the laws which were absolute to their childhood, Mr Dickens's heroes are all young for a necessity. Their courage is of the order of courage which belongs to women.[13]

For much of the nineteenth century and at least the first half of the twentieth, critical debate about Dickens and the aesthetic evaluation of his work focused on the question of whether his novels were lacking in artistry, perhaps even excluded from the domain of Art, by their proximity to 'low' journalistic or popular-culture forms, or whether they were, on the other hand, a vigorous and original contribution to the art of the novel. For every critic who found Dickens's novels to be energized by the vitality of popular culture, imaginative, linguistically dextrous, resourceful, truthful, passionate, moving, dramatic, and capacious, there was another who found them lacking in unity, defective in organization and control, distorted by the demands of serial publication, full of caricatures, mechanical, formulaic, vulgar, lacking in verisimilitude, sentimental and melodramatic. Moreover, from the 1850s to the present day, commentators on Dickens's fiction have often divided into two camps: those who think that Dickens's work is marred or distorted by its topicality and its concern with the social and moral issues of the day, and those who think that these concerns lie at the very heart of Dickens's achievement. Similarly, there has also been a division between those who think that his talents for fiction, which had produced a series of early comic masterpieces, went into terminal decline on the completion of *David Copperfield* (1850), and others who regard Dickens's early fictions as mere apprentice pieces for the major works of social and psychological analysis which began with *Dombey and Son* (1846–8). The politics of Dickens's fiction has also divided critics, between those who have seen it as radical or (at least) reforming, and those who have found it nostalgically conservative, suffused in a Pickwickian spirit of old coaching inns and a sentimental *Christmas Carol* philosophy.

II Dickens in the nineteenth century: some contemporary critical issues

> Dickens has proved his power by a popularity almost unexampled, embracing all classes. Surely it is a task for criticism to exhibit the sources of that power.
>
> George Henry Lewes, 'Dickens in Relation to Criticism',
> *Fortnightly Review,* February 1872

In attempting to 'exhibit' or account for the sources of Dickens's power, 'Criticism' has often praised his work with faint versions of the damns used by those who sought to deny or dismiss that power. George Henry Lewes, a well-known nineteenth-century commentator on the state of the art of the novel, is a case in point. In his essay on Dickens's relationship to criticism of the novel, published some twenty months after the novelist's death, Lewes managed to convert into weaknesses or faults those very qualities which other readers have seen as Dickens's strengths. In his assessment of the nature and extent of Dickens's achievement, Lewes celebrated 'the glorious energy' of the novelist's imagination, but described its vividness as having a quality 'approaching closely to hallucination' (Ford, 59), a faculty which he associates with abnormal or insane people. The sanity of Dickens and his writings was also called into question by Hippolyte Taine, who suggested that Dickens's genius was a form of madness, and that his portraits of 'eccentricities' were symptomatic of the repetitive, obsessive behaviour of a mono-maniac.[14] Margaret Oliphant also suggested that Dickens's characters were the product of an overweening and disordered mind when she compared Dickens to the archetypal mad scientist of the early nineteenth century: 'If it were possible to quicken these curious originals into life, what an odd crowd of ragamuffins and monsters would that be which should pursue this Frankenstein through the world.'[15]

One of the main problems that Dickens's fiction presented to nine-teenth-century criticism was its failure to conform to the conceptions of aesthetic realism (and particularly fictional realism) which gained ascendancy during his career. One of the clearest formulations of the mismatch between Dickens's fictional practice and nineteenth-century realist theory was provided by George Eliot, whose own novel *Middlemarch* (1871–2) later came to be widely regarded as *the* definitive realist English novel. This leading proponent of a theory of realism derived from the art historian and social commentator John Ruskin asserted that '[t]he truth of infinite value' that Ruskin taught was '*realism* – the doctrine that all truth and all beauty are to be attained by a humble and faithful study of nature, and not by substi-tuting vague forms, bred by imagination on the mists of feeling, in place of definite, substantial reality'.[16] In another essay written at the beginning of her own career as a novelist, Eliot assessed the work of the leading novelist of the previous generation as a missed opportu-nity. Dickens's novels (at least those written in the first twenty years of his career) failed to meet Eliot's requirement that fictional Art should extend the sympathies of its readers through a faithful repre-sentation of their fellow human beings, especially 'our more heavily-laden fellow-men':

> We have one great novelist who is gifted with the utmost power of rendering the external traits of our town population; and if he could give us their psychological character – their conceptions of life, and their emotions – with the same truth as their idiom and manners, his books would be the greatest contribution Art has ever made to the awakening of social sympathies. But while he can copy Mr Plornish's colloquial style with the delicate accuracy of a sun-picture ... he scarcely ever passes from the humorous and external to the emotional and tragic, without becoming as transcendent in his unreality as he was a moment before in his artistic truthfulness. But for the precious salt of his humour, which compels him to reproduce external traits that serve, in some degree, as a corrective to his frequently false psychology, his preternaturally virtuous poor children and artisans, his melodramatic boatmen and courtesans, would be ... noxious ... in encouraging the miserable fallacy that high morality and refined sentiment can grow out of harsh social relations, ignorance, and want; or that the working classes are in a condition to enter at once into a millennial state of *altruism*.[17]

Looking back at Dickens's work in its entirety (in the essay referred to earlier), Eliot's partner, George Henry Lewes, also concluded that Dickens's propensity for portraying 'human character and ordinary events ... with a mingled verisimilitude and falsity altogether unexampled' (Ford, 64) presented a problem to 'many cultivated and critical readers' – even if (indeed, even *as*) it satisfied those 'to whom all the refinements of Art and literature are as meaningless hieroglyphs' (Ford, 69). Lewes followed Walter Bagehot in regarding Dickens's power as irregular and untutored. Dickens's 'genius', Bagehot wrote in the *National Review* in 1858, was 'irregular' and 'unsymmetrical' (like Shakespeare's). It was, he suggested, characterized by 'bizarrerie', and it found voice in an 'odd style' which was 'the overflow of a copious mind ... not the chastened expression of an harmonious one' (*CH*, 391). Writing some years before the appearance of *Our Mutual Friend* (the limit case for many of Dickens's nineteenth-century reviewers), Bagehot was in many ways a more sympathetic reader of Dickens than Lewes was, but like Lewes, he saw Dickens's imagination as having an hallucinatory quality. Dickens's technique, Bagehot argued, involved a 'vivification' of 'characteristics' rather than of character (*CH*, 394). And he offered a very graphic account of what he saw as Dickens's mechanical representation of character, an aspect of Dickens's fiction also noted (and deplored) by Henry James in his review of *Our Mutual Friend*,[18] and explored by numerous critics since. Bagehot wrote:

> [Dickens] sees people in the street doing certain things, talking in a certain way, and his fancy petrifies them in the act. He goes on fancying hundreds of reduplications of that act and that speech; he frames an existence in which there is nothing else but that aspect which attracted his attention. (*CH*, 394–5)

This is a very acute nineteenth-century reading of Dickens's representation of urban character in what Walter Benjamin later described as 'an age of mechanical reproduction'.[19] Dorothy Van Ghent was among the first of the many twentieth-century critics to have placed this mode of perception and characterization as a specific response to nineteenth-century processes of reification and alienation in which 'people were becoming things, and things ... were becoming more important than people. People were becoming de-animated, robbed of their souls.'[20] With such terms as 'petrifaction' and 'reduplication', Bagehot named a distinctive modern form of aesthetic representation. However, it is a form of representation of character which Bagehot, like Lewes, viewed through a different, older, more unified conception of fictional character as a faithful representation of 'human nature', rather than (as Lewes expressed it) 'personified characteristics, caricatures and distortions of human nature' and '"catchwords" personified as characters' (Ford, 61, 65).

Bagehot's 1858 *National Review* essay (reprinted in his *Literary Studies*, 1879) repays careful rereading, because it raised in a very interesting way numerous issues which have continued to preoccupy readers and critics of Dickens. First, there is the matter of the novelist's breadth of appeal: Dickens's novels, it was asserted, were read throughout the English household and the English-speaking world, giving pleasure to servants, mistresses, children 'as well as to the master of the house' (*CH*, 390); they were regarded 'with admiring appreciation by persons of the highest culture at the centre of civilisation', as well as providing amusement for 'the roughest settler in Vancouver Island'.[21] Bagehot's assessment of this breadth of appeal was considerably more generous than those later commentators who contributed to the decline in Dickens's critical reputation following his death, by asserting that he was a writer only for the 'half-educated',[22] who was not 'regarded in the light of an artist' by any one of 'high cultivation'.[23] Bagehot also engaged with the vexed question of the unity (or disunity) of Dickens's novels: they are said to be 'miscellaneous', and 'compilations' of 'graphic scraps' – even if it is conceded that those scraps 'aim to delineate nearly all that part of our national life that can be delineated' (*CH*, 391). For Bagehot this miscellaneity was intrinsic to Dickens's mode of perception; it was a condition of his imagination. However, the author's concern with surfaces and his tendency towards caricature – his production of a gallery of oddities – are also said to work against narrative and plot: when he has 'attempted to make a long connected story, or to develop into scenes or incidents a plan in any degree elaborate, the result has been a complete failure' (*CH*, 396). Like numerous nineteenth-century critics, Bagehot found Dickens wanting in book-learning, 'sagacity', and powers of reflection, but he also acknowledged the force of that street-wiseness which Dickens himself taught his readers to admire in Sam Weller. Anticipating the late twentieth-century interest in Dickens as *flâneur*, Bagehot dwells on the author's detailed observation of street life. Bagehot also made an interesting contribution to the discussion of Dickens's political opinions. Noting that they 'have subjected him to a good deal of criticism, and to some ridicule', Bagehot located the novelist's politics in the context of the Radicalism of the 1825–45 period, concluding that Dickens's was a 'sentimental radicalism', an example of the 'extreme, perhaps excessive sensibility to human suffering' which grew up in response to 'the unfeeling obtuseness' of the early nineteenth century, but which persisted after these injustices had been removed (*CH*, 397–8).

Bagehot's Dickens was pre-eminently the novelist of nineteenth-century urban modernity in general and of London life in particular, a writer whose 'genius is especially suited to the delineation of city life', and who 'describes London like a special correspondent for posterity'. In Dickens's fiction, Bagehot acutely observed,

> London is like a newspaper. Everything is there and everything is disconnected. There is every kind of person in some houses; but there is not more connection between the houses than between the neighbours in the lists of 'births, marriages, and deaths.' As we change from the broad leader to the squalid police-report, we pass a corner and we are in a changed world ... [Dickens's] memory is full of instances of old buildings and curious people, and he does not care to piece them together. (*CH*, 394)

This is a very thought-provoking account of Dickens's representation of urban alienation, even if it does not take enough account of the way in which his fiction (particularly from the mid-1840s) is structured so as to insist on the connections between the apparently disconnected neighbours and neighbourhoods of the city.

Bagehot was not the only nineteenth-century commentator to link Dickens's fictional technique to newspapers and to journalism. In his 1864 review of the Library Edition of Dickens's novels for the *Westminster Review*, Justin McCarthy compared recent developments in fiction to the models of opinion formation usually associated with periodical journalism:

> Novels are now something more than the means of passing away an idle hour. They supply thousands of readers with a philosophy of life, and are at this moment the only form of poetry which is really popular. Time was when really serious people would have nothing to do with them ... [but now] [t]he novelist has taken rank as a recognized public instructor. Important questions of social policy, law reform, the latest invention, the most recent heresy, are formally discussed in his pages, in the most attractive manner too, with a maximum of argument and a minimum of facts. (*CH*, 447)

This transformation of the novel was mainly attributed to Dickens, and, in particular, to his response to 'the stir of the Reform movement' which was at its height when he began writing:

> Clearly, all the conditions requisite for a highly popular treatment of politics were there – an interested public and unlimited means of communicating with them. Still we doubt whether any one less gifted than Mr Dickens, or with qualifications different to his, would have succeeded in inducing half England to read books which had anything to do with the Poor Laws or Chancery reform. (*CH*, 447)

To be sure, in McCarthy's terms Dickens's was a qualified success; his fiction was 'the main instrument of the change which ... *perverted* [emphasis added] the novel from a work of art to a polemical platform for discussion and argument' (*CH*, 447). Favouring a universalist conception of Art, McCarthy acknowledged – but could not assign a wholly positive evaluation to – Dickens's concern with surface detail and with the local and topical: 'Outward peculiarities ... are at best but an imperfect index of character' (*CH*, 448).

Like Eliot, Bagehot and Lewes, McCarthy found Dickens wanting in reflection and analytical power – particularly in relation to social questions, on which he was said to overstate the case, failing to understand it, or to offer any remedy: 'It is all very well meant, but very ignorant' (*CH*, 452). Moreover, Dickens's claims 'to represent large phases of modern life', are said to be compromised by his 'trivial' belief that 'virtue is usually rewarded and vice usually punished' (*CH*, 451). For all of these reasons, and despite his many qualities, McCarthy concluded that it was impossible to think that Dickens would 'live as an English classic'; he dealt 'too much in accidental manifestations and too little in universal principles' (*CH*, 452). This question of Dickens's classic status continued to preoccupy novel criticism for a considerable part of the twentieth century, until (according to one's point of view) it had either been securely accepted or deemed no longer to be one of the more important questions to be asked about literary writing.

III   Dickens in relation to criticism in the twentieth century

> For a number of years, one of my main preoccupations ... has been the 'challenge of Dickens' – the challenge he presents to criticism to define the ways in which he is one of the greatest of writers.
> (F. R. Leavis, letter to the *Spectator*, 4 January 1963)[24]

In the twentieth century Dickens's work continued to present a challenge to critics and criticism of the novel whether or not they were mainly preoccupied with questions of 'greatness'. George Gissing (1898), G. K. Chesterton (1906) and George Bernard Shaw (in his introduction to the Waverley edition of *Hard Times*, 1912) mounted vigorous campaigns for the defence of Dickens's position among the literary greats. However, the forms of Dickens's fiction, his reputation and his readership presented a particular set of challenges to academic critics preoccupied with ideas of greatness or classic status. In 1948 F. R. Leavis famously excluded most of Dickens's fiction from *The Great Tradition* on the following grounds:

> That Dickens was a great genius and is permanently among the classics is certain. But the genius was that of a great entertainer, and he had for the most part no profounder responsibility as a creative artist than this description suggests. ... The adult mind doesn't as a rule find in Dickens a challenge to an unusual and sustained seriousness.[25]

Other twentieth-century critics were more inclined to investigate the implications of Dickens's status as a great entertainer than to use it as the reason for dismissing him from the pantheon. To this end they explored the ways in which both the subject matter and forms of his novels and his appeal negotiated various cultural divides. For example, in both *The Dialogic Imagination* (translated in 1981) and *Rabelais and His World* (translated in 1984), Mikhail Bakhtin rethought Dickens's relationship to popular traditions by inserting him in a dynamic model of cultural history in which high art is continually capturing and reworking the forms and genres of popular culture. Raymond Williams also linked what he saw as Dickens's major role in 'the critical remaking of the novel' to his involvement in 'the critical emergence of a new popular urban culture'.[26] Paul Schlicke offered us a more detailed understanding of this process in *Dickens and Popular Entertainment* (1985), an exploration of the relationship of Dickens's work to the particular forms and historical determinations of the changes that were taking place in the 'amusements of the people' in the early nineteenth century.

At round about the same time that Bakhtin was first including Dickens's *oeuvre* in an important English and European tradition of comic fiction, F. R. Leavis was, in effect, excluding from serious consideration all of Dickens's novels, apart from *Hard Times*, the only one of his works in which (according to Leavis) 'his distinctive creative genius is controlled throughout to a unifying and organizing significance', and which is not marred by 'the usual repetitive overdoing and loose inclusiveness'.[27] Whatever one thinks of Leavis's assessment of Dickens, either in the 1940s or in his subsequent revisionist reassessment, *Dickens the Novelist* published in 1970, he did describe very succinctly the outlines of the critical terrain which was mapped and fought over by some of the most influential Dickens critics in the first two-thirds of the twentieth century, as Criticism responded to the challenge posed by Dickens by finding ways of denying or accounting for the 'loose inclusiveness' and 'repetitive overdoing' of his fiction. Up until the 1960s there were three main ways of doing this: a variety of formalist approaches; (Freudian) psychoanalytic approaches; and, bridging these two, symbolist approaches.

The critical ascendancy of Henry James's (and subsequently the New Criticism's) view of the novel as an intricately inwrought aesthetic and psychological design, and a subtle balancing of formal and moral tensions, undermined Dickens's critical reputation in the interwar years. However, it subsequently produced several interesting readings of both individual novels and the Dickens *oeuvre* more generally, which strove to find ways of making the loose baggy monster seem less loose and baggy, and more designed, or alternatively, to find ways of positively evaluating its apparent inconsistencies and incoherencies. In the former vein, Leavis's appendix on *Hard Times* in *The Great Tradition* combined the New Critical emphasis on form with an organicist social critique to produce Dickens as a consciously designing artist with a moral and political purpose. The second path was taken by J. Hillis Miller, whose *Charles Dickens: The World of his Novels* (1958) explored the significance and value of the discontinuities of Dickens's novels. Miller was later to undertake an ingenious and influential deconstructive reading of Dickens, but in this earlier book he read the language and form of Dickens's work as an expression of consciousness; Dickens's writing was a process of self-fashioning, in which the author constructed himself in psychological relation to the phenomenal and social world in a series of novels which repeatedly figured the theme or motif of the search for a true and viable identity.

Unresolved questions of identity, the gaps and inconsistencies of Dickens's fiction, together with its 'repetitive overdoing' were also the subject of Edmund Wilson's earlier biographical and psycho-social essay 'Dickens: the Two Scrooges' (1941), a pathbreaking essay, whose insights continued to be deplored, explored and reworked for many years, by critics of varying persuasions. Wilson argued that an unstable dualism was the driving force of both Dickens and his novels: the author and his novels manifested a double identification with both the social insider and the outsider, but especially with the dark obsessions of the murderer and the thief. '[C]aught between two social classes in a society of strict stratifications',[28] Dickens productively mobilized his uneasy class position for aesthetic purposes into a 'study of interrelations', but it was a study, Wilson argued, whose energies were never fully controlled. Wilson's essay is a fascinating combination of bio-graphical, psychoanalytic, social and political approaches. It married Freud and Marx in a way that was symptomatic of its own moment of production, and which anticipated (indeed generated) subsequent interest in the social construction of the writer's psyche, and in cultural representations of the complex interrela-tionship of social and psychological organization. Wilson credited Dickens with the creation, in *Bleak House* (1853), of a new literary genre, 'the novel of the social group'.[29] He also offered a new way of reading recurring figures, motifs and themes in Dickens's novels, building on the discussion of the symbolism of the prison in *Little Dorrit* offered in T. A. Jackson's Marxist study *Charles Dickens: The Progress of a Radical* (1937), and later taken up in Lionel Trilling's introduction to the New Oxford Illustrated edition of *Little Dorrit* (reprinted in Trilling's *The Opposing Self*, 1955).

Dickens's study of social interrelations has, from the time of the earliest reviews of his novels, generated numerous historical or his-toricist readings; for example, Humphrey House's contextualist study *The Dickens World* (1941), and, subsequently, Philip Collins's *Dickens and Crime* (1962) and *Dickens and Education* (1963), which offered a more precisely historical exploration of Dickens's involvement in the social issues of his day. While House and Collins (and their successors) sought to clarify the ways in which Dickens's novels embodied, reflected or responded to the life of his times, John Butt and Kathleen Tillotson (*Dickens at Work*, 1957) examined them in relation to historical conditions of literary production.

Since the revolution in reading practices which resulted from the explosion of 'Theory' in the late 1960s, Dickens's novels have (among other things) been subjected to structuralist analysis; deconstructed; read through Lacanian (rather than Freudian) psychoanalysis; historicized and/or 'Marxized' in various different ways; read through Queer theory and post-colonial theory; and subjected to feminist critique. The formalist focus on the novel as autonomous art object which was favoured by the New Critics and their heirs was superseded by structuralist approaches, which (like some New Criticism) were more concerned with how texts function and how they mean (rather than with how they relate to or represent life and what they mean). Structuralist criticism viewed a fictional text (or indeed any kind of text) as a structure or construct generated by, and working within, certain systems or rules. Structuralist analyses of Dickens could thus 'discover' and explicate the deep structure that underlay the surface multiplicity and fluidity of his novels in much the same way as critics in the previous twenty years had looked for formal coherence in ostensible discontinuity.[30] Those who had earlier sought ways of making sense of the gaps, discontinuities, and sheer linguistic exuberance of Dickens's work found fresh possibilities in post-structuralist and deconstructive criticism, which focuses on the indeterminacies of language (especially literary language) and 'proceed[s] by ... the careful teasing out of warring forces of signification within the text ... [and] analyses the specificity of a text's critical difference from itself'.[31] One of the earliest and almost certainly the most widely read deconstructive reading of Dickens was J. Hillis Miller's introduction to the 1971 Penguin edition of *Bleak House*, which construed this novel as a representation or interpretation of interpreting, but one in which meaning is constantly deferred:

> *Bleak House* itself has exactly the same structure as the society it exposes. It too assimilates everything it touches into a system of meaning. ... [It] too has a temporal structure without proper origin, present or end. It too is made up of an incessant movement of reference in which each element leads to other elements in a constant displacement of meaning.[32]

Another way into some of the issues raised by Miller's reading of *Bleak House* was provided by Bakhtin's concepts of 'dialogism' (double-voicedness), 'polyphony' (multi-voicedness) and 'heteroglossia' (which 'represents the co-existence of socio-ideological contradictions between the present and the past, between differing socio-ideological groups in the present, between tendencies, schools, circles ... all given a bodily form').[33] As more of the work of Bakhtin and his circle became available in English translation in the 1980s and 1990s it provided numerous English and American critics with very productive ways of reading Dickens's multi-plotted, multi-voiced, dramatic fictions. Bakhtin located Dickens in a popular comic tradition of subversive multi-voicedness. In such novels, Bakhtin argued:

> we find a comic-parodic re-processing of almost all the levels of literary language, both conversationally and written, that were current at the time ... an encyclopaedia of all strata and forms of literary language: depending on the subject being represented, the storyline parodically reproduces first the forms of parliamentary eloquence, then the eloquence of the court, ... or forms used by reporters in newspaper articles, or the dry business language of the City, or the dealings of speculators, or the pedantic speech of scholars, or the high epic ... or Biblical style ...[34]

Bakhtin's social and historical semiotics, with its insistence that 'language is at once a system of signs and a *socially produced* system of signs',[35] corresponded to, and in some cases informed, the movement in historicist and Marxist criticism from reflectionist to mediationist and constructivist explorations of Dickens in relation to his socio-historical context. Thus, for Raymond Williams, in *The English Novel from Dickens to Lawrence*, Dickens was at once representative of and representing (constructed by and constructing) a 'new kind of consciousness' (9), a new way of seeing, knowing, and showing the crowd, the city, modern social forms and institutions, and the power of industrialism. Williams was unequivocal about the nature of the challenge that Dickens presented to criticism.

> By the standards of one kind of novel, which in England has been emphasized as the great tradition, Dickens's faults – what are seen as his faults – are so many and so central as to produce embarrassment. ... His characters are not 'rounded' and developing but 'flat' and emphatic. They are not slowly revealed but directly presented. Significance is not enacted in mainly tacit and intricate ways but is often directly presented in moral address and indeed exhortation. Instead of the language of analysis and comprehension he uses, directly, the language of persuasion and display. His plots depend often on arbitrary coincidences, on sudden revelations and changes of heart. He offers not the details of psychological process but the finished articles: the social and psychological products. (31)

Instead of following (what he saw as) the critical dead-end of trying to 'salvage' from Dickens what was compatible with the fiction of the educated minority, Williams's humanist Marxism generated a Dickens of and for modernity. This modern Dickens was simultaneously a product of the Victorian age and an unrepresentative Victorian, on the grounds that he not only articulated an emergent form of consciousness, but he also engaged critically with it and made a 'creative intervention' in it (48) by producing a way of seeing that offered his readers the possibility of moral and social agency and choice.

Some other Marxizing analyses of Dickens's fiction produced an account of Dickens's novels that was both more conflicted and more subversive than Williams's version. For example, in Terry Eagleton's Althusserian (post-)Marxist ideological critique in *Criticism and Ideology* (1976) Dickens's novels were characterized in terms of a dialogism of competing forms. Eagleton also returned to the vexed question of Dickens's realism, and the even more contentious issue of his relationship to something called 'classic realism', a label invented by late twentieth-century critics to describe (and usually proscribe) the form and ideology – indeed what many of them saw as the inherently conservative ideological form – of the nineteenth-century novel:

> In the ... earlier Dickens ... each text is a veritable traffic-jam of competing fictional modes – Gothic, Romance, moral fable, 'social problem' novel, popular theatre, 'short story', journalism, episodic 'entertainment' – which permits 'realism' no privileged status. The later 'realism' of Dickens is ... of a notably impure kind – ... dispersed, conflictual discourses which ceaselessly offer to displace the securely 'over-viewing' eye of classical realism ... [whose 'totalising' ideology] is constantly deconstructed from within by the 'scattering' effect of ... symbols of contradictory unity (Chancery Court, Circumlocution Office) which are the very principles of the novel's own construction.[36]

Many of the explorations of the ideology of fictional form in the last twenty years of the twentieth century were influenced by the work of Michel Foucault, which implicitly views language – especially rhetorical and literary language – as performative and operative: language does not merely represent the world, but it does work in the world, and operates on the world. Foucault's theorizations of how power is embodied, enacted, and deployed in and through discourse, and especially in institutional discourses, or the discourses of particular professional or social groups, have been especially influential on studies of nineteenth-century fiction. Both his earlier work on sexuality and his later work on discipline and punishment informed numerous analyses of Dickens's novels from the mid-1980s onwards, and they continue to reverberate in post-millennium Dickens criticism. The prison imagery that had preoccupied critics in the 1940s has been revisited through Foucault's work on the carceral society, the panoptical gaze, and surveillance. For example, reading *Great Expectations* in the light of Foucault's concept of a 'technology of subjection' (as well as drawing on Philip Collins's work on Dickens's own writings on the contemporary prison system), Jeremy Tambling questioned the accepted reading of this novel as a *Bildungsroman* which charts the (fictional) autobiographical subject's development into a mature autonomy, suggesting instead that it is a narrative both of and about the processes of self-imprisonment which operate in a disciplinary society.[37] D. A. Miller, one of the most influential Foucauldian readers of Dickens, focused on policing (rather than prisons) in his widely cited *The Novel and the Police* (1988), which examined the way in which the novels of Dickens and his contemporaries 'systematically participate in a general economy of policing power'. In Miller's account Dickens's novels are both a symptom and a critique of the disciplinary society; they are the site of the first appearance in English fiction of a 'massive thematization of social discipline':

> (1) an ideal of unseen but all-seeing surveillance ... partly realized in several, often interconnected institutions ... [but] identified with none; (2) a regime of the norm, in which normalizing perceptions, prescriptions, and sanctions are diffused in discourses and practices throughout the social fabric; and (3) various technologies of the self and its sexuality, which administer the subject's own contribution to the intensive and continuous 'pastoral' care that liberal society proposes to take of each and everyone of its charges.[38]

Foucault's work on the social and discursive construction of gender, sexuality and desire, and on the roles played by these constructions in the organization and management of both the individual psyche and society, has produced a proliferation of explorations of gender issues in Dickens. A number of influential books in the 1980s and 1990s focused on the interconnections between male and female sex–gender identity in Dickens's fiction, and their relationship to a wider network of meanings and associations that constitute the domains and institutions of power:[39] most notably, class, economics and empire. For example, as I discuss further in Chapter 6, Eve Kosofsky Sedgwick's *Between Men* (1985) reads *Our Mutual Friend* as a disciplinary narrative of masculine socialization in which a normative heterosexual and homophobic pattern of desire associated with the middle-class gentleman replaces a homosexual/homosocial pattern of desire associated with 'infantile need' and 'powerlessness'.[40] Nancy Armstrong's account of the history of the domestic novel as a means of constructing and disciplining the gendered subject, in *Desire and Domestic Fiction* (1987), has also been extremely influential on late twentieth-century Dickens criticism. Although she had relatively little to say about Dickens, Armstrong's Foucauldian account of the rise and development of 'respectable' domestic fiction as a site for the construction and regulation of desire, and for 'changing power relations between classes and cultures',[41] has proved very productive for reading the representation and meanings of gender and class in Dickens's fiction. *Oliver Twist* and *Hard Times* provide Armstrong with useful examples of how 'respectable fiction ... represented political conflict in terms of sexual differences' (41), and 'carried the process of suppressing political resistance into the domain of popular literature, where it charted new domains of aberrance requiring domestication' (163). This approach has subsequently been applied by other critics to the whole range of Dickens's fiction.

Like Sedgwick and Armstrong, Mary Poovey focused on the ideological work performed by the construction and representation of gender and sexuality in relation to what she describes as the wider field of cultural meanings in which Dickens's novels were produced and read, and in which they continue to be reproduced and reread. This can be seen in her discussions of *David Copperfield* and the gendering and professionalization of the writer in her 1989 book *Uneven Developments*, and in her subsequent analysis of an anxiety about the relationship between economic speculation and masculinity in *Our Mutual Friend* in *Making a Social Body* (1995). In this latter work in particular, interrelated questions of gender, class, economics, colonial expansion, and race figure prominently in Poovey's analysis of how Dickens 'mobilized the assumption that his contemporaries had only begun to question: that the identity categories we call gender and race contributed natural bases for making moral discriminations about business and everything' (157).

Poovey's attentiveness (in this case, some would argue, an over-attentiveness) to questions of race is one example of the way in which late twentieth-century postcolonialist criticism, much of it inspired by the work of Edward Said, has explored the role played by the nineteenth-century novel in both constructing and normalizing the imperialist imagination. Dickens is prominent among the nineteenth-century novelists cited in Said's *Culture and Imperialism* (1993) as contributing to 'the novel's consolidation of [imperial] authority' (92); novelists for whom ' "abroad" was felt vaguely and ineptly to be out there, or exotic and strange, or in some way or other "ours" to control, trade in "freely", or suppress when the natives were energized to overt military or political resistance'.[42] Said's work on the imperialist imaginary, together with Benedict Anderson's concept of 'imagined communities' and Homi Bhabha's model of writing the nation, has directed critical attention to Dickens's role in what Deirdre David calls the 'textual construction of empire'.[43] Noting that Dickens's fiction is pervaded by ideas about empire both in its 'large moral critique' and in its 'small acts of representation' (2), David has read *The Old Curiosity Shop* and *Dombey and Son* in the context of a broader examination of how texts 'worked to create, explain, and negotiate the difficulties attendant upon the possession of an immense and always changing empire' (8). Like Sedgwick and Poovey, David is concerned to demonstrate how the uneven and often contradictory ideological work of Dickens's texts, their role in both the construction and critique of the imperial imagination, is linked to interdependent ideas about gender and race, which conjoin 'in subordinating millions of indigenous peoples to Britannic rule and maintaining women in their private sphere' (44).

One particularly important consequence of what might broadly be described as the New Historicist interest in the wider network of connotations and associations of fictional texts and their place in the broader field of cultural meaning, has been a renewed interest in Dickens's journalism. In some cases this has meant using Dickens's essays on various subjects of the day in *Household Words* and *All the Year Round* to throw light on his fiction. Thus, both Mary Poovey's and Deirdre David's analyses of the representation of race in Dickens's fiction draw on his essay on the 'Noble Savage' in *Household Words* (11 June 1853, 337–9). Others have explored

Dickens's fiction in the light of the various campaigns that he orchestrated in his periodicals – on madhouses, sanitation, slum clearance, 'Red Tapism', and so on. In addition, partly as a result of the increasing overlap of the methods and perspectives of cultural and media studies with literary historical studies, the journalism has also been reread as an interesting and important subject for analysis in its own right, rather than as a supplement to the fiction. As Bakhtin observed in 'Discourse in the Novel':

> the boundaries between fiction and nonfiction, between literature and nonliterature and so forth are not laid up in heaven. Every specific situation is historical. And so the growth of literature is not merely development and changes within the fixed boundaries of any given definition: the boundaries themselves are constantly changing.[44]

A rereading of Dickens's work in its entirety and in the context of its moment of production affords an interesting perspective on a key moment in the history of the process in which these boundaries were being drawn.

Another fresh perspective on Dickens's journalism has come from the end-of-the-millennium interest in the figure of the *flâneur*. The changing perspectives on the spectacle of the metropolis offered by Dickens's fictional sketches in *Sketches by Boz* and *The Uncommercial Traveller*, by his essays on the 'Amusements of the People' and on the new detective police, as well as by the novels, reveal this Victorian writer as a version of Baudelaire's 'Painter of Modern Life': the 'passionate spectator', who is in his element in the crowd, 'amid the ebb and flow of movement, in the midst of the fugitive and the infinite', who, 'like a kaleidoscope gifted with consciousness ... reproduc[es] the multiplicity of life'.[45] The interest in Dickens as *flâneur* and as a painter of modern life is just one example of the curious way in which readings of Dickens seem to have come full circle. At the beginning of the twenty-first century there has been a return to Bagehot's view of Dickens as a 'special correspondent for posterity' and a poet of urban life. However, this point of return has been reached via the new route of the writings of such theorists of modernity as Georg Simmel and Walter Benjamin: viewed through these lenses Dickens has been seen as (either or both) a special correspondent for modernity and a protomodernist. Similarly, in the age of post-modern parody and magic realism in fiction we bring new reading strategies to that hallucinatory bizarrerie which Bagehot and G. H. Lewes found in Dickens's novels. Dickens does not pose quite the same problems and questions for the twenty-first century reader as he did for those nineteenth- and earlier twentieth-century readers, formed by notions of fictional realism theorized and practised by George Eliot, or by Jamesian notions of architectonic fictional form.

This study looks at Dickens's work in his time and in ours. It focuses on Dickens as a Victorian man of letters, as journalist, literary entrepreneur, and as the conductor of magazines. It looks at Dickens in relation to specifically nineteenth-century forms and modes: as the moulder of the nineteenth-century serial novel; as the manipulator of the multiple plot with its reliance on providential coincidence; as the creator of hallucinatory, mechanical, eccentrics; as an example of the melodramatic imagination. But it also looks, from the perspectives of late modernity (or post-modernity), at the modernity of Dickens's hallucinatory reduplications, his atomistic, alienated characters and social world, his representations of the exciting, vivid, bleak and/or menacing spectacle of the metropolis, or (less frequently) the industrial landscape. The following chapters, each of which focuses on the work of a particular decade in Dickens's career, attempt a contextual study which seeks to understand Dickens's work in relation both to the worlds that made him and to the worlds that his work helped to make.

2

The Making of the Novelist and the Shaping of the Novel, 1835–41

> He chose, perhaps, the worst possible medium for making his
> *entrée* – the columns of a newspaper.
>> Review of Dickens's early fiction in the *National Magazine,*
>> 1837; *CH,* 64

In a relatively brief period of quite extraordinary literary produc-
tivity in the 1830s Charles Dickens transformed himself from a
jobbing journalist and periodical essayist into a periodical editor
and producer of long, continuous narratives issued in instalments.
In the process of doing so he became a cultural phenomenon,
created a character (Pickwick) who acquired cult status, and, most
important of all, began to transform the generic contours of fiction
in ways which were to constitute a continuing challenge to criticism of the novel. Dickens began his career as a published writer
early in 1831 as a free-lance parliamentary reporter for the *Mirror
of Parliament* and subsequently for the *True Sun* (from March
1832), before joining the staff of the *Morning Chronicle* in 1834. It
will be evident, from even the most cursory reading of Dickens's
novels, that his experiences as a reporter of parliamentary proceedings during the period leading up to and immediately following the
passing of the first Reform Act (1832) were formative of both the
matter and the manner of his fiction. The parliamentary scenes
which he observed provided him with the raw material for later
satiric portraits as well as shaping his social vision and his attitudes
to bureaucracy, officialdom, and the do-nothing ruling classes.

Similarly, his mode of writing was shaped (problematically, so some critics would argue) by the techniques he developed as a parliamentary reporter and sketch-writer; methods for conveying a vivid, sharply observed, instantaneous impression of a scene, or presenting a telling mini-narrative. These techniques are much in evidence in Dickens's earliest published imaginative writing; the humorous, observant, pathetic or (occasionally) grotesque sketches and tales of (mainly) London life which he began submitting, unsolicited and unpaid, to the *Monthly Magazine* in 1833, and which he continued on an increasingly professionalized basis in the *Morning Chronicle*, the *Evening Chronicle* and *Bell's Life in London*. Dickens's peculiar rapport with his readers may also be traced to this early training as a journalist and reporter; a training which made him, as Peter Ackroyd has argued, 'at once aware of an audience which he had to address, and whose tastes he would need to satisfy, if he were to be taken seriously at all' (Ackroyd, 167).

I Street-walking with the painter of modern life: *Sketches by Boz*

> What inexhaustible food for speculation do the streets of London afford.
> 'Shops and their Tenants', *Morning Chronicle*, October 1834,
> *Sketches by Boz*, First Series, *S*, 80

> [My] object has been to present little pictures of life and manners as they really are.
> Dickens's Preface to the first edition of *Sketches by Boz*, First Series, *S*, 7

Dickens's first fictional publication was the unsigned 'A Dinner at Poplar Walk' (subsequently retitled 'Mr Minns and His Cousin'), which appeared in the *Monthly Magazine* on 1 December 1833. His first identity as a maker of fictions was that of 'Boz' (his youngest brother's family nickname), the name with which he signed the second part of 'The Boarding-House', his fifth sketch for the *Monthly Magazine* (August 1834). This was the name which appeared (increasingly in conjunction with his own) on all of his fictions up to and including *Martin Chuzzlewit*, whose monthly covers announced that it was 'Edited by "Boz"'. By the time 'Boz' made his appearance, the sketches had already begun to attract favourable reviews and the attention of other editors. The *Morning Chronicle* took five 'Street Sketches' by 'Boz' in 1834, and George Hogarth commissioned twenty 'Sketches of London' (including the series 'Seven Sketches from Our Parish') for the newly launched *Evening Chronicle* in 1835. This was followed by a series of twelve 'Scenes and Characters' in *Bell's Life in London*, which appeared over the signature of 'Tibbs' (a name used in 'The Boarding-House', and borrowed from Oliver Goldsmith's essays). Dickens revised these sketches quite considerably for a two-volume collection, *Sketches by Boz, Illustrative of Every-day Life and Every-day People*, with illustrations by George Cruickshank, which was published by John Macrone on 8 February 1836, a month before the appearance of the first number of the *Pickwick Papers*. In preparing this first series for publication in volume form, Dickens improved the style, removed some topical references and toned down the polemical and political edge of some passages. He omitted some of the sketches and tales that had already appeared and wrote three new ones: 'A Visit to Newgate', 'The Black Veil' and 'The Great Winglebury Duel'. A second series was published at the end of the. same year, when *Pickwick* had already begun to make an impact. Dickens later rewrote his own history as a writer by playing down the achievement of the *Sketches*, but it is important to remember that it was the *Sketches* rather than *Pickwick Papers* which shot Dickens to fame 'like a sky rocket'.[1] Certainly *Sketches by Boz* is just as innovative a collection as its more famous successor.

The earliest tales in the *Monthly* were humorous thumbnail sketches of the suburban pretensions of the aspiringly upwardly mobile. They have a sharp, satirical tone, and are often written in a witty, epigrammatic style, as can be seen in this description of Mr Malderton, the paterfamilias in 'Horatio Sparkins', who would reappear in a number of guises in Dickens's later novels:

> a man whose whole scope of ideas was limited to Lloyds, the Exchange, the India House, and the Bank. A few successful speculations had raised him from a situation of obscurity and comparative poverty, to a state of affluence. As frequently happens in such cases, the ideas of himself and his family became elevated to an extraordinary pitch as their means increased; they affected fashion, taste and many other fooleries in imitation of their betters, and had a very decided and becoming horror of any thing which could by possibility

be considered *low*. He was hospitable from ostentation, illiberal from
ignorance, and prejudiced from conceit. (S, 411)

As is usual in these tales, the social pretensions of Mr Malderton
and his family are ridiculed and their aspirations are punctured
and frustrated by the 'plot' (if one can use this term for the narrative structure of a short story). Later sketches satirize or expose
contemporary social evils and corruption, as in 'The Election for
Beadle' in the 'Sketches from Our Parish' series, or 'A
Parliamentary Sketch'. They also move from the parlour or
drawing room to the city streets and focus on lower-class life.

Perhaps the most striking aspects of the sketches (and some of the
tales) are their creation of a particular sense of the metropolis and of
a particular urban point of view. Dickens's contemporary, Walter
Bagehot, was one of the first to note that Dickens's 'genius is especially suited to the delineation of city life'. Dickens, wrote Bagehot in
the *National Review* in 1854, 'describes London like a special correspondent for posterity' (CH, 394). The nineteenth century was seen
by those who lived in it (as well as by later cultural historians) as the
age of great cities, and the emergent representative form of modern
subjectivity was that of the city dweller, the denizen of the city
streets. This representative modern subject was, according to some
nineteenth-century commentators (Wordsworth in his Prefaces to
Lyrical Ballads, for example), increasingly a passive spectator or consumer of the rapidly changing spectacle of urban life. It was in this
period too, as Richard Sennett observes in *The Fall of Public Man*,
that 'public behaviour' for the middle classes became 'a matter of
observation, of passive participation, of a certain kind of voyeurism'.[2]
Dickens articulated this new kind of consciousness by developing a
mode of fictional representation 'uniquely capable', as Raymond
Williams put it, 'of expressing the experience of living in cities', and
of dramatizing the hurry and confusion of modernity:

> As we stand and look back at a Dickens novel the general movement
> we remember – the decisive movement – is a hurrying seemingly
> random passing of men and women, each heard in some fixed
> phrase, seen in some fixed expression.[3]

It is, says Williams, 'a way of seeing men and women that belongs
to the street'.

Dickens's modernity, his fashioning of a new urban consciousness, was evident not just in the great social novels of his maturity

(which is what Williams was describing in the above quotation), but in all his writings throughout his career, from his earliest journalism as he was learning how to be a novelist in the 1830s and early 1840s, through to the essays he wrote as editor – or, as he preferred to call himself, 'conductor' – of *Household Words* and *All the Year Round* in the 1850s and 1860s.

Dickens himself clearly felt that the streets, and in particular the streets of London, were, in complex ways that he didn't quite understand, the source of his creativity. For example, when he was staying in Genoa and trying to write the Christmas book for 1844 (*The Chimes*), he wrote to his friend John Forster: 'Put me down on Waterloo-bridge at eight o'clock in the evening, with leave to roam about as long as I like, and I would come home, as you know, panting to go on' (*DL*, IV: 200). Or again, at another difficult moment in his writing life, when he was in Lausanne working simultaneously on his Christmas book for 1846 (*The Battle of Life*) and on the first of his great social novels (*Dombey and Son*), he wrote to Forster (3 August 1846):

> Invention, thank God, seems the easiest thing in the world. ... But the difficulty of going at what I call a rapid pace, is prodigious. ... I suppose this is partly the effect of ... the absence of streets and numbers of figures. I can't express how much I want these. It seems as if they supplied something to my brain, which it cannot bear, when busy, to lose. For a week or a fortnight I can write prodigiously in a retired place (as at Broadstairs), and a day in London sets me up again and starts me. But the toil and labour of writing, day after day, without that magic lantern, is IMMENSE!! ... I only mention it as a curious fact, which I have never had an opportunity of finding out before. *My* figures seem disposed to stagnate without crowds about them. I wrote very little in Genoa ... and fancied myself conscious of some such influence there – but Lord! I had two miles of streets at least, lighted at night, to walk about in; and a great theatre to repair to, every night.   (*DL*, IV: 612–13)

The streets, the crowds, the theatre, the city's hum and buzz of cultural implication (to borrow a phrase of Gertrude Himmelfarb's), acted as a kind of fertilizer for Dickens's imagination, an energizing, vivifying medium for his characters, a magic lantern for the imagination. He wrote to Forster in similar vein a few weeks later:

> The absence of accessible streets continues to worry me ... in a most singular manner. It is quite a little mental phenomenon. I should not walk in them in the day time, if they were here, I dare say: but

> at night I want them beyond description. I don't seem able to get rid
> of my spectres unless I can lose them in crowds. However, as you
> say, there are streets in Paris; and good suggestive streets too: and
> trips to London will be nothing then.   (*DL,* IV: 622)

The night streets, 'good suggestive streets', the locus of desire and
for the conjuring up as well as the extinction of spectres, loom
large in Dickens's imaginary. For Dickens street walking and night
walking were not just pastimes, they were a compulsion and a creative necessity.

If the city streets occupied an important part in Dickens's and in
the nineteenth century's cultural imaginary, so too did various kinds
of street walker: notably, the street hawker, the street criminal, the
prostitute, the dandy, the social investigator, the policeman and the
flâneur. Dickens was interested in all of these figures, and they
appear in various guises throughout his fiction. Recently, Dickens
himself has been represented in terms of each of these figures, or of
various combinations of them. The street hawker and the prostitute
are obviously useful figures for representing the processes of the
commercialization and commodification of literature in which
Dickens played such an important part. Moreover, as Deborah Nord
has shown, the prostitute also functions as the double for the mar-
ginal or alienated self of the male street walker or *flâneur,* or as a
connector, a carrier of the literal and symbolic diseases of modern
urban life.[4] The street-walking policeman has been used to figure the
processes of social and psychological policing and containment
which several recent cultural historians argue are embodied in
Dickens's fiction (and, indeed, in the nineteenth-century novel in
general). In the late twentieth century the street walker who has
seemed to provide the most apt figure for the Dickensian narrator,
and especially for the 'Boz' perspective, has been the *flâneur.*

For Charles Baudelaire, writing in 'The Painter of Modern Life'
in the early 1860s, the *flâneur* was both the product and expression of a specific form of urban modernity; the passionate (rather
than Wordsworth's spectre of the passive) spectator of the spectacle of the modern city:

> The crowd is his element, as the air is that of birds and water of
> fishes. His passion and his profession are to become one flesh with
> the crowd. For the perfect *Flâneur,* for the passionate spectator, it is
> an immense joy to set up house in the heart of the multitude, amid
> the ebb and flow of movement, in the midst of the fugitive and

infinite. To be away from home, and yet to feel oneself everywhere at home; to see the world, to be at the centre of the world, and yet to remain hidden from the world – such are a few of the slightest pleasures of those independent, passionate, impartial natures which the tongue can but clumsily define. The spectator is a prince who everywhere rejoices in his incognito. The lover of life makes the whole world his family, just like ... the lover of pictures who lives in a magical society of dreams painted on canvas. Thus the lover of universal life enters into a crowd as though it were an immense reservoir of electrical energy. Or we might liken him to a mirror as vast as the crowd itself; or to a kaleidoscope gifted with consciousness, responding to each one of its movements and reproducing the multiplicity of life and the flickering grace of all the elements of life.[5]

Note, in this passage, the modulation from the passionate spectator to the painter of modern life. The *flâneur*, 'the lover of universal life', like Dickens in those letters to Forster from Lausanne, 'enters into a crowd as though it were an immense reservoir of electrical energy'. The *flâneur* as painter of modern life is like a series of mobile mirrors, a kaleidoscope, reproducing and refracting the multiplicity of modernity.

According to Walter Benjamin in the unfinished study of Baudelaire on which he was engaged from the 1920s until his death in 1940, the *flâneur* was a journalistic and literary type originating in the Paris of the 1830s, when writers of *feuilletons* (serialized features sections of the Paris newspapers) and of books called *physiologies*, began to write sketches of city life from the perspective of a strolling observer of a performance, or from the perspective of 'one who goes botanising on the asphalt'.[6] The result, Benjamin argued, was a new literary genre – the panorama or diorama – and a new kind of man of letters; one who was assimilated into society as the provider of sharply observed, witty sketches of the surfaces of the spectacle of city life for the consumption of the literate classes. The *flâneur* thus functioned to reassure the urban middle class that the urban crowd was not as illegible, chaotic or threatening as it appeared to be, and that modern urban social life was more coherent than it seemed. This is indicated in the domestic imagery in Baudelaire's representation of the painter of modern life: 'it is an immense joy to set up house in the heart of the multitude ... to be away from home, and yet to feel oneself everywhere at home'.

Although the name is French, the *flâneur* is not entirely a French invention, nor is he a figure who originated in the nineteenth

century. The demeanour of the *flâneur* in many repects resembles
that of the eighteenth-century Rambler or Idler of Dr Johnson,
Oliver Goldsmith's Citizen of the world, or the Spectator or Tatler
of Addison and Steele, the periodical essayists who were Dickens's
models for so many aspects of his work (particularly *Sketches by
Boz*), and for his persona as an editor or conductor of periodicals
from *Bentley's Miscellany* in the 1830s to his own *Household
Words* and then *All the Year Round* from the 1850s. The familiar
essays of Addison and Steele, like the *feuilletons* of the *flâneurs*,
offered an amusing commentary on the urban scene. The city was
represented in their writings as discontinuous and fragmentary,
like the periodical form in which it appeared, and their observing
spectator presented himself as one who was open to the random
contingency of urban experience.[7] Like Baudelaire's and more
especially Benjamin's *flâneur*, this spectator also served to present
the city to the literate classes as a spectacle for their consumption,
while simultaneously making the city available as a public sphere
for rational and moral interaction.

By the beginning of the nineteenth century the urban sketch by
the spectating *flâneur* had become one of the shows of London,
along with the panoramas, dioramas, cosmoramas, eidophusikons,
magic lanterns, camera obscuras and other popular forms of visual
representation.[8] By the 1830s the *flâneur's* street-walking style of
urban spectatorship had become so pervasive that it seemed quite
natural for Dickens to adopt it for his earliest published works of
fiction, the *Sketches by Boz,* an English equivalent of the Parisian
feuilletons. Thus there was, in one sense, nothing particularly
novel about the Boz *Sketches*. As well as imitating some of his
favourite eighteenth-century writers, Dickens was also, in part,
imitating and improving upon the Regency fashion for comic
urban street scenes, familiar essays and periodical miscellanies as
written by William Hazlitt, Charles Lamb, Thomas De Quincey,
Leigh Hunt, Thomas Hood, Theodore Hook and Pierce Egan. The
style of the *Sketches*, like that of some of the interpolated tales in
Pickwick Papers, also owes something to the American writer
Washington Irving. Moreover, their focus on external detail,
gesture and idiosyncrasies of speech link them to the contemporary
tradition of melodrama, with which Dickens as an enthusiastic
young theatre-goer was well acquainted. Like the earlier essayists,
Dickens's purpose in his sketches seemed to be to offer amusement
and entertainment, and his persona appeared bent on exercising

and satisfying curiosity. This can be seen in the opening paragraph of 'Shops and Their Tenants' as published in *The Morning Chronicle* in October 1834:

> What inexhaustible food for speculation do the streets of London afford! We never were able to agree with Sterne in pitying the man who could travel from Dan to Beersheba and say that all was barren; we have not the slightest commiseration for the man who can take up his hat and stick, and walk from Covent Garden to St Paul's Churchyard and back into the bargain, without deriving some amusement – we had almost said instruction, from his peram-bulation. And yet there are such beings: we meet them everyday. Large black stocks and light waistcoats, jet canes and discontented countenances, are the characteristics of the race. ... Nothing seems to make an impression on their minds: nothing short of being knocked down by a porter, or run over by a cab, will disturb their equanimity.   (*S*, 80)

Or again, the opening paragraph of 'The Prisoners' Van', as it was published in *Bell's Life in London* in November 1835 (this paragraph was omitted from the collected versions of the *Sketches*):

> We have a most extraordinary partiality for lounging about the streets. Whenever we have an hour or two to spare, there is nothing we enjoy more than a little amateur vagrancy – walking up one street and down another, and staring into shop windows, and gazing about as if, instead of being on intimate terms with every shop and house in Holborn, the Strand, Fleet Street and Cheapside, the whole were an unknown region to our wandering mind. We revel in a crowd of any kind.[9]

At first glance, give or take a little brio, this might seem like famil-iar urban-sketch territory. However, from the beginning, reviewers felt that these sketches and tales were doing something new, and that, as Forster indicated in his review for the *Examiner* (28 February 1836), Dickens was opening up new literary terri-tory with a new kind of writing which took urban and suburban London as its setting and subject.

   One of the new fields that was being opened up in the *Sketches* was their creation of a particular sense of the metropolis and of a particular urban geography and mode of perception. One aspect of the modern city to which the strolling spectator consistently draws our attention is the scale and rapidity of change in the cityscape. The *Sketches* represent the different zones and the shifting social geography of London, of neighbourhoods in the process of going down or coming up. Like the French *physiologistes*, Boz represents distinctive London 'types' or phenomena: 'certain descriptions of people who, oddly enough, appear to appertain exclusively to this metropolis', types with whom one meets 'every day in the street of London, but no one ever encounters ... elsewhere' ('Shabby-genteel People', *S*, 303). Another distinctive feature of London or city life described by Boz is its peculiar secrecy and anonymity. As he writes in 'Thoughts about People', ' 'Tis strange with how little notice, good, bad, or indifferent, a man may live or die in London' (*S*, 251). A distinctive metropolitan geography and distinctive metropolitan types come together with another important 'discovery' that the amateur vagrant makes about the city in 'Seven Dials'. This is the discovery that the city is a labyrinth or maze, bewildering for the 'inexperienced wayfarer' (*S*, 94):

> Look at the construction of the place. The gordian knot was all very well in its way: so was the maze of Hampton Court ... so were the ties of stiff white neckcloths, when the difficulty of getting one on was only to be equalled by the apparent impossibility of ever getting it off again [all these things belong to the past]. But what involutions can compare with those of Seven Dials. Where is there such another maze of streets, courts, lanes and alleys. ... The stranger who finds himself in 'The dials' for the first time, and stands, Belzoni-like, at the entrance of seven obscure passages uncertain which to take, will see enough around him to keep his curiosity and attention awake for no inconsiderable time.   (*S*, 90–1)

In 'Seven Dials' it is the cityscape rather than the traveller which seems to be on the move; it is the streets and courts which get lost (rather than the traveller) as they continually elude the traveller's grasp:

> From the irregular square into which he has plunged, the streets and courts dart in all directions, until they are lost in the unwholesome vapour which hangs over the house-tops, and renders the dirty perspective uncertain and confined: and lounging at every corner, as if they came there to take a few gasps of such fresh air as has found its way so far, but is too much exhausted already ... are groups of people, whose appearance and dwellings would fill any mind but a regular Londoner's with astonishment.   (*S*, 92)

One of the interesting things about this passage is the distinction it makes between the stranger and the 'regular Londoner'. Boz is the regular Londoner *par excellence*; almost the super Londoner. The Boz persona is in part that of a special kind of reader; a special kind of reader of a new kind of text – the text of the city.

In the passage just quoted and in that dropped opening paragraph from 'The Prisoners' Van' quoted earlier, we can begin to glimpse another aspect of what the *Sketches* were opening up. Dickens's amateur vagrant is not simply an idler; rather, he anticipates Baudelaire's *flâneur*, as the painter of modern life. The 'Boz' perspective is a magic lantern which transforms the images it throws out. It is a kaleidoscope which turns the city into a phantasmagoria, making the familiar strange, rendering the real surreal by viewing Holborn and the Strand as if they were 'an unknown region to our wandering mind', or, in 'Meditations in Monmouth Street', animating whole rows of second-hand clothing into starting up from their pegs and draping themselves over imaginary wearers. If, at times, the Boz perspective presents the city as spectacle, or the space of fantasy, it also both suggests and comments upon the ways in which urban life makes everyone a spectator or observer. For example, in 'The Steam Excursion' Boz amuses himself by observing his central character, a law student who is hurrying about trying to organize an outing on the Thames, in the act of observing the other observers of the early morning street scene in which two young swells, loudly and slightly aggressively drunk, are ending their night on the town by entertaining three 'ladies' (streetwalkers) and an Irish labourer to an al fresco breakfast. This is the scene that Boz observes the student observing:

> A little sweep was standing at a short distance, casting a longing eye at the tempting delicacies; and a policeman was watching the group from the opposite side of the street. The wan looks, and gaudy finery of the wretched thinly-clad females, contrasted as strangely with the gay sunlight, as did their forced merriment with the boisterous hilarity of the two young men, who now and then varied their amusements by 'bonneting' the proprietor of this itinerant coffee-house. (*S*, 447–8)

Like many passages in the *Sketches*, this sharply observed early nineteenth-century scene has something of the perspective of the familiar sketch of the eighteenth or early nineteenth century. However, it also has something of the perspective of that urban (or more specifically metropolitan) modernity which Georg Simmel was later to anatomize in his discussions of *fin de siècle* Berlin, and

Benjamin in his anatomy of the Paris of the Second Empire. In *Sketches by Boz* Dickens begins to represent the modern urban crowd in which everyone is either unobservantly blasé (as Simmel puts it in his essay on the metropolis and mental life),[10] or suspiciously on the look-out, watching everyone else, as they pass and repass. As Walter Benjamin (quoting Simmel) noted of nineteenth-century Paris: 'Interpersonal relations in big cities are distinguished by a marked preponderance of the activity of the eye over the activity of the ear.'[11] Boz repeatedly draws upon that peculiarly ocular knowledge of the city crowd, or ' "know[ing] by sight," to use a familiar phrase', as he puts it in 'The Drunkard's Death' (*S*, 554). Ocular knowledge, or knowing by sight, involves a particular way of seeing. It is preoccupied with surfaces, and with variations in the appearance of those members of the crowd, or features of the cityscape, which for one reason or another impinge upon the consciousness of the urban passer-by. It is also, frequently, a curious, fictive form of knowledge, which constructs speculative narratives and histories to make sense of the ever-changing urban scene. This form of knowledge is very evident in 'Shops and Their Tenants', in which the speculative roamer of the city streets seeks to comprehend the urban scene by making up stories about the changing shop windows, and inventing histories for the various tenants he sees come and go. This narrator is a kind of novelist and also a kind of detective (another street walker), seeking (or inventing) causes and motives for the effects he witnesses in the surface landscape of the city. He offers a fantasy of knowledge to the perplexed spectator of urban modernity, and, perhaps, a fantasy of control.

Elsewhere, the perspective and style of the *Sketches* are those of yet another kind of street walker, the social investigator, the traveller into unknown London, reporting back to the middle classes on the subcultures of the city, as Henry Mayhew did in his reports for the *Morning Chronicle* in the 1840s. 'Gin Shops', 'The Pawnbroker's Shop', and 'Seven Dials' are all, in some respects, examples of this kind of reportage. Some of the most powerful of the *Sketches* are those in which the idler on the streets either physically or mentally removes himself from the streets and follows street walkers of various kinds indoors, or requires his readers to think about the causes and consequences of the scenes that he displays before them. In these *Sketches* the 'Boz' perspective is not simply that of the fanciful speculator, the detached spectator, or even the social reporter, but rather it seeks to co-opt the reader to a more engaged form of perception. The spectating street walker stops and looks, and makes the reader stop and look, as he bears passionate moral witness to the 'every-day' scenes and events, which he defamiliarizes through the intensity of his scrutiny. An example of this can be found in 'The Prisoners' Van', when the idler or amateur vagrant, returning from one of his lounging excursions, scrutinizes two of the passengers of the van he encounters, a sixteen-year-old prostitute and her younger sister. On this occasion Boz becomes more street preacher than street walker:

> What the younger girl was then, the elder had been once; and what the elder then was, she must soon become. A melancholy prospect, but how surely to be realized: a tragic drama, but how often acted! Turn to the prisons and police offices of London – nay, look into the very streets themselves. These things pass before our eyes day after day, and hour after hour – they have become such matters of course, that they are utterly disregarded. The progress of these girls in crime will be as rapid as the flight of pestilence, resembling it too in its baneful influence and wide-spreading infection. Step by step how many wretched females, within the sphere of every man's observation, have become involved in a career of vice frightful to contemplate; hopeless at its commencement, loathsome and repulsive in its course, friendless, forlorn, and unpitied at its miserable conclusion! (S, 317)

It was such passages which led Thomas Lister, writing in the *Edinburgh Review* (October 1838), to commend Boz's ability 'to excite our sympathy on behalf of the aggrieved and suffering in all classes; and especially in those who are most removed from observation' (*CH*, 73). The implication is that Boz is putting on display what readers of the *Edinburgh Review* might prefer to draw a veil over.

In *Sketches* such as 'The Prisoners' Van', 'The Drunkard's Death' and 'A Visit to Newgate', Dickens insists that his readers have regard for those aspects of modern city life that 'have become such matters of course, that they are utterly disregarded'. In these *Sketches* Boz seeks to combat, as he puts it in 'A visit to Newgate', 'The force of habit' that leads city workers 'day by day and hour by hour to pass and repass this gloomy depository of the guilt and misery of London, in one perpetual stream of life and bustle, utterly umindful of the throng of wretched creatures pent up within it'. In 'A Visit to Newgate', Boz self-consciously sets himself up as a special correspondent for his fellow contemporaries who has determined to visit the interior of Newgate Prison on their behalf and lay the results of this prison visit before his readers: 'what we did see, and what we thought, we will tell in our own way' (*S*, 235). Boz's way is a sketch of the architecture and geography of the prison and a series of sketches of its inmates, and, most importantly, a narrative in which Boz conjures into being a fictional inhabitant for the condemned cell he visits, and gives him a history, a wife, a dream, and a ghastly awakening to his inevitable death.

At such moments Dickens, in his Boz persona, anticipates the realist novelists of the 1840s and 1850s in the way he transforms his readers from passively consuming spectators and compels their attention to 'the lives that pass them daily in the streets' (as Elizabeth Gaskell put it in her Preface to *Mary Barton*), and in the way he 'surprises even the trivial and selfish into that attention to what is apart from themselves, which may be called the raw material of moral sentiment' (to quote from one of George Eliot's *Westminster Review* essays, in which she castigated Dickens for his failure to give a faithful representation of ordinary life). And, of course, at such moments Dickens anticipates the novelist he was himself to become in the 1840s, 1850s and 1860s, conjuring fictional characters and narratives from the city streets and transforming the representation of the city from a spectacle to a problematic space for human agency.

Dickens's first published writings, then, were a series of notes from the front line of modern urban life, scattered through the pages of daily newspapers or weekly and monthly magazines. As well as tales of the city streets and stories of suburban aspiration, they included grotesque, melodramatic tales of urban degradation and despair, such as 'The Drunkard's Death', and Gothic tales such as 'The Black Veil' (specially written for the 1836 collection), in which a woman, who describes herself as mentally ill, entreats a young surgeon to attend her 'dying' son; in a macabre twist, when the surgeon reaches the woman's home he is confronted with the dead body of the young man, who has been hanged. 'The history was an everyday one', the narrator summarizes; the poor, friendless widow had sacrificed herself to provide for her son, who, 'forgetful of the sufferings she had endured for him ... had plunged into a career of dissipation and crime. And this was the result: his own death by the hangman's hands, and his mother's shame, and incurable insanity' (*S*, 437). In 'The Black Veil', as in so many of the *Sketches*, Dickens's lifelong fascination with urban criminality, with the law and the penal system, is already much in evidence. However, 'Boz' is not only concerned with the darker side of urban life. The *Sketches* contain numerous satirical, comic and/or pathetic treatments of the 'amusements of the people' and the shows of London, as, for example, in 'London Recreations', 'Greenwich Fair', 'Vauxhall-gardens by Day', 'Astley's', and 'The River' (on the Thames as a place of entertainment).

The *Sketches* were, as Dickens announced in his Preface to the First Edition of the First Series, a young writer's 'pilot balloon', an 'experiment' in presenting 'little pictures of life and manners as they really are' (*S*, 7). It was an experiment that he intended to 'repeat ... with increased confidence on a more extensive scale' (*S*, 7), even producing 'connected works of fiction of a higher grade' (Dickens's Preface, *S*, 8). The fiction he had in mind was a projected novel entitled *Gabriel Vardon, The Locksmith of London*, which he had promised to John Macrone by the end of 1836. However, only two days after the first appearance of the first series of *Sketches by Boz*, William Hall (of Chapman and Hall) diverted Dickens from taking the direct route into a career as a novelist, by inviting him to provide the letterpress to accompany a series of Cockney sporting sketches by the artist Robert Seymour; text and sketches were to be issued monthly. Unable to resist the lure of the £14 per month which Chapman offered, Dickens embarked on what his friends told him was 'a low and cheap form of publication, by which I should ruin all my rising hopes' (Preface to 1847 edition),[12] and began writing what was to become the *Pickwick Papers*. Dickens quickly imposed his own ideas on the project, arguing that there was nothing novel in the sporting sketches idea, and that he would like to take his own way 'with a freer range of English scenes and people' (1867 Preface, *PP*, 723). Following Seymour's suicide early in the project, and his replacement by Hablot Browne ('Phiz'), the relationship between text and illustrations changed and Dickens was involved in the next stage of what turned out to be the production of a distinctive form of periodical fiction.

II   The periodical essay as novel: *The Posthumous Papers of the Pickwick Club*

> [T]he form and manner of *The Pickwick Papers* heralded a revolution in the circulation and appeal of narrative fiction.
>
> Peter Ackroyd, *Dickens* (London: Minerva, 1991), p. 190

When considering the critical issues raised by Dickens's fiction, it is important to remember that *The Posthumous Papers of the Pickwick Club*, as G. K. Chesterton observed, is neither a good novel, nor a bad novel – it is 'not a novel at all'. It is, writes Chesterton, 'something nobler than a novel'.[13] Echoing Chesterton, John Lucas has suggested that *Pickwick* is both less and more than a novel. It is less than a novel in that it lacks the organization and coherence that twentieth-century readers had come to expect of novels; an organization and coherence which, in Lucas's view, Dickens was increasingly trying to give to his series of sporting sketches as he wrote them month by month. On the other hand, *Pickwick* is more than a novel, or more than *one* novel, in the way it combines various kinds of fiction.[14] *Pickwick* is a geographical and generic adventure; 'a scatter-brained romp around the greater part of southern and eastern England and up and down and along and across the literary register'.[15] Always a favourite among readers of fiction, *Pickwick*, for much of the twentieth century, presented a challenge to theories of the novel and reading practices (derived from Henry James), 'which are marked by some adherence to the idea of organic form, that is an absence of elements in excess of those required for the work's inner aims'.[16] The renewed critical interest in *Pickwick* in recent years is unsurprising in an age which practises deconstructive readings, delights in anarchic wordplay and looks for instability, fragmentariness, and indeterminacy in its fictions.

As Dickens himself observed in his Preface to the 1867 edition, *Pickwick* was a 'monthly something'; a 'constant succession' of vividly rendered, lifelike and amusing characters and incidents. It was (he continued) 'a mere series of adventures, in which the scenes are ever changing, and the characters come and go like the men and women we encounter in the real world' . In such a work, written as 'the periodical occasion arose', Dickens unapologetically maintained (in his Preface to the first edition) that 'no artfully interwoven or ingeniously complicated plot can with reason be expected'. Certainly, it was as a periodical, or magazine, rather than as a novel that *Pickwick* was first read and reviewed. The *Sun*, for example, described it as 'amusing periodical sketches' (4 July 1836), while *Chambers's Edinburgh Journal* reviewed it as 'a series of monthly pamphlets' (29 April 1837).

In both its conception and execution *Pickwick* is a series of scenes, sketches and tales, like *Sketches by Boz*. Like its predecessor, it continues to owe a great deal to eighteenth-century periodical miscellanies such as Addison and Steele's de Coverley papers in the *Spectator*, and to earlier nineteenth-century imitations of them, such as Washington Irving's 'Geoffrey Crayon' sketches. The journalistic and periodical nature of *Pickwick* is also discernible in its references to contemporary events, such as the Norton–Melbourne case, which Dickens covered for the *Morning Chronicle* in July 1837, and which he drew upon for his representation of the court scenes in the Bardell versus Pickwick action; in the satiric treatment of the unreformed parliamentary system in the Eatanswill election; in the description of the Fleet prison; and in the sketch on literary lionhunting. Another topical aspect of *Pickwick* is Dickens's increasing use (once he had taken charge of the project and begun to shape it to his own purposes rather than those of his publisher and original illustrator) of a 'real time' plot, in which the changing seasons of the story kept pace with the season in which each monthly part appeared. The 'Boz' of the *Morning* and *Evening Chronicle* sketches is also much in evidence in the dark, Gothic, grotesque, interpolated tales which periodically interrupt the narrative, with their intimations of a dreamlike, and often violent world, in which chairs acquire the power of speech, the 'decaying skeletons of the departed mails' (in 'The Tale of the Bagman's Uncle') are restored and take on spectral passengers, and the dead come alive to instruct, terrify or simply amuse the living. These tales belong to a parallel fictional universe which interrupts, disrupts or counterpoints the 'Pickwickian' bonhomie of feasting, sporting and courting which pervades and ultimately triumphs in the main narrative.

Of course, interpolated tales are also a common device in the eighteenth-century novel, another of Dickens's models in *Pickwick*. Indeed, in so far as it is a novel, *Pickwick* is perhaps a belated version of those picaresque novels by Henry Fielding and Tobias Smollett, which Dickens read so avidly in his childhood and youth. Like them, *Pickwick* is held together by a series of journeys (many of which end in overturned carriages), involving strange meetings, mysteries and discoveries. The genial, innocent Pickwick is a man of sentiment masquerading as a man of science, a variation on Fielding's Parson Adams in *Joseph Andrews*, or, to take an older European example, a Don Quixote tilting at windmills under the watchful eye of Sam Weller, his Sancho Panza. Moreover, both *Pickwick* and its eponymous hero exemplify Smollett's wish (as expressed in the Preface to *Roderick Random*) to arouse 'generous indignation ... against the vicious disposition of the world'. As in Fielding's *Tom Jones* and *Joseph Andrews,* and Smollett's *Humphrey Clinker, Roderick Random* and *Peregrine Pickle,* the 'structural axis' of *Pickwick Papers* is, as J. H. Miller noted, 'the age-old motif of the quest. ... Quest for reality, quest for truth, it is also implicitly a quest for oneself, since one can only know oneself by knowing how one is related to the world.'[17]

In this case, the quest is set in motion through what Dickens described in a Preface, written when the novel was issued in volume form, as the 'machinery' of the Corresponding Society of the Pickwick Club. Dickens later claimed to have abandoned this device because he found it an embarrassment, but, on closer inspection, it would appear that the narrator or the editorial 'Boz' takes over Pickwick's 'corresponding' role, 'carrying the speculations of that learned man into a wider field ... extending his travels, and consequently enlarging his sphere of observation; to the advancement of knowledge, and the diffusion of learning' (1: 2) to the readers of *The Pickwick Papers.* During the course of the narrative the observers become the observed, as Pickwick and his bachelor companions Winkle, Tupman and Snodgrass (but perhaps especially Pickwick) come under the narrator/editor's lens, as they are exhibited responding to changing locations and circumstances, and interacting with a range of different types. It is this emphasis on interaction, process and change which marks out the periodical miscellany of *The Pickwick Papers* as novelistic. Particularly important is the change that occurs in Pickwick himself, as he develops from the enclosed and self-enclosed position of the cocooned innocent, and the detachment of the amateur scientist or the idly curious observer, into that of an involved actor.

Acting is much more than merely a metaphor in *The Pickwick Papers*: it is a mode both of representation and of being in the world. In *Pickwick,* as in the theatrical drama, characters are represented to the audience through speech and gesture, and some characters appear to be making themselves up as they go along. Most dramatic of all is Jingle, a character at once manic and calculating, whose quick-fire speech replicates the episodic nature and rapid pace of the narrative. If Jingle belongs, in part, to the world of pantomime, the way in which he is represented is also indicative of a newer conception of identity as fluid and unstable. Jingle, with anarchic energy, ceaselessly reinvents himself in order that he can help himself to anything that is going. On the other hand, Sam

Weller (the Cockney servant introduced with spectacular success in the fourth number) practises a more judicious form of self-help in order to survive and prosper. Sam, a streetwise, modern, urban type, belongs to the London of the *Sketches*. However, in *Pickwick* the street character has been moved from the periphery of the narrator's vision to the centre of a narrative in which he speaks for himself, in a rich and exuberant language, which enables him to engage energetically with the world and, in a curious way (rather like his creator), to seek to take control of its contingency by perceiving it through analogues and metaphors. In Sam's habitual 'Wellerisms', Dickens takes proverbial forms of speech, clichés and other standard conversational devices and injects them with a strange logic that is at once commonsensical and surreal, and which frequently combines sentiment with an almost cartoon-like violence, as in ' "Business first, pleasure arterwards, as King Richard the Third said ven he stabbed the t'other king in the Tower, afore he smothered the babbies" ' (25: 314), or ' "now ve look compact and comfortable, as the father said ven he cut his little boy's head off, to cure him o' squintin' " ' (27: 344).

Sam is the antithesis of his gullible and accident-prone social superiors – Pickwick, Tupman, Snodgrass and Winkle – having acquired worldly wisdom as a consequence of his father's rather haphazard educational philosophy of leaving him to 'run in the streets when he was very young, and shift for his-self' (20: 244). Acutely observed and an acute observer, the resourceful and upwardly mobile Sam is, in some respects, Dickens's representative in the text, casting a satiric eye on the human foibles of those he encounters, and also on social pretension and social abuses. For some critics of a psychoanalytic bent, Sam is also Dickens's representative in the text's staging of an Oedipal drama in which the author idealizes his own problematic relationship with his father. Sam, the wise child, nurtures and protects two benignly neglecting, and in some ways infantile, father-figures: Mr Weller senior, who had consigned his son to the harsh education of the streets, as Dickens's own father had done when he put him to work in Warren's Blacking Factory when he was twelve years old; and Pickwick, who, again like Dickens's father, is incarcerated in the Fleet prison as a result of stubbornness and ineptitude (leavened by a sense of justice and chivalry in Pickwick's case).

Dickens's decision to entangle Pickwick with the law, the legal profession and the penal system enabled him to draw upon his own experience as the child of an imprisoned debtor, and also on his youthful experience as a law reporter. It was also a means of bringing an element of narrative coherence to a substantial portion of Pickwick's monthly numbers. But perhaps the most important aspect of Dickens's representation of the events surrounding the Bardell versus Pickwick trial, and of the trial itself , was the fact that he began to develop further the satiric voice and social critique which he had introduced in some of the *Sketches*. This voice was given extra force and confidence by the positive response of readers and reviewers to *Oliver Twist*, whose first number appeared after the ninth number of *Pickwick*. Although with its cast of benevolent old gentlemen, prematurely middle-aged bachelors, and stereotypical old spinsters, voracious widows, pretty ingénues, and resourceful servant girls, all of whom seem to belong to a former age, *Pickwick* often seems to look back nostalgically to an eighteenth-century world of coaching inns, it also registers the energy and uncertainties of the age of reform in which it was written and set. The narrative's and the narrator's attacks on the obfuscations of the law, the duplicitous pomposity of lawyers, and the political corruption of the pre-Reform era are reinforced by Sam's urban 'outsider' irreverence and verbal dexterity. Sam is a fictional construction that embodies the possibility of resistance and change, and a better life, which is perhaps, in the end, more convincing to most twenty-first-century readers than that Pickwickian benevolence (an early form of the Dickensian 'Christmas spirit'), which seems to emanate from the Kentish idyll of Dingley Dell and finds its suburban home in Richmond.

III 'Connected works of fiction of a higher grade': *Oliver Twist* and scenes of suffering

> If the pen that designed these little outlines, should present its labours to the Public frequently hereafter; if it should produce fresh sketches, and even connected works of fiction of a higher grade, they have only themselves to blame. They have encouraged a young and unknown writer, by their patronage and approval.
>
> (Charles Dickens, 1836 Preface, *Sketches*, 8)

> The romance, novel, history, or narrative, or whatever else it may be called of 'Oliver Twist,' is assuredly an invention *per se*.

It bears no sort of resemblance to any other fiction, looking like a truth, with which we are acquainted.

(The *Atlas*, 5 November 1837, p. 713)

In May 1836, following the success of the first series of *Sketches* and shortly after the appearance of the first monthly part of *Pickwick*, Dickens signed a contract with Richard Bentley for two 3-volume novels. In early November of the same year, he entered into an agreement with Bentley to edit a new monthly magazine, provisionally entitled the *Wits' Miscellany*. Renamed *Bentley's Miscellany*, this magazine appeared under Dickens's editorship in January 1837, when *Pickwick* had completed its ninth number. *Bentley's* opened with a sketch by Dickens, 'The Public Life of Mr Tulrumble', a satire on the pompous idiocies of public officials, set in 'Mudfog' – Dickens's fictional version of Chatham in Kent, where he spent part of his childhood. In the following month Dickens published a second 'Mudfog' sketch, entitled 'Oliver Twist', in which Mr Bumble replaced Mr Tulrumble as the representative of bumbling, self-important and self-interested petty public officialdom, and the Parish Workhouse and the New Poor Law became the target for what John Kucich has described as Dickens's satiric 'parody machine'.[18] Like *Pickwick*, 'Oliver Twist' was first reviewed as a 'clever series of articles' (in the *Sun* for 1 May 1837). However, it was clear that Dickens had begun to view the project differently. Realizing that in creating the figure of the orphan abused by the state, he had hit upon a winning idea for a story, he continued the extended narrative that was to become *The Adventures of Oliver Twist, or the Parish Boy's Progress*; this 'adventure' or 'progress' was to be formally contracted as one of the two novels earlier promised to Bentley (the other was the long-projected and still to be much delayed *Gabriel Vardon, Locksmith of London*, now titled *Barnaby Rudge*).

Although the first numbers of 'Oliver Twist' were reviewed as if they were essays or pamphlets attacking Benthamite social philosophy and the New Poor Law, Dickens's contract with Bentley is an indication that *Oliver Twist* was the first of his fictions that he thought of, during the course of its composition, as a novel, or a sort of novel (at this stage Dickens still thought of the novel as something that appeared entire and in volume form rather than in 'portions' (*DL*, I: 504). What kind of novel is *Oliver Twist*? Some of its first readers might have read it as a fictionalized version of the real-life orphan tales which were popular at the time. As the story progressed, introducing its hero into London's criminal low-life, readers' expectations were likely to have been shaped by the so-called Newgate novels (based on the lives of criminals whose exploits were recorded in the *Newgate Calendar*), a form of fiction which was sensationally popular and extremely controversial in the 1830s. This Newgate vogue was given a new lease of life by the success of Harrison Ainsworth's *Jack Sheppard*, which was also serialized in *Bentley's Miscellany* between January 1839 and February 1840 with illustrations by George Cruickshank, the illustrator of *Oliver Twist*. In his 1841 Preface to the third edition of *Oliver Twist*, Dickens was at pains to dissociate his novel from romanticized versions of 'seductive' thieves, 'fault-less in dress ... fortunate in gallantry, great at a song, a bottle, a pack of cards ... and fit companions for the bravest'. His own concern, he asserted, was with 'unattractive and repulsive truth' (*OT*, liv).

Interestingly, Dickens's authorial insistence on the truth of his fiction is directly linked to his portrayal of the prostitute Nancy, who is Oliver's betrayer as well as his protector, and whose fictional fate is to be murdered for playing the woman's part in taking on this protective role. 'It is useless to discuss whether the conduct and character of the girl seems natural or unnatural, prob-able or improbable, right or wrong', Dickens wrote in his 1841 Preface, 'IT IS TRUE. Every man who has watched these melan-choly shades of life, knows it to be so' (*OT*, lvii). Dickens made this declaration in the highly wrought concluding paragraph of his Preface, in which he located the truth of his novel in the truth of Nancy, and the truth of Nancy in the truth of his own experience; a truth which he claims to have 'tracked ... through many profligate and noisome ways' long before he 'dealt in fiction' (*OT*, lvii). This proud, abused, fallen and criminal woman, who is at the heart of Dickens's first Victorian novel, remains at the centre of his art. She was to reappear in different guises in later novels, most notably in Alice Brown and Edith Dombey in *Dombey and Son*. Nancy was also resurrected with almost hysterical fervour in Dickens's public readings in the last two decades of his life.

It might be argued that a preoccupation with rogues and prosti-tutes, crime and the law is an integral part of the history of the English novel; it was certainly integral to the eighteenth-century novel, especially as practised by Dickens's favourites Defoe,

Fielding and Smollett, whose influence is clearly evident in *Oliver Twist*. Moreover, as in so many eighteenth-century novels, Oliver's progress through a series of adventures is also a journey back to origins, for Oliver does not so much make his way in the world as find his true place in it by discovering the secret of his birth. In addition, with its Bad Fairies (Fagin) and Good Fairies (Brownlow, Rose Maylie), its demons and saints, its corrupting tempters and saviours, *Oliver Twist* also adapts fairy-tale and folk-tale models. The Parish Boy's Progress through the City of Destruction towards the Celestial City (in this particular case a rural retreat) is also a secular version of Bunyan's *Pilgrim's Progress*.

If *Oliver Twist* is the work in which Dickens took a decisive step in the process of transforming himself into a professional novelist, what kind of novelist was he becoming? I want to address this question by looking at five interrelated aspects of Dickens's narrative: its representation of childhood, the city, criminality and confinement, and, implicit in all of these, the way it functions as social critique. If, as Peter Ackroyd points out, *Oliver Twist* is 'the first novel in the English language which takes a child as its central character or hero' (Ackroyd, 229), it is by no means the last of Dickens's novels to do this. Oliver is the first of a long line of actually or functionally orphaned and isolated child protagonists who people Dickens's novels. He is also the first in a succession of Dickensian innocents abroad in a wicked world. This wise child is the first of a series of meek children who, if they do not inherit the earth (as Oliver does), they do at least become the touchstone of a world that has been lost through individual and institutional self-interest, cupidity, blindness and rigidity: what Thomas Carlyle described in 'Signs of the Times' (1829) as a preoccupation with machinery. *Oliver Twist* is emphatically not a *Bildungsroman*, or novel of development, in which the hero progresses from an ignorant or innocent childhood to a maturity which consists of an experienced accommodation to the world. Oliver's progress is from an anonymous (or pseudonymous), unsettled, uncared for and innocent childhood, to a settled and secure but still innocent childhood. Oliver is haunted by his experiences, rather than shaped by them. His history is a nightmare from which Dickens's narrative permits him to awake.

In some respects Oliver prompts the question David Copperfield was later to ask about whether or not he would turn out to be the hero of his own story. Despite his shocking act of insubordination and revolt in asking for more, Oliver is less an active agent than a passive sufferer. His function is to suffer the harsh treatment that society, in the form of the Parish and the New Poor Law, metes out to its unfortunates, and thus to expose the institutionalization of man's inhumanity to man, and to act as a focus for the reader's horror and pity. Oliver is also used as a defamiliarizing device. By describing the child's innocent perspective on and response to the scenes and situations he encounters, the narrator makes the familiar strange and the strange familiar, thus destabilizing the reader's easy and habitual acceptance of the way things are.

The child Oliver is particularly important to this novel's representation of the city: in charting Oliver's arrivals in and departures from London, and his traversing of its steets as hunter or hunted, the narrator develops a particular way of writing about the city and the sense of being-in-the-city. It is a social cartography, which maps the city as a series of class-differentiated zones, charting its relationships with and to the suburbs and the country, the safe havens of the respectable classes, which are, nonetheless, threatened with invasion from the city. It also maps (and sometimes conveys something of the unmappability of) the city as psychic space: huge, labyrinthine, full of crowds. In part *Oliver Twist* returns to the mode and matter of the *Sketches*, and middle-class readers are made to dwell on a detailed representation of streets along which they would be unlikely to walk, or through which they would probably rush with eyes averted. Thus Oliver's arrival in London is described very much in the manner of 'Seven Dials'; the narrator conveys the confusion of Oliver's impressions but he (and hence the reader) sees more than Oliver does, and conveys the meanings and significance of what he sees in metaphors of pestilence and commerce (or a pestilential commerce):

> Although Oliver had enough to occupy his attention in keeping sight of his leader [the Artful Dodger], he could not help bestowing a few hasty glances on either side of the way, as he passed along. A dirtier or more wretched place he had never seen. The street was very narrow and muddy; and the air was impregnated with filthy odours. There were a good many small shops, but the only stock in trade appeared to be heaps of children, who, even at that time of night, were crawling in and out at the doors, or screaming from the inside. The sole places that seemed to prosper amid the general blight of the place, were the public-houses; and in them, the lowest

orders of Irish were wrangling with might and main. Covered ways and yards, which here and there diverged from the main street, disclosed little knots of houses, where drunken men and women were wallowing in the filth.   (8: 59–60).

In other passages Dickens uses Oliver as the means of registering what Georg Simmel was later to describe as the mental life of the metropolis. One of the most striking examples is Chapter 21, which narrates Oliver's perplexed amazement at the confusion of sights, sounds, smells and even the muddy textures of the crowded streets as he crosses London on his enforced 'expedition', with Sikes out to Shepperton. When they reach Smithfield Market:

Countrymen, butchers, drovers, hawkers, boys, thieves, idlers and vagabonds of every low grade, were mingled together in a dense mass; the whistling of drovers, the barking of dogs, the bellowing and plunging of oxen ... the cries of hawkers, the shouts, oaths, and quarrelling on all sides; the ringing of bells and roar of voices, that issued from every public-house; the crowding, pushing, driving, beating, whooping and yelling; the hideous and discordant din that resounded from every corner ... and the unwashed, unshaven, squalid, and dirty figures constantly running to and fro ... rendered it a stunning and bewildering scene which quite confounded the senses.   (21: 164)

As in the *Sketches,* the city is presented as a spectacle. It has an immense vitality, but its energy is 'hideous' and 'discordant'. As experienced by Oliver the city is a maze, an 'infernal labyrinth',[19] at the centre of which are Fagin and his criminal associates.

From the earliest reviews onwards the critical response to *Oliver Twist* has been much preoccupied with Dickens's representation of Fagin and the criminal fraternity. Rather like the Newgate novelists, some recent critics have tended to romanticize Fagin and his gang by seeing the criminal underworld as both the products of, and a more vital and communal alternative to, what David Musslewhite described as the 'vapid', individualistic world of respectable bourgeois society. Such critics place great emphasis on the novel's depiction of the feasting, the games and the punning, slangy jollity of life in Fagin's kitchen. In rejecting Fagin's world, it is argued, both Oliver and Dickens are rejecting the communal vitality of the group. The threat which Fagin's gang presents to Oliver, Musslewhite suggests, 'is not just that he might become a criminal but that he might become a member of a *group*' and that in some ways 'the burden of *Oliver Twist* is to suggest that Fagin, the Dodger, Charley Bates and the rest are not simply bound into a group by their shared criminality but that because they are a group they are to be criminalized'.[20] There is quite a lot to be said for such an argument, but in the end it is an oversimplification of Dickens's representation of crime and criminality in this novel. Fagin's gang is not simply a vital subculture, a carnivalized, communal antithesis to bourgeois individualism, but rather it is a fragile, antisocial collectivity held together by anxiety, fear and mutual suspicion.

The critical romanticization of Fagin and his band also underestimates the extent to which the novel self-consciously investigates the processes by which individuals and groups become criminalized. Despite Dickens's refusal of the Newgate label that some contemporary critics sought to attach to *Oliver Twist*, this novel does follow the Newgate model in suggesting that social conditions create crime, or as Bulwer Lytton put it in his own Newgate novel, *Paul Clifford*, 'Circumstances make Guilt'. Oliver's experiences are designed to demonstrate how the law (and especially the New Poor Law) and a classbound judiciary on the one hand, and hunger, need and social exclusion on the other, conspire to create criminals. They are also designed to elicit the readers' sympathies for the criminalized child, and to provoke their outrage at his 'criminal' mistreatment at the hands of the state. To be sure, the novel fudges the issue of the social determinations of crime, and of the processes of social determinism more generally. As numerous critics have pointed out, it is difficult to explain in social terms how a Parish Boy, born and brought up in the workhouse, brutalized by Noah Claypole during his apprenticeship to Sowerberry the undertaker, and cast among thieves in the rookeries of London, could retain preternatural goodness and such perfectly formed, grammatically correct speech.

There are several ways of accounting for Oliver's moral and linguistic purity. I will look at four interrelated explanations. The first is generic. Like so many English novels of the eighteenth and nineteenth centuries, *Oliver Twist* is a romance about an orphan of mysterious parentage. The secret of Oliver's birth is that he is, if not a nobleman, at least of superior social stock on his father's side, and superior moral stock on his mother's; like Fielding's Tom Jones and Joseph Andrews, he is one of nature's gentlemen. The second is psychoanalytic: it is easy to see why this particular romance of origins might appeal to an author who, according to the myth of selfhood which he constructed for himself and his public in the Autobiographical Fragment, was cast out of the social class into which he was born and forced to fend for himself in his own version of Fagin's kitchen – Warren's Blacking Factory. The third is theological: Dickens's Christianity provided him with ideas of innocence and Grace which would have enabled him to see Oliver's enduring purity as a realizable ideal, rather than the fantasy which it seems to be to so many (perhaps most) modern readers. The fourth way of reading Dickens's representation of Oliver is to see it as a failure of nerve or imagination, or a form of bad faith, which is closely and complexly connected to Dickens's liminal class position as the son of an insecurely lower middle-class father, and as an upwardly mobile young man who was in the process of making himself as a professional writer. While writing *Oliver Twist* Dickens was consolidating his own class position and establishing his own agency as a husband, a father, a breadwinner, and a professional writer, but, Richard Dellamora argues, 'he had no way at hand of turning "the orphan of a workhouse" into a man who could convert purity into respectability while continuing to represent the classes among whom he had been born'.[21]

The final aspect of the novel that I want to examine is its treatment of confinement. Dickens's first novel (as opposed to a collection of sketches) is suffused with a sense of claustrophobia and with images of imprisonment and confinement. It begins with the literal and metaphorical confinement of Oliver's mother, who is incarcerated in the workhouse for her confinement (in the sense of giving birth) of her child. Oliver is thus born into a world of confinement, and, I would suggest, he is never out of it. In part, the novel's use of metaphors of confinement is an effect of its Romantic treatment of the child. Oliver is the Wordsworthian child of nature around whom the shades of the prison-house of society close. He is also the Blakean innocent, constrained by the 'mind-forg'd manacles' of early nineteenth-century philosophical and theological systems and social institutions. But Dickens's preoccupation with confinement in this novel goes further than the use of a Romantic metaphor. It is the beginning of his habitual fictional representation of what a number of critics, following Michel Foucault in *Discipline and Punish*, describe as the carceral.

Oliver's early training could serve as a text-book example of the regime of discipline and punishment which Foucault saw as instrumental in the construction of post-Enlightenment subjectivity. Throughout the novel Oliver is mentally and physically confined: first in the workhouse where his body is disciplined through its severe dietary regime, and where his questioning of that regime is met with confinement in a coal cellar (2: 5) and a 'dark and solitary room' (3: 15). Subsequently, apprenticeship to Sowerberry also involves confinement in the coal cellar (4: 30) and being made to sleep surrounded by coffins in a confined space 'that looked like a grave' (5: 32). After making his escape to London he is repeatedly confined in crumbling, labyrinthine buildings and in airless, windowless rooms by Fagin and Sikes. Even when he is under the protection of Brownlow, Oliver is confined in darkened rooms and fed a light diet. Indeed, it might be argued that Oliver's 'progress' simply involves the exchange of one kind of confinement for another, albeit in a more benign and domestic form. In this sense the novel itself functions, in Foucauldian terms, as a technology of discipline. It is an example of what Nancy Armstrong describes as 'a display of social redemption through the domestication of desire'. After dismantling the criminal sub-culture and expelling it from the world of the novel, Dickens incarcerates Oliver in a bachelor household, presided over (from a slight distance) by a married Rose Maylie 'who is neither mother, nor sister, nor lover, but who has displaced all of these roles'.[22]

IV 'Detachable sketches and artificial *bits*': *Nicholas Nickleby*

[I]n our new work, as in our preceding one, it will be our aim to amuse, by producing a rapid succession of characters and incidents, and describing them as cheerfully and pleasantly as in us lies.
(Boz's 'Proclamation' on *Nicholas Nickleby*, 28 February 1838, *NN*, 780)

[T]he periodical essayist commits to his readers the feelings of the day, in the language which those feelings have prompted. As he has delivered himself with the freedom of intimacy and the cordiality of friendship, he will naturally look for the indulgence which those relations may claim.

(Henry Mackenzie, *The Lounger*, no. 101, 6 January 1787,
quoted in Dickens's Preface to the 1839 edition of *Nicholas
Nickleby, NN,* 3)

Dickens began work on another narrative containing a 'rapid succession of characters and incidents' half-way through the serial
publication of *Oliver Twist,* and at the end of March 1838
Chapman and Hall published the first of the twenty monthly parts
of *The Life and Adventures of Nicholas Nickleby, Containing a
Faithful Account of the Fortunes, Misfortunes, Uprisings,
Downfallings and Complete Career of the Nickleby Family, edited
by 'Boz'.* The prefatory material accompanying the early editions of
this narrative tell a story about Dickens's self-fashioning as a professional author. The first edition of *The Pickwick Papers* had been
dedicated to Serjeant Talfourd for his work in the cause of authors'
copyright. The monthly publication of *Nicholas Nickleby* was pre-
faced by a proclamation on the authorial rights of Boz, in an (un-
successful) attempt to claim ownership and forestall imitations and
dramatizations. By the time of *Nickleby*'s publication in volume
form, the title page announced its author as Charles Dickens.
Boz/Dickens was in the process of constructing himself as an
author, but one who described himself not as a novelist, but rather
as 'the periodical essayist, the Author of these pages', *NN,* 5).

In *Nicholas Nickleby* Dickens cemented his contemporary popu-
larity and reputation by repeating what had rapidly become a
winning formula with readers: a picaresque narrative in which a
central character encounters a range of comic and grotesque types
in town and country settings; some London 'sketches'; a cocktail
of pathos and melodrama, comic parody and general social satire;
and a sharp attack on specific social evils of the day. In the case of
Nicholas Nickleby the main targets of Dickens's satiric focus were
the Yorkshire Schools, and the culture of speculation – in particular in the episode of the United Metropolitan Improved Hot
Muffin and Crumpet Baking and Punctual Delivering Company.
As usual, reviews of the work during the course of its part publication often appeared under the 'magazine' section, and consisted
mainly of the reproduction of lengthy extracts from the work
under review. Thus the *Mirror* reproduced two extracts to which it
gave the titles 'London Lodgings' and 'A Party in Lodgings',
announcing that its 'plan is to detach sketches and artificial *bits,*
with which Mr. Dickens's writing generally abounds' (21 July

1838, p. 60). Many subsequent readers and critics have been all too ready to agree that *Nicholas Nickleby* consists of detachable sketches and 'artificial bits', and that this bittiness makes it one of Dickens's least successful novels. But is it really any less coherent than *Pickwick* or *Oliver Twist*? Or are charges of lack of coherence a consequence of reading *Nicholas Nickleby* through a perception of Dickens as the kind of novelist he was to become in the mid-1840s, rather than as the creator of narrative entertainments that he was in 1838?

One source of the novel's disparate energies and its potential for incoherence is its theatricality. It is, in part, a novel about the professional theatre, but more importantly, it is also a profoundly theatrical novel. None of Dickens's other novels, J. Hillis Miller argues, 'is closer in plot, characterization, and constantly asserted moral, to the conventions of the decadent drama and the popular novel of Dickens's day'.[23] Like the popular theatre of the early nineteenth century, *Nicholas Nickleby* mixes styles, modes and genres, and has little regard for unity of design. Like many of Dickens's later novels, *Nickleby* is about performance: the performance of class, gender, familial and emotional roles. However, in this novel performance and role-playing are not only very near the surface, they are particularly self-conscious. The characters in *Nicholas Nickleby* form their identity or become themselves by impersonating real or imaginary models of those they wish to be, engaging in a form of novelistic self-construction: Mr and Mrs Squeers egregiously impersonate middle-class virtue, their daughter constantly rehearses the role of the heroine of a sentimental romance, and the Mantalinis (formerly known as Muntle) borrow their roles from the novel of fashionable high life, as does Mortimer Knag, the brother of their assistant:

> a wonderfully accomplished man reads every novel that comes out; I mean every novel that – hem – that has any fashion in it, of course. The fact is, that he did find so much in the books he read applicable to his own misfortunes, and did find himself in every respect so much like the heroes – because of course he is conscious of his own superiority, as we all are, and very naturally – that he took to scorning everything, and became a genius; and I am quite sure that he is at this very present moment writing another book.   (18: 220)

As Steven Marcus has pointed out, almost everyone in the novel is 'consciously engaged in appropriating certain manners of behaviour', and 'engaged in a perpetual activity of self-creation through imitation, emulation or acting'.[24] All of this is mediated through the ironic gaze of 'Boz', who makes fun of the performers and their performance, and at the same time parodies the dramatic and literary sources for their role(s).

Indeed, the whole narrative of *Nicholas Nickleby* is a kind of parody in the way that it rewrites the eighteenth-century picaresque novel, and it is perhaps more closely modelled on this earlier fictional form than any other of Dickens's fictions. Nicholas, its eponymous hero, a young man reduced to poverty by the speculations of his father and 'cast upon a rough world and the mercy of strangers' (58: 711), like Smollett's Roderick Random, might have 'laid claim to the character of a gentleman by birth, education and behaviour; and yet (so unlucky had the circumstances of my life fallen out) I should find it a very hard matter to make good my pretensions even to these'.[25] Nicholas's adventures, however, are considerably less colourful and sexy than Roderick's, and his fate is significantly different. Roderick's brawling and bawdy life as a ship's surgeon turns out to have been a prelude to his being reunited with his father (now a wealthy merchant), and married to a Lady. Nicholas's attempt to run away to sea, on the other hand, ends in his becoming part of a theatrical company in which he is employed as a writer, before moving on to learn how to become a benevolent businessman with the Cheeryble brothers. When Nicholas is united with his heiress (Madeline Bray), he invests her fortune in the Cheeryble firm, and in due course becomes 'a rich and prosperous merchant' (65: 775), the self-made man who buys the family home that his father had lost through his careless business speculations and gradually fills it with 'a group of lovely children': 'it was altered and enlarged, but none of the old rooms were ever pulled down, no old tree was rooted up, nothing with which there was any association of bygone times was ever removed or changed' (65: 777). As Robin Gilmour has pointed out, in *The Idea of the Gentleman in the Victorian Novel* (1981), there is an interesting and complex class shift in the movement from the world of *Tom Jones* and *Roderick Random* to that of *Nicholas Nickleby*. In the latter novel the idea of the hero and the gentleman has changed. These roles are no longer merely a matter of aristocratic birth, manners, marriage to a woman of aristocratic lineage, and adherence to a stylized chivalric code of honour. They are in the process of being moralized and transferred to the middle class. The son of a gentleman of very modest means, Nicholas is a gentleman by virtue of the scrupulosity and (usually) prudent generosity of his moral conduct, his conception of and behaviour towards women, and his conception of the family. Nicholas is the gentleman at the head of the bourgeois family and the family firm.

Nicholas Nickleby is a novel about the middle class, or perhaps, more accurately, about the making of the nineteenth-century middle class. It is, among other things, a novel about commerce and business, about prudence and speculation, about what it means to make one's way in the world. In other words, it is a very early novel about what have come to be known as 'Victorian Values', anticipating Samuel Smiles's doctrine of 'self-help' by some twenty years. *Nicholas Nickleby* simultaneously satirizes and valorizes middle-class pieties. It satirizes the middle-class family through its depiction of the Squeers's grotesque parody of the ideal family, and their canting hypocrisy. It satirizes the middle-class 'virtues' of work, prudence and accumulation, through its depiction of the excessive dedication to these values of Ralph Nickleby, 'the capitalist'. But it also satirizes aristocratic idleness, prodigality and profligacy in its depiction of Sir Mulberry Hawk, Sir Frederick Verisopht, and the Mantalinis. On the other hand, work, prudence and accumulation, when combined with generosity, caring for others and redistribution, are positively evaluated. If Ralph Nickleby is the unacceptable face of bourgeois capitalism, then the Cheeryble brothers and their scrupulously methodical, punctual and fiercely loyal clerk, Tim Linkinwater, are the sunny justification of its possibilities.

The Cheeryble brothers belong, in part, to the utopian world of the fairy or folk tale, and hence have presented problems to readers whose conceptions of fiction have been developed in relation to the realist novel. As if by magic, when Nicholas is scanning the window of the Register Office in search of employment opportunities, Brother Charles appears at his elbow:

> with such a pleasant smile playing about his mouth, and such a comical expression of mingled slyness, simplicity, kind-heartedness, and good-humour, lighting up his jolly old face, that Nicholas would have been content to have stood there and looked at him until evening, and to have forgotten meanwhile that there was such a thing as a soured mind or a crabbed countenance to be met with in the whole wide world. (35: 428)

Critics of this novel commonly dismiss the Cheeryble brothers as sentimental exemplars of Dickensian twinkle-eyed benevolence (the Pickwickian precursor of the Christmas spirit), who jointly perform the role of Fairy Godfather to Nicholas. Certainly they do perform this role, and not only in relation to Nicholas's story. Like every other performance in this novel of performances, the Fairy Godfather role is precisely that: a role, a performance, an act. The Cheeryble brothers masquerade as magicians, who relieve distress, find people employment, or furnish their houses with a wave of their wand, without appearing to be involved in these matters at all. However, the power of the wand depends on the human agency which has built up their business, and the social and moral choices that they make in dispersing its profits. Moreover, as with virtually all the roles performed in this novel, the fairy godfather role as performed by the Cheerybles has an element of the grotesque. Cheeryble philanthropy (like the 'tele-scopic philanthropy' which Dickens was later to castigate in *Bleak House*) subsists on the misfortunes of others. There is something macabre in the relish with which Charles Cheeryble savours Nicholas's situation – '"Bad thing for a young man to lose his father. Widowed mother, perhaps? Brothers and sisters too – eh?"'; something macabre, too, in the way he metaphorically rubs his hands at the latest case brought to their attention by Trimmer (a sort of disaster hunter): '"Smashed by a cask of sugar, and six poor children – oh dear, dear, dear!"' (35: 429–30). The Cheerybles also derive from another folk tale, one that Dickens rewrote in various forms throughout his career: they are Dick Whittingtons who never forget that they came barefoot to the 'wilderness' of London, before succeeding in business. London, the city of damnation in *Oliver Twist*, is thus transformed into a city of entrepreneurial opportunity in which the poor are not inevitably consigned to the slums but can make their way in the world.

In this novel of family businesses – the Squeers's school, the Crummles's theatrical troupe, the Mantalinis' millinery business – the Cheerybles run their business like a family, even like a home. Their counting-house is described in positively domestic terms as 'a sufficiently desirable nook' (37: 445), in which everything is snug and orderly, and both Tim Linkinwater and his employers live on the premises. Is this a merely nostalgic representation of a world in which industry and commerce existed alongside the domestic and familial space, a world which was rapidly disappearing by the late 1830s?[26] Or is it, on the other hand, a form of representation which is attempting self-consciously to resist the separation of the domestic from the commercial, the private from the public? Perhaps it is both. There is something motherly as well as fatherly about the Cheeryble brothers, and their feminized, domesticated world of commerce is more productive and fertile, in this narrative, than is the arid, masculine, depersonalized world of Ralph Nickleby, which damages or destroys both his own unacknowledged child and the families of others.

The Cheerybles, however, are only part of the story of humanely successful commerce. Nicholas's story takes him in a different direction, away from London. When he has become 'a rich and prosperous merchant' he renovates his father's house in Devonshire, where he brings up his numerous family in close proximity to his sister Kate and her husband, the Cheerybles' nephew, Frank. London is a place to which both families repair only 'when the cares of business oblige [them] to reside there' (65: 777). The movement from the firm of Cheeryble Brothers to 'Cheeryble and Nickleby' is another chapter in the process of the domestication of culture described by Nancy Armstrong, in which the household is detached from politics and commerce to become their 'complement and antidote, the "counter-image" of the modern marketplace'. Armstrong sees this as the creation of 'an apolitical realm of culture within the culture as a whole'.[27] While the account of the ending of the novel that I have just given might seem to support Armstrong's thesis, an attempt to engage with the disparate energies of this novel would complicate it. Each family among the wide range of families displayed in *Nicholas Nickleby* has its own complex internal politics and each in turn exists in a complex relation to the wider social and material world in which it is located. Moreover, if Nicolas's story ends in a family homecoming, the story of his illegitimate cousin Smike would seem to suggest both that families are the source of many of the problems that the *idea* (or ideal) of the family is meant to solve, and that some forms of social damage cannot be repaired by domesticity. The family, in the form of the Squeers family and his own rejecting father, is quite literally the death of Smike. Metaphorically, however, the death of Smike is his ultimate homecoming, and as such it is an early example (Oliver's friend from the workhouse is another) of a long line of 'child' deaths that have caused Dickens's readers to weep, laugh or sigh according to temperament.

V   A retrospective turn: *Master Humphrey's Clock*

In many ways *Nicholas Nickleby* is a generic hybrid, a palimpsest in which elements from all of Dickens's earlier works are embedded. Dickens's next project also took a retrospective turn and demonstrated a similar generic hybridity and instability. In July 1839, shortly before the appearance of the seventeenth number of *Nicholas Nickleby*, he outlined his idea for a new weekly publication, which was to consist 'entirely of original matter'. It was to be modelled on the eighteenth-century periodicals, *The Tatler, The Spectator,* and Oliver Goldsmith's *Bee,* but would be 'far more popular both in the subjects of which it treats and its mode of treating them' (*Life,* I: 113). The projected new weekly would draw on other eighteenth-century publications, notably Swift's *Gulliver's Travels* and *The Citizen of the World,* which would be the models for 'a series of satirical papers purporting to be translated from some Savage Chronicles, and to describe the administration of justice in some country that never existed', so as to 'keep a special lookout upon the magistrates in town and country, and never leave those worthies alone' (*Life,* I: 113). The new periodical, whose working title was *Old Humphrey's Clock,* or *Master Humphrey's Clock,* would also look back to the earlier sketches, replacing 'Boz' with 'Gog and Magog', whose 'Relaxations' were to consist of a series of papers 'containing stories and descriptions of London as it was many years ago, as it is now, and as it will be many years hence' (*Life,* I: 113). It was also designed to look back to Dickens's earlier success *The Pickwick Papers,* as he indicated to his friend John Forster:

> I should propose to start, as *The Spectator* does, with some pleasant fiction relative to the origin of the publication; to introduce a little club or knot of characters and to carry their personal histories and proceedings through the work; to introduce fresh characters constantly; to reintroduce Mr. Pickwick and Sam Weller, the latter of whom might furnish an occasional communication with great effect; to write amusing essays on the various foibles of the day as they arise; to take advantage of all passing events; and to vary the form of the papers by throwing them into sketches, essays, tales, adven-

tures, letters from imaginary correspondents and so forth, so as to diversify the contents as much as possible.   (*Life*, I: 112–13)

Although the first number of the new weekly sold some 60,000 copies when it appeared on 4 April 1840, *Master Humphrey's Clock* was one of Dickens's few failures with both reviewers and readers. One reason for this failure was that the project was based on an idea whose time had passed; to borrow a phrase of Elizabeth Barrett Browning, the world was becoming 'too old and fond of steam' for a return to the eighteenth-century periodical.[28] Just how well Dickens learned that lesson became evident in the 1850s when he went on to occupy a commanding position in the new middle-class magazine culture with *Household Words*. Secondly, the project as initially conceived failed to satisfy the demand, which Dickens had himself created, for continuous narrative. Sales of the periodical fell off considerably when readers realized that it contained no serial novel. They revived quite spectacularly only when Dickens began to develop Master Humphrey's story of his night-time meeting with Nell and his visit to the old curiosity shop from what was planned as a short sketch into a serial narrative which filled the whole of each issue of *Master Humphrey's Clock*. After the third chapter of what was to become *The Old Curiosity Shop* (in the eighth number of the *Clock*), Master Humphrey, the erstwhile narrator of Nell's story, disappeared from view until the concluding stages of the narrative, when he reappeared briefly to reveal himself as Nell's great uncle, the Single Gentleman, and to introduce *Barnaby Rudge*, which succeeded *The Old Curiosity Shop* as the single item of each weekly issue. When *Barnaby Rudge* reached the end of its run *Master Humphrey's Clock* ceased publication.

Dickens announced the imminent demise of his weekly periodical in an address to the readers of *Master Humphrey's Clock* in September 1841. This address is worth quoting at length, since it is not usually reproduced in modern editions and it gives an interesting perspective on both Dickens's relationship with his readers, and his thoughts, at the beginning of the 1840s, on the limitations of writing for weekly publication:

> DEAR FRIENDS,
>   NEXT November, we shall have finished the Tale [*Barnaby Rudge*], on which we are at present engaged; and we shall have travelled together through Twenty Monthly Parts and Eighty-seven

Weekly Numbers. It is my design, when we have gone so far, to close this work. Let me tell you why.

I should not regard the anxiety, the close confinement, or the constant attention, inseparable from the weekly form of publication (for to commune with you in any form, is to me a labour of love), if I had found it advantageous to the conduct of my stories, the elucidation of my meaning, or the gradual development of my characters. But I have not done so. I have often felt cramped and confined ... by the space in which I have been constrained to move. I have wanted you to know more at once than I could tell you. I have sometimes been tempted ... to hurry incidents on, lest they should appear to you who waited from week to week, and had not, like me, the result and purpose in your minds, too long delayed. In a word, I have found this form of publication most anxious, perplexing, and difficult ...

Many passages in a tale of any length, depend materially for their interest on the intimate relation they bear to what has gone before, or to what is to follow. I sometimes found it difficult [with weekly publication] ... to sustain in your mind this needful connection.[29]

Notwithstanding 'considerations of immediate profit', Dickens resolved to return to monthly publication as 'a better means of communication between us'.

VI Walks on the wild side: *The Old Curiosity Shop*

> Night is generally my time for walking ...
> I have fallen insensibly into this habit ... because it affords me greater opportunity of speculating on the characters and occupations of those who fill the streets.
>
> *The Old Curiosity Shop*, 1: 3

During its run in *Master Humphrey's Clock*, the weekly parts of *The Old Curiosity Shop* were more successful than any of Dickens's previous serials, with over 100,000 sales for each issue. As well as expanding Dickens's British readership, *The Old Curiosity Shop* also extended his international readership. The novel's success with American readers was one of the reasons for Dickens's first visit to the USA in 1842. Although there were some negative reviews in Britain, more positively inclined reviewers compared Dickens's work with that of Homer, Spenser, and Shakespeare. However, by the time of Dickens's death in 1870 tastes had changed, and *The Old Curiosity Shop* was consigned to the lower ranks of Dickens's work on account of its excessive pathos and sentimentality – a ranking which persisted well into the twentieth century. Of all Dickens's novels, Steven Marcus noted in 1965, 'The Old Curiosity Shop is least likely to be read with sympathy today. The modern reader is inclined to believe that in this novel Dickens is most cruelly dated. Its very intensities – of sentiment, of the desire for moral and sexual purity, of the public indulgence of private sorrow – are those least suited to command the attention of the modern literary mind.'[30] Subsequent historical reassessments of nineteenth-century sentiment, the melodramatic imagination and the grotesque, as well as various psychoanalytic and political readings of the social and sexual energies and the death impulses in this novel, have provided new contexts in which to read it, stripped away some of its critical baggage, and made it available in new ways to turn-of-the-millennium readers.

The relatively lowly critical status of The Old Curiosity Shop for much of the twentieth century is partly due to the fact that it is a difficult novel to categorize and pin down. This is partly a matter of its origins in a periodical miscellany as outlined above. As Dickens developed the narrative, which gradually engrossed all of the pages of Master Humphrey's Clock, he incorporated into it the kind of material that he had intended to include in the weekly miscellany. The Old Curiosity Shop thus became 'a miscellany within a miscellany' (Brennan, World's Classics, xii), and was, according to some critics, even 'more of a muddle' than Nicholas Nickleby.[31] At least one recent critic, however, has sought to demonstrate that, if The Old Curiosity Shop is a muddle, that muddle is symptomatic of a broader social and cultural muddle. Sue Zemka has argued that there is a certain aesthetic and thematic coherence in the way in which four of the novel's 'seemingly disconnected motifs' – the Punch and Judy Show, the travelling waxworks, Gothicism and gambling – focus on various class issues: 'class position, class mobility, and the class status of various cultural practices'. These interlinked motifs and preoccupations, Zemka suggests, provide 'a tight symbolic organization that underlies the disorder of the plot'. At the same time, however, the tensions or discrepancy between the novel's symbolic and narrative economy are symptomatic of 'contradictions inherent in the ideological interleaving of Protestantism and capitalism in early Victorian England'.[32]

One of the challenges or difficulties that The Old Curiosity Shop poses for modern readers is its hybridity and polarization. It is a novel of sharp contrasts, and contrast is intrinsic to its moral scheme and affective method. It is also a novel which eclectically combines contrasting modes, genres and registers. It combines or moves between: melodrama (with its excesses of sentiment and sharp moral polarization); tragedy; comedy; allegory; pastoral; urban realism; folk or fairy tale (Nell as Beauty to Quilp's Beast, or Quilp as the Yellow Dwarf); pathos, and the grotesque. References to and parallels with high culture jostle with those from popular culture. There are frequent allusions to Shakespeare, most notably, for some critics, in the similarities between Quilp and Richard III, and between the deaths of Nell and King Lear's faithful and mistreated daughter Cordelia. The whole narrative is an allusion to Bunyan's *Pilgrim's Progress*, a book 'over which [Nell] had pored whole evenings, wondering whether it was true in every word, and where those distant countries with the curious names might be' (15: 121): Nell is the pilgrim who leaves the City of Destruction and travels through the Slough of Despond and other Bunyanesque locations until she reaches the country of Beulah and ultimately the Celestial City. There are equally numerous references to popular entertainment in the form of Dick Swiveller's songs (which combine Shakespearean allusions with popular tradition), and the representation of the various entertainers and show people encountered by Nell on her travels – most notably Mrs Jarley with her waxworks and Codlin and Short the Punch and Judy men.

For many readers the most problematic aspect of *The Old Curiosity Shop* is its representation of its child-heroine as a figure of pathos, a victim, an innocent, a figure of unalloyed purity, whose 'progress', like that of Oliver Twist, represents a 'Principle of Good surviving through every adverse circumstance',[33] but whose unearthly goodness is unable to survive in this earthly vale of sin and tears. As my reference to *Oliver Twist* indicates, Nell is a common enough Dickensian type; the wise child who is its own parent, and who acts in a parental role to its inadequate actual parent or parent-substitute (in this case Nell fulfils this role in relation to her grandfather who is addicted to gambling). As Deirdre David points out, one of the most pervasive figures in Dickens's early fiction fuses the 'literary tropes of the pilgrimage and the picaresque' in the image of 'the child trudging along the road to his or her destiny'.[34] Whereas Oliver's or David Copperfield's function in this pattern is to survive and find a place in society through the discovery of family and a vocation or profession,

Nell's is to die a pathetic and lingering death after helping others to find family, vocation or profession. Such self-sacrificial goodness has proved an irritant to later readers. Swinburne dismissed Nell as 'a monster as inhuman as a baby with two heads', and, in one of the most quoted put-downs in the history of criticism, Oscar Wilde announced that one would need a heart of stone to read the death of little Nell without laughing.[35] In the latter half of the twentieth century some critics sought to understand rather than mock Nell's life and death by situating it in various historical, socio-economic, cultural and biographical contexts. The most obvious context for Nell is biographical: Nell is yet another lament for the lost childhood and betrayal by the adult world which Dickens experienced when he was put to work in Warren's Blacking Factory. She is also Dickens's idealization of his seventeen-year-old sister-in-law Mary Hogarth, who died while he was working on *Oliver Twist* and *Nicholas Nickleby*. Several critics and biographers have explored Dickens's representation of Nell's life and death as the author's way of coming to terms with or displacing his sexual feelings for his young sister-in-law, his guilt about those feelings and his grief at her death. The pathos or sentimentality of Nell's representation also has a cultural history as well as a personal one. It belongs to an historically specific form of sensibility, dating from the eighteenth century, whose transformation Philip Collins traced in *From Manly Tear to Stiff Upper Lip: The Victorians and Pathos* (1974). Nell's pathos also belongs to the English Romantic tradition of childhood. Like Wordsworth's Lucy, Nell dwells among the untrodden ways, and when she is in her grave Dickens's reader, like the lyric voice of Wordsworth's poem, is meant to feel 'the difference to me'. More interestingly, perhaps, Nell's pathos may also be linked to the pathos and social meaning of some of Wordsworth's solitary figures. Like the Old Cumberland Beggar, the mendicant Nell becomes a focus for Christian sentiment in the reader and for charitable feelings and actions in the text, and a test case for contemporary conceptions of society and community.[36]

Nell's retreat from London and her mendicant wanderings in the countryside can be read as figuring a retreat from the cash nexus of capitalism,[37] and Nell can be seen as an instrument of social critique. London is a prison, a place of financial corruption and sexual danger, from which Nell flees to the supposed safety of the countryside. Nell's natural innocence is thus pitted against the forces of culture and modernity. Nell's journey out of London with her grandfather in some ways replicates Oliver's journey to Shepperton with Bill Sikes: they pass through the various zones of the city, 'the labyrinths of men's abodes', 'the haunts of commerce', 'a straggling neighbourhood, where the mean houses parcelled off in rooms told of the populous poverty that sheltered there'. However, the description of Nell's journey is more precisely focused on the poverty and suffering of the city dwellers:

> The shops sold goods that only poverty could buy, and sellers and buyers were pinched and gripped alike. Here were poor streets where faded gentility essayed with scanty space and shipwrecked means to make its last feeble stand ...
> ... Damp rotten houses, many to let, many yet building, many half-built and mouldering away ... children scantily fed and clothed ... scolding mothers ... shabby fathers, hurrying with dispirited looks to the occupation which brought them 'daily bread' and little more – mangling-women, washerwomen, cobblers, tailors, chandlers driving their trades in parlours and kitchens and back rooms and garrets, and sometimes all under the same roof – brick-fields skirting gardens paled with staves of old casks, or timber pillaged from houses burnt down, and blackened and blistered by the flames – mounds of dock-weed, nettles, coarse grass and oyster-shells, heaped in rank confusion – small dissenting chapels to teach with no lack of illustration, the miseries of Earth, and plenty of new churches, erected with a little superfluous wealth, to show the way to Heaven. (15: 119–20)

Both Nell and the narrative make a move from the urban nightmare towards pastoral, and both moves are problematic and compromised. First, Dickens's narrative is constructed so as to demonstrate to Nell and the reader that one cannot escape the City of Destruction or the forces of capitalism simply by removing oneself from London. The world of greed, gambling and speculation which Nell had thought to leave behind is not confined to London. Moreover, the wasteland of commercial London has its nightmarish counterpart in the unreal city in the industrial Midlands, with its Frankenstein monsters, the factories and the Chartists. Again, it is worth quoting at length:

> On every side, and as far as the eye could see into the heavy distance, tall chimneys, crowding on each other, and presenting that endless repetition of the same dull, ugly, form, which is the horror of oppressive dreams, poured out their plague of smoke, obscured

the light, and made foul the melancholy air. ... [S]trange engines spun and writhed like tortured creatures; clanking their iron chains ... and making the ground tremble with their agonies. ... Men, women, children, wan in their looks and ragged in attire, tended the engines, fed their tributary fire, begged upon the road, or scowled half-naked from the doorless houses. Then came more of the wrathful monsters ... screeching and turning round and round again; and still, before, behind, and to the right and left, was the same interminable perspective of brick towers, never ceasing in their black vomit, blasting all things living or inanimate, shutting out the face of day ...

But, night-time in this dreadful spot! – night, ... when every chimney spirted up its flame; ... when the noise of every strange machine was aggravated by the darkness; when the people near them looked wilder and more savage; when bands of unemployed labourers paraded the roads, or clustered by torch-light round their leaders, who told them in stern language, of their wrongs, and urged them on to frightful cries and threats; when maddened men, armed with sword and firebrand, spurning the tears and prayers of women who would restrain them, rushed forth on errands of terror and destruction, to work no ruin as surely as their own – night, when carts came rumbling by, filled with rude coffins (for contagious disease and death had been busy with the living crops); when orphans cried ... when some called for bread, and some for drink to drown their cries ... who shall tell the terrors of the night to the young wandering child!   (45: 346–8)

These are indeed what Carlyle described as 'Signs of the Times'. The creator and narrator of this scene is both fascinated and appalled by the demonic energy of the death-in-life of the industrial Midlands, and the young wandering child whom he places in the scene is bemused and terrified. Both narrator and child retreat from the ferocious energies of the industrial town into a nostalgic rural past and the life-in-death of Nell's final resting place. The innocent child at the centre of this narrative is violated and destroyed by urban modernity, but it is a narrative in which social critique gives way to consolatory fictions. The novel's heavy investment in Nell's grace and her rebirth into life eternal gives imaginative and emotional force to the standard evangelical message that social injustice and suffering in this life will be redeemed in the hereafter. In this life, the life of the novel's narrative present, social injustice and human suffering are 'magically' ameliorated by the purging of destructive forces (such as Quilp), and the redistributive efforts of a fairy godfather (the single gentleman), who has traced

the footsteps of Nell and her grandfather and looked after everyone who had helped them on their way ('trust me, the man who
fed the furnace fire was not forgotten' (73: 570).

As well as being read as a figure in a critique of the domestic
economy and the forms of social organization which it produces
and by which it is supported, Nell has more recently been reread
in the context of an exploration of the ways in which ideas about
gender, in conjunction with ideas about race and class, were put to
work in the writing of empire in the nineteenth century. Deirdre
David, for example, has examined the way in which Dickens's representation of Nell appropriates ideas about gender in order to
negotiate 'the advantageous but also disruptive "getting and spend-
ing" made possible by Britain's burgeoning colonial wealth'. It is,
David argues, primarily through the suffering of the 'civilized/
pale/female' Little Nell at the hands of the 'savage/dark/male'
Quilp and a 'heathen' barbaric society', that 'Dickens manages
acceptance and critique of empire'.[38]

This reading offers a new way of decoding the dualism at the
heart of *The Old Curiosity Shop*: the dualism of Beauty/Beast;
angel/monster; good/evil; body/spirit; vitality/passivity. This polar-
ized duality comes from melodrama, and it is deeply ingrained in
Dickens's mode of representation in this novel – nowhere more so
than in the pairing of Nell and Quilp, who are inextricably bound
together in the novel's pattern of figuration. If Nell has been the
source of most critical carping about the novel from Dickens's
death until the mid-twentieth century, Quilp has been the source
of much critical inventiveness. Since the 1960s, Freudian critics in
particular have 'read the novel as a Quilpiad, finding an
affirmation of phallic vitality in the cigar-smoking dwarf',[39] and a
fictional release of Dickens's incestuous passion for Mary Hogarth,
which is atoned for by the exquisite death of Nell. Certainly Quilp
is a figure of fierce erotic drives and attraction. According to the
wife whom he terrorizes, the demonic, diminutive Quilp 'has such
a way with him when he likes, that the best-looking woman here
couldn't refuse him if I was dead and she was free, and he chose to
make love to her' (4: 33).

Quilp is a grotesque who has escaped from the containment of
the interpolated tales of *Pickwick Papers* or the criminal underworld of *Oliver Twist*. He is a lecherous, sado-masochistic, appeti-
tive creature, possessed by a restless, destructive energy, who, after

a night of tyrannizing over his wife (and keeping a cigar alight throughout the proceedings), breakfasts off

> hard eggs, shell and all, devoured gigantic prawns with the heads and tails on, chewed tobacco and water-cresses at the same time and with extraordinary greediness, drank boiling tea without winking, bit his fork and spoon till they bent again, and in short performed so many horrifying and uncommon acts that [his wife and mother-in-law] were nearly frightened out of their wits and began to doubt if he were really a human creature.   (5: 42)

Daniel Quilp is a subversive as well as a repulsive figure, a figure of *ressentiment*, who is, perhaps, as John Carey has suggested, 'Dickens's way of avenging himself upon the sentimental set-up of *The Old Curiosity Shop*, upon all that part of his nature that revelled in angelic, plaster heroines, the deaths of little children'.[40] Quilp is also a mythic figure, a subterranean creature, a 'primitive', referred to variously as an imp, ogre, goblin, demon, will-o'-the-wisp, savage, African chief and Chinese idol. He is a metamorphic creature, who is described as (among other things) a dog, monkey, salamander, mole, weasel, hedgehog and bluebottle. Quilp's demonic and protean energy is a positive charge which both energizes Dickens's prose and propels the narrative. Quilp is, indeed, the villain of the piece, but his restless and diabolical energy also signifies the force and energy of the docklands and the dark commercial city that lie at the heart of Dickens's London.

Quilp's savagery may also be linked to early Victorian myths about barbarism and the way in which these myths were deployed in the construction, defence and critique of empire. The representation of Quilp and of his persecution of Nell thus becomes the means by which Dickens registers his 'discomfort with empire as it was developing in early Victorian culture'.[41] Quilp and Nell are symbols of lewd and demonic evil on the one hand, and pristine purity on the other, but they are also racialized figures. Nell is by descent a 'Good Angel' of the civilized white race; Quilp, on the contrary, seems to belong to the savage dark races. He is compared to an 'African chief' seated on a piece of matting 'regaling himself with bread and cheese' and (to judge from the number of empty porter pots) large quantities of beer (13: 108). He is also described as dining off a beefsteak, 'which he cooked himself in somewhat of a savage and cannibal-like manner' (67: 19). Quilp is thus a 'symbolic cannibal, roaming the domestic spaces of early Victorian

Britain in search of human food'.[42] He is an abhorrent figure, like the Bushmen exhibited for public entertainment, whom Dickens described in his later *Household Words* piece, 'The Noble Savage' (1853), an essay which attacks the sentimentalization of the savage in Romantic myth. 'I have not the least belief in the Noble Savage', Dickens was to declare in this essay. 'I consider him a prodigious nuisance, and an enormous superstition … [He is] cruel, false, thievish, murderous; addicted more or less to grease, entrails, and beastly customs; a wild animal … [He] has no moral feelings of any kind … and his "mission" may be summed up as simply diabolical' (*DJ*, III: 143).

However, if Quilp is an ignoble savage (a Caliban) and a cannibal, and thus a representative of the colonized races, he is also a *rentier*, an entrepreneur and a usurer, and thus a representative of the colonizing race:

> He collected the rents of whole *colonies* of filthy streets and alleys by the water-side, advanced money to the seamen and petty officers of merchant vessels, had a share in the ventures of divers mates of East Indiamen, smoked his smuggled cigars under the very nose of the Custom House, and made appointments on 'Change with men in glazed hats and round jackets pretty well every day … On Quilp's Wharf, Daniel Quilp as a shipbreaker …   (4: 38, emphasis added)

Quilp thus represents not only native savagery, but also colonial rapaciousness. In the early nineteenth-century writing of empire, Deirdre David suggests, both of these are forces which can be tamed, contained or eradicated only by forfeiting female life, or by the self-sacrifice of Englishwomen.

Although David's reading offers a new way into what other critics have seen as the primitive moral duality of *The Old Curiosity Shop*, its exclusive focus on Nell and Quilp ensures that it remains locked within that dualism. One way out of the impasse of the apparently irreconcilable polar opposites of Nell and Quilp is provided by Dick Swiveller. Dickens saw Swiveller as a key character whom 'I mean to make much of' (*DL*, II: 70). In some respects Swiveller is a recycled character: he has a touch of Jingle and more than a dash of Sam Weller. However, in other ways he is a new departure, an early, comic version of Eugene Wrayburn of *Our Mutual Friend* – the no-good young man with expectations, who blames his parents for his lot in life, but is redeemed by experience, illness and the care of and for a good lower-class woman whom he rescues from her class and servitude. Swiveller begins, like so many of Dickens's characters, living in his own self-enclosed world of fantasy, but as the narrative progresses he comes to occupy the space between the moral polarities of Nell and Quilp, and his habitual patter, richly strewn with quotations from high art and popular culture, functions as a 'subversive commentary' on both of them. If Quilp represents the manic, demonic force that energizes the narrative and perhaps acts as an emblem of the force that energizes Dickens's writing, then Swiveller is a more benign figure of imaginative energy. Interestingly, Swiveller and Quilp share a common interest: the object of desire for both of them is a vulnerable young girl. However, whereas the barbaric Quilp harries Nell to death, Swiveller civilizes himself, and sends the Marchioness to school until she is 'full nineteen years of age – good-looking, clever, and good-humoured' (73: 568), and fit to be his wife. Nell and the Marchioness/Sophronia Sphynx, the self-sacrificial, desired, dead child-woman and the trained-up wife, is another dualism which was to reappear repeatedly in Dickens's fiction.

VII History through the keyhole: *Barnaby Rudge*

> Chroniclers are privileged to enter where they list, to come and go through keyholes, to ride upon the wind, to overcome, in their soarings up and down, all obstacles of distance, time and place.
> Dickens, *Barnaby Rudge*, chap. 9, p. 71

> In these real times, when all the Fairies are dead and buried ...
> Dickens, *Barnaby Rudge*, chap. 31, p. 240

Barnaby Rudge is, by almost common consent, the least read of Dickens's books. Relatively poor sales (declining from 70,000 per week at the outset of its serialization to 3000 at the close) and a lukewarm reception by its first reviewers (when it was reviewed at all), suggest that contemporary readers found it lacking in the inventiveness and spontaneity which they had already come to expect from Dickens. It has continued to pose problems for readers, and for most of the twentieth century critics tended to 'ignore it, brush it off ... refer to it as a mere pot-boiler, or excuse it as a misguided attempt to write a costume drama in the manner of Lytton or Ainsworth'.[43] Generic hybridity and an unusual narrative structure might also be included among the possible reasons for the lengthy period of critical neglect of this novel. *Barnaby Rudge* mixes fiction with fact, murder mystery with a history of the Gordon Riots, and the personal with the political. Its narrative structure is also curiously bifurcated, with a five-year interval between the two parts of the novel. However, in the last twenty years or so, *Barnaby Rudge* has been the subject of some interesting rereadings and reassessments, as critics have engaged more seriously with the genre of the historical novel and with the nature and significance of Dickens's engagement with history. An early example of this can be found in Steven Marcus's reading of the novel, which interestingly combines historical contextualization with a psychoanalytic focus on fathers and sons, and commends the intelligence with which *Barnaby Rudge* represents and investigates the connections between 'authority in political and social relations' and 'personal and social ones'.[44] Later, Michael Hollington re-examined it as a representation and exploration of 'the grotesque in history' (*Dickens and the Grotesque*, 1984), and Myron Magnet devoted more than half of his study of *Dickens and the Social Order* (1985) to an exploration of the novel's representation of the competing forces of aggression and civilization – a reading which puts Dickens very firmly on the side of a rather conservative conception of social order. A similar conclusion was reached via a very different route by Natalie McKnight in her Foucauldian study, *Idiots, Madmen, and other Prisoners in Dickens* (1993), which argues that Dickens's conservatism works to silence and contain the 'idiot' Rudge. More recently, Steven Connor has offered a more radical reading, which analyses the novel's representation of the disturbance of social space, making use of theories of the constructed nature of social space developed in anthropology and cultural studies.[45] *Barnaby Rudge* has thus increasingly come to be seen as a complicated and complex historical novel. It also has a complicated and complex history.

The period between the original conception and the publication of *Barnaby Rudge* was probably longer than for any of Dickens's other novels. Its planned mode of publication also underwent several metamorphoses. Under its original title of *Gabriel Vardon, the Locksmith of London*, it was promised to Macrone, the publisher of *Sketches by Boz*, for publication at the end of 1836 in three volumes ('unlike the low cheap form of publication' of the serially issued *Pickwick*). It is clear from his letters that Dickens intended *Gabriel Vardon* to be a serious work of literature 'on which I might build my fame' (*DL*, I: 165). In September 1837, its title now changed to *Barnaby Rudge, A Tale of the Riots of '80*, it was promised (still as a novel in volume form) to Bentley for delivery in October 1838. Owing to pressure of work on *Oliver Twist* and *Nicholas Nickleby* this plan was shelved in favour of projected monthly serialization in *Bentley's Miscellany* in 1839. This scheme was also abandoned and publication 'as a novel, and not in portions' (*DL*, I: 504) was scheduled for January 1840. By the following July the novel was offered to Chapman and Hall as containing 'matter sufficient for ten monthly numbers' (*DL*, II: 93) before it finally appeared in threepenny weekly numbers in *Master Humphrey's Clock* from 13 February to 27 November 1841. This protracted and complicated genesis is more than just a minor episode in the history of publishing, and it has more than passing biographical interest; it is a significant moment in the process of shaping the kind of novelist Dickens was to become, and hence in the shaping of the nineteenth-century English novel.

It is clear from Dickens's preface that the Gordon Riots of 1780 – hitherto unrepresented in fiction and 'presenting very extraordinary and remarkable features' (1841 Preface, *BR*, xxxiii) – were at the centre of his original conception of his novel. He thus set out to write a serious historical novel, with which he sought to emulate and challenge the achievement of Sir Walter Scott. It was undoubtedly Scott's depiction of the Porteous Riots and the storming of the Tolbooth in *The Heart of Midlothian* (1818) that provided the literary inspiration for his central riot scene, and it was Madge Wildfire and David Gellatley in Scott's *Waverley* (1814) who provided the models for Barnaby. During the five years of its gestation, however, Dickens's tale of the riots of 1780 outgrew its origins in the Scott tradition. It also established some distance between itself and the historical romances of Scott's prolific early Victorian heirs, Bulwer Lytton and Harrison Ainsworth. *Barnaby Rudge* is one of the first of those Victorian historical novels which use their setting in the recent past as a way of exploring contemporary issues and anxieties, investigating the relationship between past and present, and examining the process of history and of social change. In the end *Barnaby Rudge* perhaps owes less to Sir Walter Scott's historical novels than it does to Thomas Carlyle's *History of the French Revolution* (1837) and *Chartism* (1839). It is less a tale of the 1780s than a history of the 1830s. It is less about the 'No Popery' Gordon Riots than about the fears unleashed in the middle classes by the 'no property' riots of the 1830s: the Poor Law riots, the Chartist risings at Devizes, Birmingham and Sheffield, and the attempts to release Chartist prisoners in the Newport rising of 1839.

If *Barnaby Rudge* is an historical novel, what view of history does it offer? What kinds of relationship between the past and present does it envisage? First, it is concerned with those kinds of history that we would now describe as 'total history' and 'history from below'. It is concerned with the history and politics of personal relationships and with the connections between these histories and this politics and broader social and political movements and events. It is concerned, too, with the histories of 'ordinary' people and the ways in which they become involved or caught up in the process of History. Then there is the question of Dickens's use of real historical events. It is difficult to see how readers in 1841 could have avoided drawing comparisons between recent and current social disturbances and the Riots at the centre of Dickens's novel. Dickens surely encouraged such analogies with the rhetoric he employed to represent the riot scenes, and by the way in which he represented some of the insurgents. Sim Tappertit and his 'Prentice Knights, for example, seem (among other things) to be a parody of aspects of Chartism and Unionism. But what does it mean to use the fanatical puritanism of the 'No Popery' campaign of 1780 (and also to exaggerate its fanaticism by emphasizing Gordon's unstable mental state) as an analogue for the working-class and Chartist risings of the 1830s? Is this to distort or misrepresent history? To put it crudely, shouldn't Dickens, the 'sentimental radical', the critic of the New Poor Law and of Newgate Prison, have been on the side of those who challenged authority, rather than – as the case appears to be – demonizing them as a mob, and coming out on the side of order and authority? I want to address some of these questions by looking briefly at the ways in which this novel represents the past, and also at the ways in which it approaches the issue of change and engages both with the forces of authority and order and with challenges to them.

Interestingly, *Barnaby Rudge*, which itself turns the clock back to 1775 and 1780, repeatedly focuses on 'the absurdity of turning the clock back'.[46] It offers a series of comic, satiric, tragic, Gothic and/or grotesque portraits of people who are haunted by or in thrall to the past. The lives of two characters,

Haredale and Mrs Rudge, are distorted by a violent act in the past (the murder of Haredale's older brother by Mrs Rudge's husband). This act scars and haunts them and also leaves its mark on Barnaby, whose birth was induced by his mother's shock at discovering the identity of the murderer. Three of the novel's most unsympathetically represented characters are depicted as deludedly backward-looking. Sir John Chester's patrician worldliness and his concept of gentlemanliness – which is based on Lord Chesterfield's *Letters to His Son*, first published in 1774 – are made to seem ludicrously outmoded even in the 1780s. The Hangman Ned Dennis's nostalgia for a sterner penal regime is grotesquely so. The comic-grotesque Sim Tappertit's insurgent 'Prentice Knights are also backward-looking, espousing as they do a bogus chivalric code based on presumed ancient rights, and seeking to overthrow the present order in favour of a return to a mythic version of 'Old England', which is a carnival-esque world-turned-upside-down:

> 'prentices had, in times gone by, had frequent holidays of right, broken people's heads by scores, defied their masters, nay even achieved some glorious murders in the streets, which privileges had been gradually wrested from them ... the degrading checks imposed upon them were unquestionably attributable to the innovating spirit of the times, and they united therefore to resist all change, except such change as would restore those good old English customs. (*BR*, 8: 68)

Sim's retrospective utopianism has a distinct echo of some Chartist rhetoric. The manifesto of the Chartist Convention of 1839 asserted that the 'principles of our Charter were the laws and customs of our ancestors, under which property was secure and the working people happy and contented'.[47]

The novel opens with what, at first sight, might appear to be an idealized picture of Old England and old English customs, in the form of a lengthy description of 'a house of public entertain-ment called the Maypole', as it was 'in the year 1775' (1: 3). The Maypole is a building and an institution suffused with a spirit of the 'days of yore' and 'times gone by'. On closer inspec-tion, however, it is unclear whether 1775 is the best or the worst of times for the Maypole, one of the key locations in the novel. The Maypole is an ancient hostelry, steeped in legends of the Virgin Monarch, and it has its own invented traditions and order, all maintained and presided over by the landlord, John

Willet. This ancient building is so well established in its Epping
Forest setting that whole colonies of birds have made their nests
in its ancient fabric. There is a sense of ripeness and harmony:

> It was a hale and hearty age though, still: and in the summer or
> autumn evenings, when the glow of the setting sun fell upon the
> oak and chestnut trees of the adjacent forest, the old house, partak-
> ing of its lustre, seemed their fit companion, and to have many years
> of life in him yet.   (1: 4)

But the Maypole is also a building in its dotage: it 'looked as if it
were nodding in its sleep'; its brickwork, 'originally ... a deep dark
red ... had grown yellow and discoloured like an old man's skin;
the sturdy timbers had decayed like teeth'. There is something
curiously grotesque about this picturesque building. It is excessive
and fantastical, with 'more gable ends than a lazy man would care
to count on a sunny day; huge zig-zag chimneys, out of which it
seemed as though even smoke could not choose but come in more
than naturally fantastic shapes'. It is 'gloomy' and 'ruinous', with
many disused rooms, and the ubiquitous birds and their nests are
as much a sign of a building reverting to a state of nature as one
existing in close harmony with it (1: 4).

The Maypole represents an apparently Pickwickian world of
comfort, order and harmony, with its 'fragrant grove' of lemons,
'goodly loaves of snowy sugar', 'punch idealised beyond all mortal
knowledge', 'drawers full of pipes', and numerous cupboards and
presses 'all crammed to the throat with eatables, drinkables, or
savoury condiments' (19: 153). However, this earthly paradise and
those who frequent it are also represented as constituting a self-
enclosed, self-satisfied, ossified world of custom, habit and superstition. John Willet's Maypole may be 'the very snuggest, cosiest,
and completest bar that ever the wit of man devised', but it is also
the site of a backward-looking, tyrannical *ancien régime* in which
the law of the father is absolute:

> Silence, sir!' roared [Joe Willet's] father. 'When your opinion's
> wanted, you give it. When you're spoke to, you speak. When your
> opinion's not wanted and you're not spoke to, don't give an opinion
> and don't you speak. The world's undergone a nice alteration since
> my time certainly. My belief is that there an't any boys left ... that
> there's nothing now between a male baby and a man – and that all

the boys went out with his blessed Majesty King George the Second!
(1: 11)

This outburst in the opening chapter signals the novel's pervasive
concern with relationships between fathers and sons: between
John and Joe Willet, Sir John Chester and his legitimate and illegitimate sons, Barnaby and his reappearing father, and Sim Tappertit
and his surrogate father Gabriel Varden. Indeed, as Steve Marcus
pointed out in *Dickens: From Pickwick to Dombey*, problematic
father–son relationships, tensions between the older and younger
generations, and authority and challenges to authority, comprise
the central structuring oppositions of this novel. These oppositions
are a focus for the novel's representation and investigation of the
abuse or neglect of parental and/or social duty, the proper use of
authority, and the legitimacy or illegitimacy of challenges to
authority. John Willet's obstinate refusal to admit his son into the
full citizenship of adulthood, and Sir John Chester's snobbish
attempts to order the life of his legitimate son have both a structural and a political function: structurally, they serve as the
obstructive, repressive mechanism, traditional to comedy, by
which a corrupt or decaying older generation frustrates the energies and desires of the younger generation, and politically they
provide a context in which a challenge to (misused) authority can
be seen as legitimate.

One of the novel's most malign characters, Chester's illegitimate
son, the unsocialized malcontent Hugh (the Maypole's ostler), also
seems to have legitimate grounds for his hatred of authority.
Dickens uses Hugh as a way of raising questions about the consequences of aristocratic profligacy and neglect (what Carlyle, in *Past
and Present*, was to describe as 'do-nothing dilettantism'). He is
also used as a figure for 'the bitter discontent grown fierce and
mad' of the neglected lower classes.[48] Like Jo the crossing sweeper
in *Bleak House*, Hugh 'don't know nothink'. Abandoned by his
father (as far as Hugh is concerned an unknown 'gentleman'),
taken away from his mother when she is imprisoned and subsequently hanged for passing a forged note, Hugh, in John Willet's
words, 'can't read or write, and has never lived in any way but like
the animals he has lived among, [he] *is* an animal' (11: 90). Hugh
is just as much a victim of social neglect as Jo is, but whereas the
latter character (despite his inadvertently deadly role in spreading
smallpox) was to be mobilized in Dickens's rhetoric of reform,

Hugh is mobilized as the spectre of insurgent terror; he is one of those for whom 'if something be not done, something will do itself one day, and in a fashion that will please no-one'.[49] Sim Tappertit is in some ways Hugh's parodic other, and his resentment of Gabriel Varden's benign exercise of a quasi-parental authority over his apprentice is satirized as an illegitimate *ressentiment* against authority in general.

The most contentious aspect of Dickens's concern with authority and the challenge to authority in *Barnaby Rudge* is his representation of the Riots in scenes depicting the burning of Newgate and the Warren, the burning and pillaging of houses and businesses in various quarters of London, and the spoliation of the Maypole. Dickens's fictionalizing of the Gordon Riots, and especially his treatment of Gordon and his manipulative secretary Gashford, have been criticized as historically inaccurate. Perhaps the most important historical fact about Dickens's representation of mob violence is that it was written after the French Revolution, and, like much English writing in the first half of the nineteenth century, is haunted by the spectre of this great European trauma. The riots in *Barnaby Rudge* are, in part, a Carlylean phantasmagoria of the manifold causes of social unrest, and its uncontrollable, hydra-headed nature once it is unleashed. It is difficult to decide whether Dickens's delineation of the forces of established order and those who challenge it is seeking to be even-handed, or whether it is simply contradictory. The novel is satirically and sometimes bitterly critical of the blindness and inefficacy of the Magistracy, Parliament, and City worthies who are unable to protect the citizenry from the mob – a dissident body which the forces of law and order have created; 'the very scum and refuse of London, whose growth was fostered by bad criminal laws, bad prison regulations, and the worst conceivable police' (49: 375). On the other hand, the riots are represented as both a crazy carnival in which an unjust world is turned upside down by the socially oppressed, and – this is the more forceful impression – a nihilistic and ultimately self-destructive dance of death by those who cry 'down with everything!'

> If Bedlam gates had been flung open wide, there would not have issued forth such maniacs as the frenzy of that night had made [at the burning of the Warren]. There were men there, who danced and trampled on the beds of flowers as though they trod down human enemies ... who rushed up to the fire, and paddled with it in their

hands as if in water; and others who were restrained by force from plunging in, to gratify their deadly longing. (55: 425)

In the passage just quoted Dickens demonizes the mob, but a few chapters earlier he had psychologized it:

> A mob is usually a creature of very mysterious existence, particularly in a large city. Where it comes from or whither it goes, few men can tell. Assembling and dispersing with equal suddenness, it is as difficult to follow to its various sources as the sea itself; nor does the parallel stop here, for the ocean is not more fickle and uncertain, more terrible when roused, more unreasonable, or more cruel.
>
> The people who were boisterous at Westminster upon the Friday morning, and were eagerly bent upon the work of devastation in Duke-street and Warwick-street at night, were, in the mass, the same. Allowing for any chance accessions of which any crowd is morally sure in a town where there must always be a large number of idle and profligate persons, one and the same mob was at both places. (52: 396)

In this passage, the mob is both a force of nature and a product of culture – a distinctively urban phenomenon. The setting of *Barnaby Rudge* may be 1780, but Dickens's representation of the crowd is what we would now recognize as distinctively nineteenth century. It is a mode of representation which has led Steven Connor to suggest, in his account of space, place and 'the body of riot' in this novel, that 'Dickens is, in a sense, the first modernist in his representation of the city as a psychological space, organised according to psychopolitical investments and projections.'[50]

One of the main problems of Dickens's depiction of the mob is the way in which his narratorial persona seems to get caught up in it. If *Barnaby Rudge* is a novel about the challenging and transgressing of boundaries, then its narrative point of view seems, at points, to dissolve boundaries. In a letter written as the novel was ending its serialization, Dickens expressed this as a problem of both perception and representation:

> In this kind of work the object is, – not to tell everything, but to select the striking points and beat them into the page with a sledgehammer. And herein lies the difficulty. No man in the crowd... No looker-on from a window ... beheld an Individual, or anything but a great mass of magistrates, rioters and soldiery, all mixed up together. Being always in one or other of these positions, my object has been to convey an idea of multitudes, violence and fury;

and even to lose my own dramatis personae in the throng.
(*DL*, II: 218)

For both spectators and those caught up in it, the mob destroys
perspective and dissolves individuality. It dissolves the present and
wipes out the past. It has been suggested that *Barnaby Rudge*
retreats from revolutionary violence – however justified its causes –
and takes refuge in the past, or merely reinstates old injustices in
new forms. Certainly *Barnaby Rudge* is a novel *about* revolution
(or more correctly insurrection), rather than a revolutionary novel.
It is a novel which is concerned with the nature of social change,
and with the passing of power from one generation to the next. It
is even, perhaps, a novel about progress and the kinds of questioning and challenge which are necessary to progress. It is here that
the two parts of the novel are brought together. The rebellious
sons, Joe Willet and Edward Chester, play a crucial role in righting
the wrongs caused by the actions of the merely disaffected sons –
Sim Tappertit and Hugh, and the alienated son Barnaby.

   Barnaby Rudge is in many ways Dickens's farewell to the eighteenth century and to the fictional models of an older generation of
novelists. Throughout these early years of Dickens's self-transformation from a writer of occasional sketches (*Sketches by Boz*), to a
writer of connected sketches (*Pickwick*), and longer narratives
which had their origins in sketches (*Oliver Twist* and *The Old
Curiosity Shop*), Dickens had been rewriting and re-forming the
eighteenth-century periodical essays and picaresque novels that
had constituted his own childhood reading. In the lengthy period
of the gestation and writing of *Barnaby Rudge* he sought to
emulate the fictional model of Sir Walter Scott, the major male
novelist of the early nineteenth century and a dominant influence
on the male novelists writing at the time when Dickens was beginning his own career of authorship. Although Dickens was to return
to the form of the historical novel in the 1860s, and although
Fielding and Smollett were to continue to resurface in his work
(particularly in *David Copperfield*), *Barnaby Rudge*, with its rewriting of the past, in effect marks the end of Dickens's attempts to
reproduce the fiction of the past.

3

Travails in Hyper-Reality, 1842–48

I 'Here be monsters': *Martin Chuzzlewit*

> '....we never knows wot's hidden in each other's hearts; and if we had glass winders there, we'd need keep the shetters up, some on us, I do assure you!'
>
> (Dickens, *Martin Chuzzlewit*, chap. 29, 400)

From the point at which he joined the staff of the *Morning Chronicle* in 1834 until the appearance of the concluding number of *Barnaby Rudge* in November 1841, Dickens was constantly engaged in writing sketches, stories and serial narratives for immediate publication. Exhausted by this regime, anxious to avoid the perils of over-production (which he felt had blighted Scott's career as a novelist), and eager to meet his American readers and to consolidate his position in America, Dickens took a break from writing for immediate publication when he had finished *Barnaby Rudge* – although not before he had secured a monthly salary of £150 from his publishers Chapman and Hall, to be drawn from his share of the profits of his next novel. This novel was *Martin Chuzzlewit*, the first of whose twenty monthly numbers came out in January 1843, shortly after the publication of Dickens's impressions of his disappointing and disillusioning travels in America, *American Notes for General Circulation* (October 1842). *Martin Chuzzlewit* was in many respects a return to the *Pickwick* formula of presenting 'a rapid succession of characters and incidents', as Boz put it in his 'Proclamation' on *Nicholas Nickleby* on 28 February (*NN*, 782), organised around the *Nickleby* motif of a young man who is forced by adverse family circumstances to make his way in the world. Dickens was very pleased with the result: 'I think Chuzzlewit in a hundred points immeasurably the best of my stories ... I feel my power now, more than I ever did ... I have greater confidence in myself than I ever had' (*DL*, III: 590). Despite the fact that in Mr Pecksniff and the anarchically loquacious nurse Sairy Gamp, Dickens had created two of his most extraordinary comic grotesques, sales of the monthly numbers were disappointing.[1] The serial also received relatively little critical attention during the course of its nineteen-month run, and the few reviews that appeared were mostly negative and complained of Dickens's exaggeration and caricature. Reviews of subsequent editions in book form were rather more positive and, on the whole, although it was not a notable commercial success, *Martin Chuzzlewit* increased Dickens's critical reputation.

Later critical opinion on *Martin Chuzzlewit* has tended to be sharply divided. It has been designated as a landmark novel, and seen variously as the first novel of Dickens's mature phase or, alternatively, as the high point of his early comic genius: it is the 'strangest, most demanding and funniest of Dickens's earlier fictions', argues John Bowen, 'and one of the most important of all nineteenth-century novels'.[2] For some critics *Chuzzlewit* is the last novel of the creatively dynamic 'Boz' phase, and the work which marks Dickens's descent into self-commodified authorship. David Musslewhite, for example, has argued (in *Partings Welded Together*, 1987) that its opening genealogy of the Chuzzlewit family (parodic though it is) and its dynastic plot mark *Chuzzlewit* as the novel in which the familial structure (which was to dominate the later novels) triumphs over the looser, more capacious and more heterogeneous patterning of the earlier novels. For Steven Marcus, on the other hand, this parodic and self-parodic work, in which Dickens makes fun of his own sentimental style, was quite simply 'a great novel', in which Dickens began to develop the consciously mannered style that was to mark his mature novels. It offered 'a supreme dramatization of selfishness in all its varieties, and of certain ways in which the modern self develops ... a panoramic vision of the direction in which modern society was moving'.[3] For others, it was a transitional novel, which showed Dickens's 'awareness of the possibilities of an overriding theme', but also demonstrated that he was 'not yet fully at ease either in the degree of extreme black and white acceptable or in the process of presenting moral regeneration in its flawed hero'.[4] *Chuzzlewit* has also been designated as a crisis novel, because Dickens experienced a number of difficulties with the structuring and pacing of his tale during the process of writing – difficulties which led to his determining to plan his work more carefully in future. In *From Copyright to Copperfield: The Identity of Dickens* (1988), Alexander Welsh argued that *Chuzzlewit* was both a transitional and a crisis novel: it was the product of a crisis of identity, born of a crisis in Dickens's self-definition as a man and a writer. This double crisis was precipitated partly by Dickens's response to America and partly by his reaction to the charges of self-interestedness which British and American commentators levelled at his interventions on the cause of international copyright in speeches he gave during his American journey. As a result of this journey, Welsh argued, Dickens experienced 'just enough identity confusion ... to have a valuable and lasting effect on his fiction writing'.[5] However, it might also be argued that *Martin Chuzzlewit* is less the product or symptom of identity confusion, than a novel which is more or less self-consciously preoccupied with questions of identity and the confusions of identity in the modern world. John Bowen's recent deconstructive reading attributes the unpopularity of this novel with some readers in both the nineteenth and twentieth centuries to the fact that it is – in its structure, language and dominant preoccupations – 'a key harbinger of modernism',[6] a novel whose central concerns are the problems of modernity: the social and psychological implications of commodification, capitalism and urbanism.

As with many of Dickens's novels, much of the critical debate has focused on *Martin Chuzzlewit*'s design, or lack of it. George Orwell famously declared that it had 'wonderful gargoyles [and] rotten architecture',[7] and John Lucas (in an enthusiastically appreciative account of the novel) described it as 'something of a marvellous mess', a directionless novel, whose author seems unable to decide whether he is writing a 'realistic study or a moral and prescriptive fable'.[8] All this despite the fact that there is evidence that the early numbers were very carefully planned, and that Dickens's own account of the genesis of this novel emphasized 'design'. For example, he insisted in the Preface to the first volume edition that he had endeavoured 'to resist the temptation of the current Monthly Number, and to keep a steadier eye upon the general purpose and design', which, he announced, was to be that of 'exhibiting, in various aspects, the commonest of all the vices' (*MC*, xiii).

Some of the critical and readerly reservations about *Martin Chuzzlewit* may be attributed to the fact that both its form and its content constitute a kind of assault upon its audience. In his satiric representation of both English and American life in this novel, Dickens seems to have engaged in the high-risk strategy of biting the hand that fed him. Something of the nature of Dickens's satiric project may be glimpsed in the motto which John Forster dissuaded him from adding to the title page of the volume edition: 'Your homes the scene, yourselves the actors here!' *(Life*, I: 296). Having relinquished this stinging motto, Dickens underscored his satiric intent in successive Prefaces in which he implicitly elaborated on Jonathan Swift's dictum, in his Preface to *The Battle of the Books* (1704), that 'Satire is a sort of glass, wherein beholders do generally discover everybody's face but their own.' Thus, he made the point contained in the discarded motto (and, at the same time, countered some early objections to his novel) by observing: 'It is almost needless to add, that the commoner the folly or the crime ... an author endeavours to illustrate, the greater the risk ... of being charged with exaggeration' (1844 Preface, *MC*, xxiii). The point was underscored in a later Preface, in which he wrote that '[a]ll the Pecksniff family upon earth are quite agreed, I believe, that no such character as Mr Pecksniff ever existed' (1850 Preface, *MC*, 717). Later still, Dickens asserted that '[w]hat is exaggeration to one class of minds and perceptions is plain truth to another' (1867 Preface, *MC*, 719).

What kind of satire did Dickens write in *Martin Chuzzlewit*, and what were its targets? Forster saw *Chuzzlewit* as a change of satiric direction, in which satiric attacks on the 'vile' abuses of debtors' prisons, 'parish Bumbledoms', and Yorkshire schools were replaced by a satiric focus on 'something much more pestiferous':

> [H]e had not before so decisively shown vigour, daring, or discernment of what lay within reach of his art, as in taking such a person as Pecksniff for the central figure in a tale of existing life. Setting him up as the glass through which to view the groups around him, we are not the less moved to a hearty destestation of the social vices they exhibit, and pre-eminently of selfishness in all its forms ... *(Life*, I: 296)

One of the novel's late twentieth-century editors distinguished *Chuzzlewit* from Dickens's earlier work by describing it as a moral rather than social satire.[9] It is easy to see why. Dickens's claims in his Prefaces that his project was to exhibit human vice and folly, and abstract and universal human foibles such as selfishness and hypocrisy, invite comparison with the moral satire of the seventeenth-century playwright Ben Jonson and eighteenth-century satirists such as Joseph Addison, Richard Steele, Jonathan Swift and Alexander Pope. However, it would be difficult to avoid the conclusion that *Martin Chuzzlewit* is concerned with particular nineteenth-century forms of these human vices, and that it has a typically nineteenth-century concern with money, mammonism and the spread of speculative capitalism. In other words, Dickens, like Thomas Carlyle, was concerned to exhibit, explore and deplore some of the signs of the times, in which 'cash payment' was rapidly becoming 'the sole nexus of man to man'.[10]

Most prominent among the common vices that *Martin Chuzzlewit* both exhibits and exposes are the vices of selfishness, pride and hypocrisy. In one sense there is nothing new in this; they are to be found among Dickens's satiric targets from the earliest tales and sketches. However, in this novel they come under sharper scrutiny, foreshadowing the intensity of focus that they will receive in later novels such as *Dombey and Son* and *Our Mutual Friend*. In *Chuzzlewit* selfishness, pride and hypocrisy reach monstrous proportions in such characters as Pecksniff, Old Martin and Jonas Chuzzlewit. In parodic form these vices are even seen to invade such a benignly comic character as Mark Tapley, who constantly seeks for a way of finding some credit for his jolly constitution: 'one of my hopeful wisions is, that there's a great deal of misery awaitin for me; in the midst of which I may come out tolerable strong, and be jolly under circumstances as reflects some credit' (48: 628). In *Martin Chuzzlewit* the forms of self-division, selfishness and egotism seem to proliferate to such an extent that egocentric isolation is represented as the condition in which most people live in a modern acquisitive society. Jonas Chuzzlewit, for example, is both an idiosyncratic grotesque and a typical product of an individualistic, materialistic society:

> The education of Mr Jonas had been conducted from his cradle on the strictest principles of the main chance. The very first word he learned to spell was 'gain', and the second (when he got to two syllables), 'money'. But for two results, which were not clearly foreseen perhaps by his watchful parent in the beginning, his training may be said to have been unexceptionable. One of these flaws was,

that having been taught by his father to over-reach everybody, he had imperceptibly acquired a love of over-reaching that venerable monitor himself. The other, that from his early habit of considering everything as a question of property, he had gradually come to look, with impatience, on his parent as a certain amount of personal estate, which had no right whatever to be going at large, but ought to be secured in that particular description of iron safe which is commonly called a coffin, and banked in the grave.   (8: 105–6)

If Jonas's irredeemable selfishness is the result of familial and social example and conditioning, so too is the redeemed selfishness of the young Martin Chuzzlewit. Martin's is the selfishness and self-centredness born of great expectations: ' "I have been bred up from childhood with great expectations," ' he explains, ' "and have always been taught to believe that I should be, one day, very rich" ' (6: 83). Martin is thus the first of a long line of Dickens's studies of the socio-psychology of expectation in young middle-class men, whose lives are (mis)shaped by their expectations of future wealth and social position and by the expectations of others about them. Other examples of this particular line include Steerforth in *David Copperfield*, Richard Carstone in *Bleak House*, Henry Gowan in *Little Dorrit*, Pip in *Great Expectations*, Eugene Wrayburn in *Our Mutual Friend*, and Edwin Drood in Dickens's final and unfinished novel.

Perhaps the most self-obsessed individual in the novel is Mr Pecksniff. In this character the novelist of the English middle classes turns his satiric fire upon the English middle-class vice of hypocrisy, and, in particular, on the selfishness and hypocrisy involved in affecting an unselfish, forgiving morality. Hippolyte Taine first called attention to Pecksniff's essential Englishness in an essay written in 1856 in which he claimed that there were no Pecksniffs in France, since his own countrymen were more inclined to affect vice than virtue. Commenting after Dickens's death on the changing American response to his representation of their countrymen, Forster similarly called attention to the quintessential Englishness of Pecksniffery:[11]

> The confession is not encouraging to national pride, but this character is so far English, that though our countrymen as a rule are by no means Pecksniffs the ruling weakness is to countenance and encourage the race. When people call the character exaggerated ... they only refuse, naturally enough, to sanction in a book what half their lives is passed in tolerating if not worshipping. ... [Dickens has exposed a great danger] in showing the larger numbers who, desiring to be thought better than they are, support eagerly pretensions

that keep their own in countenance, and without being Pecksniffs, render Pecksniffs possible. (*Life*, I: 294)

Dickens's representation of Pecksniff is designed to satirize and interrogate the social meanings and manifestations of the 'moral' and of 'morality'. Neither of these words is used in anything other than an ironic sense in *Martin Chuzzlewit*. The essence of Pecksniffery and Pecksniffian morality is revealed in Pecksniff's first appearance in Chapter 2, and is merely expanded and intensified as the novel proceeds. Here is the reader's introduction to Pecksniff:

> Mr Pecksniff was a moral man: a grave man, a man of noble senti-ments and speech ... Perhaps there was never a more moral man than Mr Pecksniff: especially in his conversation and correspon-dence. It was once said of him ... that he had a Fortunatus's purse of good sentiments in his inside. In this particular he was like the girl in the fairy tale, except that if they were not actual diamonds which fell from his lips, they were the very brightest paste, and shone prodigiously. He was a most exemplary man: fuller of virtu-ous precept than a copy-book. Some people likened him to a direc-tion-post, which is always telling the way to a place and never goes there: but these were his enemies; the shadows cast by his bright-ness; that was all. (2: 10–11)

Everything about Pecksniff, from his throat to his 'soft and oily' manner, and his 'plain black suit, and state of widower ... all tended to the same purpose, and cried aloud, "Behold the moral Pecksniff!"' (2: 11). This is a man for whom morality is a rhetori-cal performance, whose habitual mode of discourse involves 'using any word that occurred to him as having a good sound, and round-ing a sentence well, without much care for its meaning' (2: 13); a man who is able to derive a moral lesson even from the act of eating ham and eggs, for even eggs 'have their moral', and that moral is that every 'pleasure is transitory. We can't even eat, long. ... When I say we, my dear ... I mean mankind in general; ... There is nothing personal in morality my love' (2: 12).

Pecksniff's cant on the impersonality of morality is true in one sense: moral actions usually do involve a sacrifice or denial of self in the interests of the other. However, Dickens constructs Pecksniff as a grotesque distortion of this truth. Like so many of the characters in the novel, Pecksniff is represented as practising a form of self-splitting in order that he can become the beneficiary of his own self-denial and the object of his own benevolence. Thus he warmed his hands at the fire 'as benevolently as if they were someone else's, not his' (3: 32). It is perhaps significant that the name 'Pecksniff' echoes 'Pickwick', since Dickens's egregiously 'moral man' is a curious inversion of his earlier benevolent man. Pecksniff is a hollow echo of Pickwickian sentiment.

Even Pecksniff's profession is a form of pretension, an affectation. He is an architect who has never designed or built anything, and a land surveyor only in the sense that he is in the habit of surveying with self-satisfaction the 'extensive prospect [that] lay stretched out before the windows of his house' (2: 11). Pecksniff's real profession and his 'genius' lies not in the practice of architecture, but in 'ensnaring parents and guardians', and 'pocketing premiums' for architectural pupils (2:11). It is an indication of Dickens's concern for topicality in this novel that he should have made Pecksniff a man with a profession, and that the specific profession should be that of architect. The rebuilding of the House of Commons (which had been destroyed by a fire in the mid-1830s), the building of the new railway stations, and the expansion of London made the architect one of the central and most controversial figures of the period in which Dickens was writing *Chuzzlewit*. Thus it is perhaps not surprising that 'when he needed a figure to represent the commercialism and vainglory of his own age, he found an architect' (Ackroyd, 409–10).

If Pecksniff is one example of a self-deceiver, then Sairey Gamp is another. Like Pecksniff, Sarah Gamp becomes the object of her own benevolence through the good offices of her invented friend, Mrs Harris. Like Pecksniff, Mrs Gamp is a monster, but, with her huge appetites for ale, gin, pickled salmon and cucumbers, she is a monster of Rabelaisian energy. Michael Slater has argued that if Mrs Nickleby is 'an anti-woman joke developed out of masculine exasperation', Mrs Gamp is an anti-woman joke 'developed out of masculine fears ... a clear literary expression of a dread of the female'.[12] Certainly Mrs Gamp is sinister and terrifying, but she is also a gloriously energetic reversal of that model of self-sacrificial femininity which Dickens idealizes in the figure of Ruth Pinch in this novel, and in countless other female characters throughout his fiction. Mrs Gamp is a nurse who nurses herself and who sacrifices her patients' comfort in favour of her own. She presides indiscriminately over life and death, as, 'setting aside her natural predilections as a woman, she went to a lying in or a laying-out with equal zest and relish' (19: 269). If Nurse Gamp disturbs the peace of the sick and dying with her (self-)ministrations, she also disturbs the peace of the English language with equal zest and relish. Her freely associative, inventive, syntactically anarchic language – what Chesterton described as her 'unctuous and sumptuous conversation' – took the novel 'to places it would not visit again until Joyce'.[13] Pecksniff and Gamp are just two of a host of deceiving, self-deceiving and/or self-alienated characters in *Martin Chuzzlewit*. Indeed, the novel is marked by a new kind of preoccupation with deception, duplicity and secrecy, and with the fraud and crime with which they are so intricately connected. Several of these preoccupations coalesce around the figure of Nadgett, who is the most interesting early example of Dickens's enduring fascination with detectives and detection, and a prototype for the secretive detective of the sensation novels and the developing crime novel in the 1860s. Nadgett is a distinctive modern, urban type, an example of what Wilkie Collins later described as 'the confidential spy of modern times ... the necessary detective attendant on the progress of our national civilization'.[14] He is a man who belongs 'to a class; a race peculiar to the city; who are secrets as profound to one another, as they are to the rest of mankind' (27: 386):

> [Nadgett] was born to be a secret. He ... seemed to have secreted his very blood. ... How he lived was a secret; where he lived was a secret; and even what he was, was a secret. In his musty old pocket-book he carried contradictory cards, in some of which he called himself a coal-merchant, in others a wine merchant, in others a commission agent, in others a collector, in others an accountant: as if he really didn't know the secret himself. He was always keeping appointments in the city, and the other man never seemed to come. ... [H]e often secretly indited letters in corner boxes ... but they never appeared to go to anybody, for he would put them in a secret place in his coat, and deliver them to himself weeks afterwards, very much to his own surprise.   (27: 385–6)

Walter Benjamin traced the origins of the social content and meaning of the fictional detective and of the detective story to 'the obliteration of the individual's traces in the big-city crowd'.[15] Dickens's novels chart the processes of that obliteration but they also, for the most part (and certainly in *Martin Chuzzlewit*), retrieve the individual's traces and (through the complex multiple plot and the use of coincidence) make visible the lines of connection between apparently atomistic individuals. The modern city, as

viewed from Todgers's boarding house in Chapter 9, may be a dis-
orientating, labyrinthine maze, but Dickens's narrative goes on to
insist that the inhabitants of the modern metropolis are connected
in all sorts of ways. Even characters who appear to inhabit entirely
different worlds turn out to be linked to each other:

> As there are a vast number of people in the huge metropolis of
> England who rise up every morning, not knowing where their heads
> will rest at night, so there are a multitude who shooting arrows over
> houses as their daily business, never know on whom they fall. Mr
> Nadgett might have passed Tom Pinch ten thousand times; might
> even have been quite familiar with his face, his name, pursuits, and
> character; yet never once have dreamed that Tom had any interest
> in any act or mystery of his. Tom might have done the like by him.
> … But the same private man [Jonas Chuzzlewit] out of all the men
> alive, was in the mind of each at the same moment … when they
> passed each other in the street.   (38: 505)

Nadgett's secrecy and the multiple identities (and absence of
identity) signalled by the numerous and contradictory cards which
he carries in his pocket-book are replicated in Montague Tigg's
self-transformation into Tigg Montague, Director of the Anglo-
Bengalee Disinterested Loan and Life Insurance Company. In Tigg
and his far from disinterested business dealings, Dickens reworks
the satire on the United Metropolitan Improved Hot Muffin and
Crumpet Baking and Punctual Delivery Company, 'a great Joint
Stock Company of vast national importance', which he had developed in Chapter 2 of *Nicholas Nickleby*. Writing in the wake of a
series of bank crises and the spectacular collapse of various bubble
companies, Dickens, in *Martin Chuzzlewit*, represents fraud and
swindling as *the* distinctive modern crimes. They are institutional-
ized forms of deception which are both the symptom and the
product of the way we live now (to appropriate the title of
Trollope's novel of 1874–5, which features the fraudster and
confidence trickster Augustus Melmotte). Just as Pecksniff gives
the appearance of morality, so, too, the Anglo-Bengalee Company
gives the appearance of substance. However, this appearance of
substance is an elaborate confidence trick based on the confidence
inspired by the material trappings of Victorian commerce, which
provide a simulacrum of a going concern:

> Business! Look at the green ledgers with red backs, like strong
> cricket-balls beaten flat; the court-guides, directories, day-books,

> almanacks, letter-boxes, weighing-machines for letters. ... [L]ook at
> the iron safes, the clock, the office seal – in its capacious self, secu-
> rity for anything. Solidity! Look at the massive blocks of marble in
> the chimneypieces. ... Publicity! Why, Anglo-Bengalee Disinterested
> Loan and Life Insurance Company, is painted in the very coal-scut-
> tles. (27: 373)

In *Martin Chuzzlewit*, Dickens's satiric representation of modern
English society is paralleled and intensified by his representation of
America. 'I have seen the future; and it works', wrote the
American journalist Lincoln Steffens following a visit to the Soviet
Union in 1919.[16] In the novel's American episodes Dickens, in
effect, announces that he has seen the future and it doesn't work.
Dickens's own disillusioning travels in America are reworked in
the experience of the young Martin Chuzzlewit and Mark Tapley,
and in particular in Martin's adverse reactions to the public nature
of American life, to the abstraction and journalistic rhetoric of
American speech, to the despotism of public opinion, and to the
lack of individuality:

> [W]herever half a dozen people were collected together there, in
> their looks, dress, morals, manners, habits, intellect, and conversa-
> tion, were Mr Jefferson Brick, Colonel Diver [etc.] ... over, and
> over, and over again. They did the same things; said the same
> things; judged all subjects by, and reduced all subjects to, the same
> standard. (21: 301)

And underlying everything is the ubiquitous obsession with
money: 'All their cares, hopes, joys, affections, virtues, and associations, seemed to be melted down into dollars ... men were
weighed by their dollars, measures gauged by their dollars; life was
auctioneered, appraised, put up, and knocked down for its dollars'
(16: 235).

To Dickens's youthful radicalism America had seemed like the
country of the good revolution (as opposed to the violence and
chaos of the French Revolution), and the harbinger of a future
society, a brave new world which would regenerate an ossified
England. 'What are the Great United States for if not for the
regeneration of man?' an American asks Martin (21: 300). In
America man is said to exist 'in a more primeval state' (21: 299),
and nowhere is this primeval state more in evidence than in the
description of Martin's journey to and arrival in Eden, a section of
the novel which owes something to the romance quest, something

to the Bible and something to Milton's *Paradise Lost*. In the new settlement of Eden the 'waters of the Deluge might have left it but a week before: so choked with slime and matted growth was the hideous swamp which bore that name' (23: 325). In Dickens's narrative America turns out to be no promised land and no Eden. Ironically, however, Dickens uses the country which was the site of the loss of his own early radicalism as the locus of the origins of his hero's redemption from selfishness. While nursing Mark Tapley through the illness which the servant had contracted when tending his master, Martin begins to confront his own selfishness, and 'to think how it was that this man who had had so few advantages, was so much better than he who had had so many' (33: 451). If Dickens the man was not persuaded that the purpose of the Great United States was the regeneration of mankind, Dickens the novelist did at least represent America as the site of the beginning of the regeneration of one man, as Martin's redemption from selfishness prepares him for reintegration into civilized society. Redemption, regeneration and social (re)integration were to become prominent and increasingly problematic preoccupations in Dickens's fiction. They were at the very heart of the Christmas books which he wrote between 1843 and 1848, books on which so much of Dickens's dubious reputation as the guardian of the heart's affections has been built.

II Redemptive fictions in 'a whimsical kind of masque': the Christmas Books, 1843–8

> My chief purpose was, in a whimsical kind of masque which the good humour of the season justified, to awaken some loving forbearing thoughts, never out of season in a Christian land.
> Dickens, Preface to *The Christmas Books*, 1852, *CB*, p. xxxix

Perhaps more than any other author, Dickens is associated in the popular imagination with Christmas. From his evocation of the magic, kindness and benevolence of Christmas time in 'A Christmas Dinner' in *Sketches by Boz*, through his depiction of festive scenes in *Pickwick*'s Christmas at Dingley Dell, and especially through his Christmas books and Christmas stories, Dickens made a particular, and some would argue extremely sentimental, version of Christmas his own. However, as Sally Ledger has recently reminded us, Dickens's 'celebration of the domestic ideal amidst winter festivities' in the Christmas books always exists in an uneasy tension with their 'staging' of 'the threats posed to domesticity by a society ill at ease with itself' in the Hungry Forties (*CB*, xxvii and xxx).

The five Christmas books, published separately between 1843 and 1848, mixed elements of the folk and fairy tale with the ghost story or tale of the supernatural to teach a moral lesson about memory, forgiveness, human sympathy and social responsibility. Dickens claimed that these books offered a new kind of story, invented by himself, in which a 'little dreaminess and vagueness is essential to [the] effect' (*DL*, V: 466). The Christmas books belong to that period of restlessness and crisis of self-definition in which *Martin Chuzzlewit* was produced, and which persisted after its publication, exacerbated, to some extent, by its initially lukewarm reception (and that of *American Notes*) by both readers and reviewers. During this period, as his letters to Forster and others indicate, Dickens experienced great difficulty in settling down to write. It was also a period in which he had numerous struggles with publishers over terms and conditions, and in which his finances were strained as a result of the relatively poor sales of *Chuzzlewit* and the increasing demands on his finances from his growing family, his financially wayward father, and others making claims on his charity. Largely as a result of these financial problems, Dickens spent extensive periods living and travelling in Europe during the five years in which he published the Christmas books, a fact which may, in part, account for their relative lack of temporal and spatial specificity.

There is some evidence to suggest that during this period in which he was geographically removed from the sources of his inspiration Dickens was unsure of the direction his life and work should take. In the winter of 1845–6 he was involved in setting up the *Daily News*, a morning paper which was to be (as the advertisement on 1 December 1845 put it) of 'Liberal politics and thorough Independence'. He was appointed its editor at £2000 a year in November 1845, but resigned in early February 1846, having found the pressures of editing a daily paper uncongenial, and also having come under fire for being unable to keep up with the details of the political and economic debates of the day. After resigning the editorship he nevertheless continued to contribute articles on various subjects, including 'Travelling Letters', which were later included in his *Pictures from Italy* (1846). In the summer following his abandonment of the editorship of the *Daily News*, Dickens seems to have been considering a public role outside of literature, but based, in part, on his reputation as a campaigning writer. 'I have an ambition for some public employment', he wrote to Lord Morpeth on June 20 1846:

> some Commissionership, or Inspectorship, or the like, connected with any of those subjects in which I take a deep interest, and in respect of which the Public are generally disposed to treat me with confidence and regard. On any questions connected with the Education of the People, the elevation of their character, the improvement of their dwellings, their greater protection from disease and vice – or with the treatment of Criminals, or the administration of Prison Discipline, which I have long observed closely – I think I could do good service ... I have hoped, for years, that I may become at last a Police Magistrate, and turn my social knowledge to good practical account from day to day. (*DL*, IV: 566–7)

The Christmas books were one of the ways in which Dickens sought to exercise 'some Commissionership' connected with the subjects in which he took a deep interest, as T. A. Jackson suggested in his socialist analysis of the author's work. It was in his Christmas books in particular, Jackson argued, that Dickens

> revealed his gathering hatred of that which lies at the heart of the bourgeois system of society – the subordination of all men, and of every human capacity to the tyrannical dominance of a vast, impersonal process of *money-gaining*. ... The whole series of Christmas books can, therefore, be regarded quite fairly as 'escape fantasies' – projections of Dickens's desire for a way out of the conflicts and crises of class struggle and revolution which had culminated in concrete political explosions – in the mad year of 1848 – just before the last of the series was written.[17]

A Christmas Carol (subtitled 'A Ghost Story of Christmas'), the first, best-known, best-loved, and most frequently and variously adapted of Dickens's Christmas books, was written in October and November of 1843 while he was still struggling with the writing of *Chuzzlewit*. The idea of a small festive book for the Christmas season was conceived in order to make good the financial disappointment of the current serial, and the preoccupations and characters of *A Christmas Carol* are closely linked to those of the novel. Scrooge is a more fantastical version of the unreformed old Martin, and Bob Cratchit is an older Tom Pinch, who has acquired a wife and children. The *Carol* is thus a 'dream reworking' of *Martin Chuzzlewit*, in which selfishness, money, greed, and the commercialized society that is produced by and reproduces them, are represented in 'condensed and fantastic form' (Ackroyd, 431). Formally this first example of Dickens's new sort of story returns, in part, to the mode of the interpolated tales of *Pickwick*, as it reworks, at greater length, the story of Gabriel Grub, the curmudgeonly old man who is visited by goblins who show him images of the past and future. In fact, like most of Dickens's fiction, the *Carol* (and the other Christmas books) is a generic hybrid. In this particular case it combines the supernatural hauntings and carceral images of Gothic, the violence and hyperbole of pantomime, and the magical transformations of fairy tale.[18] This generic hybridity and the blending of realism and fantasy to focus on social questions was to become Dickens's habitual mode in his later full-length novels.

A Christmas Carol had its origins, as Kathleen Tillotson noted, in Dickens's deepest personal and political concerns. By means of the ghost story and fairy tale, the author revisited in covert form the childhood experiences he also addressed (semi-secretly) in the autobiographical fragment which he wrote a few years later (1847). Dickens's personal feeling about the abuses of his own childhood are replicated by both broader and more specific political concerns about the social conditions of children. Angered by the conditions of the children he had seen at work in the Cornish tin mines, an anger which was intensified by his reading of the second report of the Commissioners enquiring into child labour in March 1843, Dickens first planned to write 'a very cheap pamphlet called an "Appeal to the People of England on behalf of the Poor Man's Child"', but decided to hold his fire until Christmas when 'a Sledge hammer' would 'come down with twenty times the force' (*DL*, III: 459, 461). In September of the same year he took up the cause of the Ragged Schools, arguing that in the 'prodigious misery and ignorance of the swarming masses ... the seeds of ruin are sown'.[19] *A Christmas Carol* is used to solicit the readers' sympathy for the causes (and Cause) of 'Ignorance and Want', and the unreformed Scrooge is used to expose the horror of Utilitarian thought, *laissez-faire* economics and Malthusian population theory.

In both its content and its form *A Christmas Carol* underlines Dickens's belief in the human capacity for redemption from selfishness to sympathy, and his sense of the urgent social necessity for this capacity to be made operative. This tale for Christmas underscores the role that representation and fiction can play in this process. One of the lessons that the *Carol* teaches is E. M. Forster's lesson of 'only connect'. In this case, the path to redemption involves learning to connect the self with the other, the personal with the social, the past with the present, and present actions with future consequences. Dickens's story of the education and redemption of Scrooge also explores its own educative and redemptive procedures. As J. Hillis Miller pointed out in his 1993 essay on the *Carol*, Scrooge's visions are 'a hyperbolic form of the normal procedures of Victorian fiction'. The visions variously presented by the ghosts of Christmases past, present and future work in the same way that fiction does: '[t]ranscending time, space, and the opacity of households or persons is just what novels with omniscient narrators do. They take us into a realm based on the real world but a transformation of it'.[20] Despite its origins in Dickens's social outrage and his anger at the unwillingness of government to deal with specific social iniquities, the implication of Scrooge's story would seem to be that no structural social change is necessary for the amelioration of the conditions of the poor and the ending of the alienation of the rich. The message of *A Christmas Carol* is that these things can be achieved if everyone acquires a sympathetic humanity and practises Christian charity. Moreover, narrative, and perhaps especially the storytelling of the novel or tale, seems to have an important role to play in this transformative process. In other words it is possible to read both the form and content of *A Christmas Carol* as embodiments of the 'change-of-heart' credo that can be found in virtually all of Dickens's novels, and thus it has become a kind of test case for critical debates about whether Dickens's fiction offers its readers a sentimental radicalism or a sentimental conservatism.

Latterly critics interested in the role of representation in a developing commodity culture have offered a different view of Scrooge's 'progress', and of the *Carol*'s status as a 'culture-text'. *A Christmas Carol*, it has been suggested, is a self-referential text about the circulation of images: Scrooge is presented not with real life but with images of real life, and the reader is presented with images of images of real life. The reader is positioned as a spectator of a Scrooge who is, in turn, a spectator of the images which are presented to him by his ghostly visitants, and those images always focus on the denial and/or enjoyment of the pleasures of consumption. By focusing on this form of 'spectatorship' as the mechanism of Scrooge's conversion, *A Christmas Carol* thus 'tells the story of a Victorian businessman's interpellation as the subject of a phantasmagoric commodity culture in which laissez-faire economics is happily wedded to natural benevolence'.[21] In his miserly mode Scrooge has sought to acquire money rather than the goods that it can buy, and to impose on others his own lack of desire for or pleasure in consumption. Scrooge's redemption or progress consists of his learning how to become a good consumer, and how to keep money and goods in (benevolent) circulation. To complete this virtuous circle of consumption the Christmas book which tells the story of Scrooge's progress becomes itself an object of pleasurable consumption, 'an endlessly sympathetic commodity',[22] involved in a circular process of fulfilling the desires which it has itself created.

The 'progress' or 'conversion' in the second of the Christmas books, *The Chimes* (1844), subtitled 'A Goblin Story', is that of a lowly ticket porter, Trotty Veck. This conversion is effected by means of an horrific vision of the future, provided on New Year's Eve by the goblins who inhabit the bells whose chimes habitually punctuate Veck's days and nights. As a result of the pronouncements of various statistically-minded Aldermen, Magistrates and Politicians with whom he comes into contact during the course of the last day of the year, Veck becomes convinced that he and his class are 'Wrong every way! ... Born bad. No business here!' ('The First Quarter', *CB*, 115). It is the function of the spirits of the chimes to disabuse Veck of this personal and social despair, and to teach him (and the reader) that 'we must trust and hope, and neither doubt ourselves, nor the good in one another'. Although *The Chimes* ends with the New Year celebrations and the wedding of Veck's daughter, and contains idealized images of lower-class domestic life similar to those in *A Christmas Carol*, it is less genial than its predecessor. Whereas the first Christmas book attacked contemporary social philosophy and economic theory in indirect and allegorical forms, *The Chimes* satirizes specific historic individuals, such as Sir Peter Laurie (fictionalized as Alderman Cute), the London magistrate notorious for passing harsh sentences on the poor, and Lord Brougham (Sir Joseph Bowley in *The Chimes*), who supported a number of philanthropic causes, but in many instances demonstrated a complete indifference to the sufferings of the poor. Malthusianism is satirized through Mr Filer, whose view of society is refracted (and distorted) through statistics which enable him to 'demonstrate' that (among other things) tripe, the poor man's food, is 'without an exception the least economical and the most wasteful article of consumption that the markets of this country can possibly produce':

> The loss upon a pound of tripe has been found to be, in the boiling, seven eighths of a fifth more than the loss upon a pound of any other animal substance whatever. Tripe is more expensive, properly understood, than the hothouse pine-apple… . You snatch your tripe, my friend, out of the mouths of widows and orphan. ('The First Quarter', CB, 108)

The figures of authority are sharply satirized, and the consequences of their social philosophy and (in)action are vividly dramatized in Trotty's harrowing dream-vision of his daughter's suffering and suicide. However, these authority figures are left untouched and unchanged, while it is the confused little ticket porter who is required to undergo a conversion. In this respect *The Chimes* might be described as dispensing the 'Carol philosophy' of 'cheerful views, sharp anatomisation of humbug, jolly good temper … and a vein of glowing, hearty, generous mirthful beaming reference in everything to Home and Fireside' (*DL*, IV: 328), which Dickens outlined as the aims of a new periodical, 'The Cricket', which he projected in July 1845.

This periodical project was abandoned (on Forster's advice), but Dickens developed its leading ideas into the Christmas book for 1845, *The Cricket on the Hearth*. In this 'Fairy Tale of Home', the Cricket acts as the supernatural agent who preserves the romance of home by reassuring the 'lumbering, slow, honest' John Peerybringle, a Carrier in his 'burly middle-age' ('Chirp the First', *CB*, 192, 193), of the faithfulness of his young wife Dot. Like many fairy tales *The Cricket on the Hearth* explores serious adult issues, such as deception, illusion, sexuality, and relations between the sexes, but it does so in a way which many readers have found to be excessively sentimental. 'Exaggerated, absurd, impossible sentimentality'[23] were also charges levelled at *The Battle of Life: A Love Story* (1846), the only one of the Christmas books not to use a supernatural agency. *The Battle of Life*, described by Dickens as a tale about 'quiet victories and struggles, great sacrifices of self, and noble acts of heroism … done everyday in nooks and corners, and in little households, and in men's and women's hearts',[24] is the complicated story of two sisters, Grace and Marion Jeddler, who both love the same man, and who both attempt to disguise their feelings and to sacrifice their own happiness for each other. It is this spectacle of female self-sacrifice which effects the conversion at the heart of this book: the conversion of the girls' father, Dr Jeddler, a disaffected sceptic who treats life as a joke. The complications of his daughters' stories are put to work so as to change Jeddler's philosophy, and lead him to acknowledge that, 'It's a world full of hearts ... a serious world ... full of sacred mysteries' ('Part the Third', *CB*, 362–3). *The Battle of Life*, like the other Christmas books, thus reverses the mid-Victorian grand narrative of competitive individualism, which plots life as a struggle for economic and/or evolutionary dominance.

'Forget and Forgive' is the injunction with which *The Battle of Life* closes. In contrast, the last of the Christmas books, *The Haunted Man* (1848), returns to the '*Carol* philosophy' of *remember* and forgive. The haunted man of the title, a chemist and academic called Redlaw, is a solitary figure who is embittered by his memory of past suffering and injustice. Redlaw makes a Faustian bargain, accepting the gift of forgetfulness of all his past suffering which is offered by the phantom double who mysteriously appears to him, only to discover that this gift is, in fact, a curse which he must pass on to everyone he meets. The only exceptions to the influence of his 'gift' are the maternal Millie Swidger, and a monstrous child of the slums to whom she offers shelter. Like Scrooge, Redlaw is redeemed, in part, by being given a vision of the future: the condition attached to the granting of his wish for forgetfulness enables him to see enacted the awful consequences of fulfilling this desire, and makes him desire something different. Redlaw is also redeemed through the intervention of Milly, who seeks to put to sympathetic use her own memories of suffering and grief, most notably the memory of the death of her child. Christmas is the catalysing moment of Redlaw's redemption. At Christmas the Phantom returns, accompanied by a shadowy female form, and puts into a more general social context Redlaw's selfish desire for delivery from the burdens of suffering and the consequences of his own and others' past actions. The Phantom preaches to both Redlaw and the reader on the subject of individual and social responsibility, concluding with the injunction that Redlaw should behold, in the monstrous boy, 'the perfect type of what it was your choice to be. ... He is the growth of man's indifference; you are the growth of man's presumption':

> 'No softening memory of sorrow, wrong, or trouble enters here, because this wretched mortal from his birth has been abandoned to a worse condition than the beasts. ... All within this desolate creature is barren wilderness ...'
> 'There is not,' said the Phantom, 'one of these – not one – but sows a harvest that mankind MUST reap. From every seed of evil in this boy, a field of ruin is grown that shall be gathered in and garnered up, and sown again in many places in the world, until regions are overspread with wickedness enough to raise the waters of another Deluge. Open and unpunished murder in a city's streets would be less guilty in its daily murder, than one such spectacle as this.' (3: 446–7)

In the passage just quoted, as in so many places in the Christmas books, we see something of the rhetoric of social critique which is developed further in the novels that were to follow. In these novels, as in the Christmas books, Dickens continued to exploit his interest in and fondness for old nursery tales. What Forster wrote of the Christmas books could (for good and ill) be equally applied to almost any of Dickens's subsequent novels, and certainly to his next novel, *Dombey and Son*:

> The social and manly virtues he had desired to teach, were to him not less the charm of the ghost, the goblin, and the fairy fancies of his childhood. ... What were now to be conquered were the more formidable dragons and giants that had their places at our own hearths. ... With brave and strong restraints, what is evil in ourselves was to be subdued; with warm and gentle sympathies, what is bad or unreclaimed in others was to be redeemed; the Beauty was to embrace the Beast ... the star was to rise out of the ashes ... and we were to ... bring ... [our wilder brothers] back with brotherly care to civilization and happiness. (*Life*, I: 301)

4

Mid-Victorian
Self-Fashionings, 1846–50

I   Making the family firm? *Dombey and Son*

The Times, whose reviewer had panned the first two Christmas books, also ran an extremely hostile notice of *Pictures from Italy* (Dickens's sketches of his impressions of France and Italy during his travels to and residence in Italy in 1844–5). The reviewer in this latter piece pointed out Dickens's present shortcomings – a penchant for 'the literary ventriloquial', disgraceful punctuation, over-reliance on capital letters and illustrations – and offered him advice on his future direction. Noting Dickens's acknowledgement (in the Preface to *Pictures from Italy*) of his mistake in breaking off old relations between himself and his reader, the reviewer cautioned the author against being too eager to resume those relations: 'He has not only to sustain his past reputation, but to repair the mischief which we assure him has been done by his latest publications' (*The Times*, 1 June 1846, *CH*, 141).

Dickens repaired the mischief in quite spectacular fashion with his next novel on an English subject, *Dombey and Son*, which appeared in twenty monthly parts between October 1846 and April 1848. *Dombey* was an immediate success with readers, whose appetites had been whetted by the extensive advertising campaign that Dickens's new publishers, Bradbury and Evans, had conducted from late August onwards. The first number had an initial print run of 25,000, followed by two more of 5000 and 2000, and sales of the subsequent numbers never fell below 30,000.[1] High sales were, in this case, matched by critical acclaim, including praise from the novelist who was coming to be regarded as Dickens's chief competitor. After reading the number narrating the death of Paul, Thackeray asserted: 'There's no writing against such power as this – One has no chance! Read that chapter describing young Paul's death: it is unsurpassable – it is stupendous.'[2]

Dombey and Son received a great deal of attention from twentieth-century critics, many of whom saw this novel as a literary landmark, which signalled a new direction not only for Dickens, but also for nineteenth-century fiction more generally. What kind of landmark is *Dombey*? It has become commonplace to regard this novel as both formally and conceptually more coherent than Dickens's earlier fictions (in short as more of a *novel* than his earlier fictions). This coherence has been attributed to the careful advance planning that Dickens undertook during his preparation for and composition of *Dombey*, as can be seen in his surviving working plans for the individual numbers, and in his involvement in the design of the cover for the serial parts, which gave a clear indication, from the outset, of the scope of the entire novel. As Kathleen Tillotson argued in 1954, *Dombey* was not only the earliest example in Dickens's work of 'responsible and successful planning', but it was also the first of Dickens's novels to have both 'unity ... of action', and unity of 'design and feeling'. Perhaps more importantly, it was also the first of Dickens's novels 'in which a pervasive uneasiness about contemporary society takes the place of an intermittent concern with specific social wrongs'.[3]

Dombey has been widely acknowledged as the first of Dickens's novels to deal with Victorian society in its entirety, and the first to engage self-consciously with modernity. In *Dombey and Son*, wrote Humphrey House in 1941, '[t]he people, places and things become "modern" '.[4] In short, *Dombey and Son* has been generally heralded as the first novel of Dickens's mature phase, the first example of a positively evaluated 'late Dickens'. Numerous other critics, however, have regarded *Dombey* as exemplifying Dickens's decline into his repetitive late phase, yet another stage in the process by which he created himself as a modern, professional author and commodified both himself and his fiction, completing the apotheosis of Boz which was begun in *Martin Chuzzlewit*. 'In creating Dombey', Gabriel Pearson wrote in 1962, Dickens 'partly created himself as Dombey, the linear, purposive, selfish architect of a unique destiny'. In thus relinquishing the spontaneity of the 'Boz' persona, Pearson argued, Dickens introduced into the writing process a 'division of labour' between the Dickensian 'professional craftsman' and Boz's 'more capacious and public identity as mime, manipulator and performer'.[5] Developing this argument further, David Musslewhite claimed that Dickens paid too large a price for this division of labour and for the new focus on the inner conflict of his characters, sacrificing 'a radically subversive talent for exploring and registering the varied and variegated complexities, human and social, of a society at a critical moment of its development and change', and trading it for 'a lamentable obsession with familial strains and neurotic introspection'.[6]

Much of the plethora of criticism that was devoted to *Dombey and Son* in the latter third of the twentieth century was concerned with this relationship between Dickens's 'obsession with familial strains' and introspection, and his representation of and attitudes to 'society at a critical moment of its development and change'. On the one hand, Dickens's representation of familial tensions and the introspective was seen as a way of engaging with the human, social and political complexities of a society at a critical moment of development and change. On the other hand, the focus on familial relationships and introspective states came to be regarded as a means of displacing or evading the social and political complexities of historical change. There are two main orders of change in this novel. First, there are the great life changes of births, deaths and marriages, which are associated in the novel's symbolism with the sea and with 'what the waves were always saying', as in the title of Chapter 16. These have been identified by some critics as representing a natural, feminine principle. The other order of change is social, cultural and material. It is associated with the masculine world of business, and it is summed up in the words of Sol Gills, 'competition, competition – new invention, new invention – alteration, alteration' (4: 40). The chief figure for this latter order of change is the railway, whose impact is charted through the changing face of Stagg's Gardens (in Chapters 6 and 15) and, more importantly, which is registered as a radical transformation of the sense of time and space, as well as of social relations. *Dombey and Son* marks the birth of the 'Railway world':

> There were ... railway journals ... hotels, coffee-houses, lodging-houses, boarding-houses; railway plans, maps, views, wrappers, bottles, sandwich-boxes, and time-tables; railway hackney-coaches and cab-stands; railway omnibuses, railway streets and buildings,

railway hangers-on and parasites and flatterers. ... There was even railway time observed in clocks, as if the sun itself had given in ...

To and from the heart of this great change, all day and night, throbbing currents rushed and returned incessantly like its life's blood. ... Wonderful Members of Parliament, who, little more than twenty years before, had made themselves merry with the wild railroad theories of engineers ... went down into the north with their watches in their hands, and sent on messages before by the electric telegraph, to say that they were coming. Night and day the conquering engines ... advancing smoothly to their journey's end, and gliding like tame dragons into [their] allotted corners, stood bubbling and trembling ... as if they were dilating with the secret knowledge of the great powers yet unsuspected in them, and strong purposes not yet achieved.   (15: 213–14)

In his depiction of the railway Dickens placed himself, as John Ruskin put it, as 'a pure modernist – a leader of the steam-whistle party *par excellence*'.[7] In *Dombey and Son* the railway is vital and transformative. It brings work and prosperity to the Toodles family and to their neighbours, subtly altering class relations in the process. As if by magic, and at great speed, the railway world transforms the nondescript landscape of Stagg's gardens to a brighter, busier (if rather clapboard) place of work and habitation. It is the embodiment and symbol of humankind's (and, feminist critics would argue, especially man's) warring with rude nature. It is one of the many aspects of modernity which challenge and change both humankind's relationship to and conception of 'Nature' and the natural: 'It might be worthwhile, sometimes,' opines the narrator 'to inquire what Nature is, and how men work to change her, and whether in the enforced distinctions so produced, it is not natural to be unnatural' (47: 622). The railway is associated with upheaval and renewal, but also with death. It provides a spectacular nemesis for Carker, the Manager, who is killed by an express train. Perhaps more interesting still is the chapter describing Dombey's railway journey to Leamington, in which the prose mimics the speed and rhythm of the train as it represents Dombey's alienated sense of dislocation (this latter chapter also offers an interesting perspective on class and race relations in its representation of Dombey's angry encounter with Toodle, whom he suspects of being 'a bidder against him' in his grieving for his recently dead son, Paul, and in its description of Major Bagstock's treatment of his black servant):

> Away, with a shriek and a roar, and a rattle, from the town, bur-
> rowing among the dwellings of men and making the streets hum,
> flashing out into the meadows for a moment, ... through the fields,
> through the woods, through the corn, through the hay, through the
> chalk, through the mould, through the clay, through the rock,
> among objects close at hand and almost in the grasp, ever flying
> from the traveller, and a deceitful distance ever moving slowly with
> him: like as in the track of the remorseless monster, Death!
> ...
> Louder and louder yet, it shrieks and cries as it comes tearing on
> resistless to the goal; and now its way, still like the way of Death, is
> strewn with ashes thickly. ... There are dark pools of water, muddy
> lanes, and miserable habitations far below. There are jagged walls
> and falling houses close at hand, and through these battered roofs
> and broken windows, wretched rooms are seen, where want and
> fever hide themselves in many wretched shapes ... as Mr Dombey
> looks out of his carriage window, *it is never in his thoughts that the
> monster who has brought him there has let the light of day in on these
> things: not made or caused them.*   (20: 272–4, emphasis added)

Here, as in the phantoms, spirits and goblins of the Christmas
books, Dickens uses Dombey's self-imprisonment in an introspective world to provide a nightmare vision of psychological and
social alienation. The railway – as it is represented here – is potentially the means by which Dombey and the middle-class reader
might be brought into contact with a social reality which they
would rather avoid looking at; a social reality which – if they will
look, listen, learn and act – it is in their power to change.

Like *A Christmas Carol* and *The Chimes*, which preceded it,
Dombey and Son is a 'condition-of-England' narrative, and one in
which Dickens began to develop the metaphors and narrative
methods which he was to use in his great social novels of the 1850s
and 1860s. The much-discussed narratorial excursus in Chapter 47 is
a case in point. Shot through with Carlylean images of disease, this
chapter is central to the novel's social analysis and requires very
careful reading and rereading. It is worth quoting at some length:

> Those who study the physical sciences, and bring them to bear upon
> the health of Man, tell us that if the noxious particles that rise from
> vitiated air, were palpable to the sight, we should see them lowering
> in a dense black cloud above such haunts, and rolling slowly on to
> corrupt the better portions of a town. But if the moral pestilence
> that rises with them ... could be made discernible too, how terrible
> the revelation! Then should we see depravity, impiety, drunkenness,

theft, murder, and a long train of nameless sins against the natural affections and repulsions of mankind ... creeping on, to blight the innocent and spread contagion among the pure. Then should we see how the same poisoned fountains that flow into our hospitals and lazar-houses, inundate the jails, and make the convict-ships swim deep, and roll across the seas, and over-run vast continents with crime. Then should we stand appalled to know, that where we generate disease to strike our children down and entail itself upon unborn generations, there also we breed, by the same certain process, infancy that knows no innocence, youth without modesty or shame, maturity that is mature in nothing but suffering and guilt.
(47: 623)

This passage fuses Dickens's interests in criminality and its social causes and consequences, prison reform, sanitary reform, and the reform of 'fallen women'.[8] It anticipates the rhetorical mode of *Bleak House* with its stance of seeking to open the eyes of the middle-class reader with prophecies of doom. It also anticipates the later novel's imagery of a creeping fog or miasma of disease that connects the different social zones of the city and the different classes of society, and which continues to reap its harvest in successive generations.

In this passage, as in the novel as a whole, Dickens constructs his narratorial persona in the mode of one of the night-time visitants or benevolent shades of the Christmas books. He is (or aspires to be) the 'good spirit', invoked by the narrator:

Oh for a good spirit who would take the house-tops off ... and show a Christian people what dark shapes issue from amidst their homes, to swell the retinue of the Destroying Angel as he moves forth among them! For only one night's view of the pale phantoms rising from the scenes of our too-long neglect; and, from the thick and sullen air where Vice and Fever propagate together, raining the tremendous social retributions which are ever pouring down, and coming ever thicker! ... men, delayed no more by stumbling-blocks of their own making ... would then apply themselves like creatures of one common origin, owning one duty to the Father of one family, and tending to one common end, to make the world a better place! (47: 623–4)

Dickens is here projecting himself as the novelist-as-spirit of the yet-to-come, whose function is to transform not only Dombey, but also the bourgeois reader, with his nightmare vision of the physical and moral contagion hidden in the heart of Victorian London.

Thus far my analysis of Dickens's representation of change in *Dombey and Son* has – quite deliberately – focused on the novel as

(more or less) self-conscious social critique. Like many of his contemporaries, Dickens wrote with a purpose, and conceived of his
novels as a form of intervention in the social and political world.
Much recent criticism of *Dombey*, however, has tended to focus
on the novel as cultural or psycho-social symptom, using various
combinations of psychoanalytic, materialist, historical, historicist
and feminist perspectives to investigate the complexities of
'Dickens's intertwining of literal and symbolic economies', and of
the novel's representation and investigation of the politics of the
family and gender politics.[9] The centrality of gender politics to this
novel is evident in its title, and in the suppressed alternative title
which surfaces in Miss Tox's observation at the end of the fifth
number (signalled in advance in a letter to Forster on 25 July
1846), that 'Dombey and Son' is 'a Daughter after all' (*DL*, IV:
589–90).

These two titles, 'Dombey and Son' and 'Dombey and Daughter
(after all)', are important signposts in the novel's mapping of nineteenth-century gender roles and the complexities of their interconnections with capitalism. Dickens's juxtaposition of the House of
Dombey (the firm) with Dombey's (and Florence's) house and with
other versions of the home places the separate spheres of men and
women at the centre of the novel's structure. *Dombey and Son* is
organized around a series of gendered polarities which are associated with Florence and Dombey: private/public; domestic/
commercial; nature/culture; organic/mechanical; influence/power;
sea/railway. It is perhaps tempting to read the novel in the light of
Miss Tox's declaration as a victory of the feminine over the masculine, of love over pride, of influence over power, and of the
domestic over the commercial. However, such a reading would
radically oversimplify the novel's exploration of both social and
gender economies. Certainly, this is a novel which, like much mid-
Victorian fiction by men and women, works towards a model of
gender complementarity in its representation of the companionate
cross-class marriage of Florence and Walter Gay. However, the
narrative strategies and representational modes it deploys on the
way to this ending explore – or sometimes just *reveal* – the fault-
lines of mid-Victorian constructions of gender, and particularly of
the 'separate spheres' ideology.

Dombey, for example, is not, like Pecksniff, a Jonsonian portrait of hypocrisy, selfishness and pride. Rather he is a representation and exploration of the limitations and contradictions of a

particular version of bourgeois masculinity, which is defined through action, competition, commerce, and through securing the male succession. In their different ways Dombey and his son are the vehicles for an exploration of the crippling effects of this version of masculinity: Dombey Senior is almost destroyed by seeking to inhabit this role, and the death of Dombey Junior, in part, signifies his inability to occupy it. The Dombeyan version of masculinity constructs femininity as reproductive (rather than pro-ductive), and in its gendered division of labour all emotional work is consigned to women. Although Dickens's novel could not be described as espousing the women's cause, it does, nevertheless, explore the issue of women's place in a rapidly changing world – an issue which was being addressed in numerous pamphlets and tracts appearing in the 1840s. *Dombey and Son* explores these issues through its representation of a range of female characters, and, most importantly, through its juxtapositioning of Florence Dombey's submissive vulnerability (which is represented in the dis-course of fairy tale) and her stepmother Edith's self-aware, self-dramatizing, passive resistance (which is represented in the mode of melodrama), as alternative female survival strategies which expose the complexities of gender politics, and the contradictions of mid-Victorian constructions of femininity.[10] In particular, Dickens's representation of Florence exposes some of the contra-dictions of the ideology of the separate masculine and feminine spheres, and of the contemporary worshipping of the angel in the house. Paradoxically, Florence is most hated by her father when she most closely approximates the Victorian feminine ideal of exerting moral influence and inspiring love and devotion through her own self-sacrificial love. Conversely, she is most loved by him, most influential in his moral redemption, and most effective as a domestic angel when she has rebelled against the law of the father, left the patriarchal home, married a man from a lower class, spent her honeymoon on a trading voyage to China, and helped her husband to build up his business – and, it should be added, when she has also become a mother, the mother of a son (another Paul, but crucially not another Dombey).

If Florence is an instinctive angel both in and out of the house, her sometime stepmother, Edith Grainger-Dombey, is a woman whose knowledge of the world has given her a proto-feminist awareness of the economics and power-politics of middle-class marriage, as demonstrated in her speeches and in her demeanour to Dombey, to her exploitative mother Mrs Grainger, and to Dombey's Manager, Carker (Dombey's instrument of choice for her subjugation and humiliation). This proto-feminist is also represented as a fallen woman (in opposition to Florence, the virgin/madonna), and is thus linked to Alice Brown, the prostitute, who (in a typically Dickensian coincidence) turns out to be her cousin. Edith is also linked to Alice through Carker the Manager: Alice's descent to prostitution had begun with her seduction and betrayal by Carker, and it is Carker who also plots Edith's seduction, only to discover that he has merely been used as the instrument of her revenge on Dombey. This pairing of Edith and Alice works in a number of contradictory ways. It is yet another device for linking together the disparate social spheres of the novel, and it is also, as Deborah Nord has pointed out, a possible means of mounting 'a powerful critique of a proud and mercenary patriarchy'. However, the nature of this critique is complicated and also, to some extent, diminished by the fact that, as dangerous and tainted women, both Edith and Alice are marginalized and ultimately banished from the narrative, with the consequence that the text 'wavers between the desire to marshal the spirit of reform and the urge to protect the sanctity of middle-class life'.[11]

Dombey and Son has been of particular interest to feminist critics precisely because it takes as one of its main subjects the gendered division of labour and scrutinizes 'the masculine world of public value through the values of the feminized private sphere'.[12] The novel's investigation of the separate spheres and the politics of gender is also intricately linked to its mixing of genres and narrative modes . Helen Moglen, for example, has read the novel as two 'distinct but interdependent narratives': Dombey's story, 'an anxious critique of the economical and ethical forces transforming Britain', which is cast in the mode of social realism, and Florence's story, which takes the form of social realism rewritten as a pastoral romance of woman and nature. Both stories and both modes of representation are complicated by being subjected to what Moglen describes as 'melodramatic and sentimental interrogations'. In the sentimental mode (often a fairy-tale mode), the narrator speaks for the less privileged and those who can't speak for themselves. On the other hand, in the melodramatic mode, active rebellious self-dramatizing characters (such as Edith) speak for Dickens, or perhaps speak more than Dickens consciously knows, articulating an awareness that oppression is not merely individual and personal but also general and social.[13]

Another area in which this novel might be said to speak more than it consciously knows is in its treatment of sexuality. Several feminist readings of the novel in the 1970s noted its tendency either to deny or repress sex and sexuality or to equate them with death and incest. Robert Clark's frequently cited materialist-psychoanalytic essay also began with the novel's equation of sexuality, death and incest, proceeding from the proposition that the 'only way to have sex and survive [in *Dombey*] is, in effect, to have it as Walter and Floy do, innocently and incestuously, as brother and sister', and going on to argue that the novel represents 'economic exchange entangling with the sexual' in an attempt to answer 'the riddle of the arbitrary taboo on women's participation in the economic order'. Like most materialist readings of Dickens's middle and late period fiction, Clark's reading of *Dombey* located the novel in its socio-economic context – Free Trade debates, the railway mania of 1835–7 and 1845–7, the banking crises of the 1840s, and the general shift from mercantile capitalism to venture capitalism. More speculatively, it also sought to establish a psychoanalytic context for the novel by uncovering (what Clark argued was) its masked Oedipal structure, in which Dombey is castrated by the loss of his son and his business, and ends the novel 'impotent, emasculated, superseded' by his daughter.

Dombey and Son is, in this account, not simply a novel about repression, but it also enacts its own patterns of repression, in which radical questions or insights are repressed by residual patriarchal prejudices – in other words, this is a novel which seeks to repress or suppress what it really knows. *Dombey*'s mapping of the transformation to Free Trade, Clark argues, raises the question of free trade *for* women, and both economic and sexual equality for wives and daughters, but the radical implications of this question are converted 'into a free trade in women (incest, prostitution)', and subsequently into a recognition that 'a free trade in women will abolish the family', by (as it were) deregulating the actions of seducers, or removing 'the incest taboo that makes the family what it is'. Thus the text's 'libidinous desire' for these radical implications confronts a repressive mechanism:

> for the fear must always be that if conservation and appropriation, alliance and sexuality, are allowed to merge, then the maintenance

of working capital will be impossible. ... In order that this should not be, sexuality must be completely banished from the family.[14]

Patterns of blindness and repression have also featured prominently in post-colonialist critiques of *Dombey and Son*, which have been concerned to unmask what Suvendrini Perera has described as 'the repressed second half'[15] of the novel's title – 'Wholesale, Retail and for Exportation' – by redirecting attention to the work that Dickens's representation of gender, the family and economic change performs in the construction, maintenance and management of the British imperialist imagination. It would be a very obtuse critic indeed who did not note that Dombey himself is presented, right from the outset, as the type of the imperialist imagination:

> The earth was made for Dombey and Son to trade in, and the sun and moon were made to give them light. Rivers and seas were formed to float their ships; rainbows gave them promise of fair weather; winds blew for or against their enterprises; stars and planets circled in their orbits, to preserve inviolate a system of which they were the centre. (1: 4)

Dombey and Son is self-evidently a critique of empire and of the imperial imagination, but it is a form of critique which also serves to construct and perpetuate the imperial imagination. The novel's story of the fall and subsequent regeneration of a mercantile House and a family, together with its reworking of the Dick Whittington tale in Walter Gay's rise from humble shipping clerk, via a marvellous voyage and marriage to a high-born maiden, to be the head of the new Dombey and Son, is in part a critique of the old-style commerce which was at the heart of empire. However, it is also a story of imperial enterprise, and a story about the formation of the imperial subject. This story (or the interrelationship of these various stories) separates out and suppresses the links between British capital and the domestic economy, on the one hand, and colonial adventure, the processes of colonization and the politics of colonialism, on the other. Colonialism and the operations of mercantile capital are thus represented in terms of their impact on the family and sexual relations, and also on (and in) the metropolis, rather than in terms of their impact on and in the colonized countries. Thus, as Deirdre David has pointed out, Dombey is criticized by Dickens for his explict ill-treatment of women and children in the home, rather than for the implicit mistreatment of colonized peoples upon which his trading empire is built. He is punished – with the loss of his empire and family – not for his inequitable and (by association) violent dealings with 'native peoples', but for his pride, poor parenting, and his bad judgement in failing to recognize feminine moral authority and regarding his daughter as 'a mere piece of base coin that couldn't be invested – a bad Boy – nothing more' (1: 5).[16] Both Dombey's redemption and the rebuilding of his House depend on the 'movement from rejecting "a bad Boy" to accepting a good daughter', and on Dombey's (and the reader's) recognition of the importance of the home in counterbalancing the (business) House. *Dombey and Son* is indeed a Daughter after all, but its future is only assured when the Firm is softened and feminized. Only then can it trade with moral authority. The gender and moral authority of trade (this time the trade of authorship) is also one of the key concerns of Dickens's next novel, *David Copperfield*.

II   The gendered subject of writing: *David Copperfield*

If, as I have indicated in the previous section, *Dombey and Son* has been seen (from various points of view) as the watershed novel, which marks the advent of 'late Dickens', *David Copperfield* has all too often been seen, as Simon Edwards has argued, as 'a mere sport or holiday', a self-enclosed and self-referential offshoot of Dickens's suppressed autobiographical fragment,[17] that attenuated act of self-explanation (published in Forster's *Life*) which describes the author's early life and the shame and pain of his employment in Warren's Blacking Factory. *David Copperfield*, which is generally agreed to be the most personal of Dickens's novels, has been read (often dismissively) as an *apologia pro vita sua*, an act of authorial self-justification, and a complex wish-fulfilment narrative in which Dickens plays out various familial and psychological dramas, including fantasies about his first love affair, his marriage, and his complex sentimental (and possibly sexual) feelings for his wife's sisters.

David Copperfield was published in monthly parts between May 1849 and November 1850. Like *Dombey and Son*, its predecessor, *Copperfield* begins with the birth of a child, but this time the birth is preceded by the demise of the father rather than succeeded by the immediate death of the mother. This novel is thus the story of

a fatherless boy, a 'posthumous child' (1: 2), who must learn to be
the father of the man into whom he grows. *David Copperfield* was
the first of Dickens's novels to be narrated in the first person. Like
the later *Great Expectations*, its form is that of a fictional autobiography. Like *Nicholas Nickelby* and *Martin Chuzzlewit* it is a
Bildungsroman, that is, a narrative that traces the hero's quest for
identity as he develops from childhood to maturity. Echoing
Laurence Sterne's narrator in *Tristram Shandy*, who begins his
story with the hour of his conception, David Copperfield begins
his narrative with the 'day and hour of my birth'. David proceeds
to tell the story of his Edenic early life with his 'poor mother'
Clara and their servant Peggoty, followed by his expulsion from
this maternal Eden with the arrival of a stepfather, Murdstone, the
birth of a brother and the death of his mother. The rest of the narrative rehearses the orphan's subsequent wanderings in a world in
which he encounters all manner of heroes and villains, angels and
monsters and undergoes various trials, before coming to rest in his
discovery of a profession or vocation and his second marriage to
Agnes. *David Copperfield* is a rite-of-passage tale, which (like
Dombey) draws on the tradition of the fairy tale with its evil step-
parents, ogres and fairy godmothers. It is a sort of *Pilgrim's
Progress*. It is also, in part, Dickens's *Jane Eyre*: David's five-day
confinement to his room by Murdstone and his being made to
wear, at Salem House, a placard announcing 'Take care of him.
He bites' (5: 74), echo the early experiences of discipline and punishment in the Red Room and at Lowood School, which Charlotte
Brontë had invented for the heroine of her first novel published
just two years earlier. *David Copperfield* is also Dickens's portrait
of the artist as a young man, a *Kunstlerroman*, which traces the
growth and development of a nineteenth-century novelist, as
Dickens writes his own version of Carlyle's history of the hero as
man-of-letters.

David Copperfield occupies a distinctive place in Dickens's work.
Its publication marks the mid-point of his novelistic production:
seven novels preceded it, and seven were to follow (if we count the
unfinished *Edwin Drood*). Admired by other novelists (notably
Tolstoy), *David Copperfield* was the favourite novel of Sigmund
Freud – a fact which should not surprise us, given that this novel
(as Alexander Welsh has pointed out) helped 'to codify the very
assumptions that bring psychoanalysis into being'. [18] Dickens's own
most cherished work has also long been a firm favourite with

readers. As is so often the case, John Forster's assessment of the novel – despite its sanctimonious tone – gives an indication of Dickens's own sense of his novel, and also speaks for generations of readers:

> That the incidents arise easily, and to the very end connect them-selves naturally and unobtrusively with the characters of which they are a part, is to be said perhaps more truly of this than of any other of Dickens's novels. There is a profusion of distinct and distinguish-able people, and a prodigal wealth of detail; but unity of drift or purpose is apparent always, and the tone is uniformly right. By the course of events we learn the value of self-denial and patience, quiet endurance of unavoidable ills, strenuous effort against ills remedia-ble; and everything in the fortunes of the actors warns us, to *strengthen our generous emotions and to guard the purities of home.* It is easy thus to account for the supreme popularity of *Copperfield*, without the addition that it can hardly have had a reader, man or lad, who did not discover that he was something of a Copperfield himself. Childhood and youth live again for all of us in its marvel-lous boy-experiences. ... It is the perfection of English mirth.
>
> (*Life* II: 106–7, emphasis added)

David Copperfield's recreation of the childhood state ('marvellous boy-experiences'), its 'perfection of English mirth', and the lessons it teaches about the value of patience, self-denial, endurance, and the need to cultivate 'the generous emotions' and 'guard the puri-ties of home', are qualities which have endeared this novel to readers, and to those mid-twentieth-century critics who were con-cerned to explore the moral art of nineteenth-century fiction. One of the most influential mid-twentieth-century accounts of the moral art of *David Copperfield* was Gwendolyn Needham's reading of the narrative dynamic of David's story as one of emotional growth, in which the insecure and too-pliant young protagonist learns how to be the hero of his own life by discarding the example of those – such as his mother, his aunt Betsey, Steerforth, Little Emily and Rosa Dartle – who have suffered or caused suffering as a result of their undisciplined hearts.[19] Having followed his own youthful and untutored heart by making an unsuitable marriage with the childlike Dora, David's change of direction begins, according to Needham, when he takes note of the terms in which Annie Strong clears up a misunderstanding with her husband, a man many years older than herself. Annie thanks her husband for saving her from marriage to her cousin, Jack Maldon, and thus saving her 'from the first mistaken impulse of my undisciplined heart' (45: 647). These words, and Annie's assertion that there 'can be no disparity in marriage like unsuitability of mind and purpose' (45: 646–7), echo in David's mind 'as if they had some particular interest, or some strange application that I could not divine' (45: 643), and he begins to discipline his own heart by accepting responsibility for the consequences of his marriage to Dora, before eventually – after Dora's death and a further period of wrestling with his undisciplined heart amidst the sublime landscapes of Switzerland – becoming worthy of marriage to Agnes.

Notwithstanding, or possibly as a result of, the influence of this morally schematic reading, *David Copperfield* was relatively neglected by mid-twentieth-century critics, who were much more interested in the later, darker, social-problem novels. However, with the advent of feminist, New Historicist and psychoanalytical criticism, *David Copperfield* came to be regarded not only as central to Dickens's *oeuvre*, but also as one of the central texts of nineteenth-century culture. With the advantage of hindsight it is easy to see why *Copperfield* should have come under such close scrutiny in the 1980s. A glance back to my summary of the novel's plot and at Needham's reading of it will indicate why this fictional autobiography of the transformation of an orphaned boy into both a professional writer and a middle-class husband should have proved to be such fertile ground for Foucauldian interrogations of the operations of power and discipline, New Historicist investigations of bourgeois self-fashioning, feminist examinations of the representation of women and the construction of gendered and classed identities, and psychoanalytic explorations of Oedipal dramas and narratives of maternal lack. Under the gaze of this body of criticism a novel that had been regarded by many of Dickens's readers and critics as one of his least complex, has been reread as a 'multi-layered work', which addresses many of the central mid-Victorian fears, anxieties and concerns about the self and its relation to society, about the economic and political structure of society, and about gender roles.[20] As is so often the case in Dickens's novels, these fears, uncertainties and attempts at definition are played out in the representation of the home, the family, the neglected, bereaved, or abandoned child, the Angel in the House and the fallen woman. In addition to these familiar Dickensian figures, and existing in an extremely complex relationship to them, *David Copperfield* adds, for the first and only time in his fiction, the figure of the writer, and specifically, the novelist. In doing so it becomes a novel which both embodies and investigates the making of the modern novelist, and the making of the modern novel and of a novelistic mode of subjectivity.

Published in the same year as *The Prelude*, *David Copperfield*, like Wordsworth's poem, is about memory and the growth of the writer's mind. It both consists of and reflects upon the 'childish recollections and later fancies, the ghosts of half-formed hopes, the broken shadows of disappointments dimly seen and understood, the blending of experience and imagination' (46: 647–8) which form its hero as both a man and a writer. Of course, all of Dickens's fiction leading up to *David Copperfield* is, in some way, retrospective, but from *A Christmas Carol* onwards Dickens became increasingly preoccupied with memory both as a psychological entity and as a moral process which might move the moral subject to an understanding of 'what you might have been, and what you are ... and ... what you may be yet!'[21] Unlike the Christmas books, however, *David Copperfield* specifically foregrounds the connections between memory, the writer and writing. As the narrator reminds his readers in Chapter 58, 'this narrative is my *written* memory'; and written memory, like all forms of writing, both conceals and reveals 'the most secret current of my mind' (58: 796; emphasis added).

The shaping of the writer, by experience and especially the experience of maternal lack, abandonment and suffering, is fairly minutely detailed in the early stages of the novel. David escapes into narrative when, 'shut out and alienated' from his mother as a result of her marriage to the stern Victorian patriarch, Murdstone, he discovers his dead father's books with their tales of such heroes as Roderick Random, Peregrine Pickle, Humphrey Clinker, Tom Jones, The Vicar of Wakefield, Don Quixote, Gil Blas and Robinson Crusoe (4: 52–3). He first turns storyteller when he recounts (and often improvises upon) the narratives of his childhood reading at the behest of his schoolfellow Steerforth, in order to beguile the nights and early mornings in the dormitory of Mr Creakle's school. The older narrating David likens this early storytelling to that of the Sultana Scheherazade in the *Arabian Nights*, and describes it as an experience which encouraged 'whatever I had within me that was romantic and dreamy' (7: 90). Later, David's period in the bottling warehouse, like Dickens's in the blacking factory, is represented as a source of fiction-making:

> When my thoughts go back, now, to that slow agony of my youth, I
> wonder how much of the histories I invented for such people [as he
> observed in his wanderings] hangs like a mist of fancy over well-
> remembered facts! When I tread the old ground, I do not wonder
> that I seem to see and pity, going on before me, an innocent roman-
> tic boy, making his imaginative world out of such strange experi-
> ences and sordid things!   (11: 164)

There is a similarly detailed representation of the preparatory
stages of David's formation as a professional writer, when he
determinedly applies himself to learn shorthand, having 'heard
that many men distinguished in various pursuits had begun life by
reporting the debates in Parliament' (36: 512). Dickens's narrator
presents his younger self as a model of self-effacing, but earnest
and arduous self-help:

> I feel as if it were not for me to record, even though this manu-
> script is intended for no eyes but mine, how hard I worked at that
> tremendous shorthand, and all the improvement appertaining to it.
> ... I will only add, to what I have already written of my persever-
> ance at this time of my life, and of a patient and continuous energy
> which then began to be matured within me, and which I know to be
> the strong part of my character ... that there, on looking back, I
> find the source of my success. I have been very fortunate in worldly
> matters; many men have worked much harder, and not succeeded
> half so well; but I never could have done what I have done, without
> the habits of punctuality, order, and diligence, without the determi-
> nation to concentrate myself on one object at a time ... which I then
> formed. ...   (42: 590)

The novel is much less detailed, however, in its representation of
its hero's actual work as a reporter and his subsequent transformation into a writer of magazine pieces and, later still, into a novelist.
The most important stages in David's progress as a writer are narrated in the novel's 'retrospective' chapters. For example, in
Chapter 43 ('Another Retrospect'), we first learn of his employment 'reporting the debates in Parliament for a Morning
Newspaper', and just a paragraph later he announces his 'coming
out' as a magazine writer, in a seamless transition from putting pen
to paper to achieving the financial success that enables him to
marry Dora: 'I have taken with fear and trembling to authorship. I
wrote a little something, in secret, and sent it to a magazine. Since
then, I have taken heart to write a good many trifling pieces. Now
I am regularly paid for them. Altogether, I am well off' (43: 610).

David's transformation into a writer of fictions is also narrated retrospectively, and in a rather throwaway manner:

> I must have been married, if I may trust to my imperfect memory for dates, about a year or so, when one evening, as I was returning from a solitary walk, thinking of the book I was then writing – for *my success had steadily increased with my steady application,* and I was engaged at that time upon my first work of fiction. ...
>
> (56: 647, emphasis added)

The successful completion of this book is announced (if that is not too emphatic a term) in the chapter entitled 'Domestic'. It is worth quoting this passage at some length, since it offers a very good example of the way in which this novel constructs the figure of the professional writer. It will also allow me to begin to examine some of the ideological work (to borrow a phrase from Mary Poovey) which this figure performs:

> I laboured hard at my book, without allowing it to interfere with the punctual discharge of my newspaper duties; and it came out and was very successful. I was not stunned by the praise which sounded in my ears, notwithstanding that I was keenly alive to it... . It has always been in my observation of human nature, that a man who has any good reason to believe in himself never flourishes himself before the faces of other people in order that they may believe in him. For this reason I retained my modesty in very self-respect; and the more praise I got, the more I tried to deserve.
>
> It is not my purpose, in this record, though in all other essentials it is my written memory, to pursue the history of my own fictions. They express themselves, and I leave them to themselves. When I refer to them, incidentally, it is only as part of my progress.
>
> Having some foundation for believing, by this time, that nature and accident had made me an author, I pursued my vocation with confidence. Without such assurance I should certainly have left it alone, and bestowed my energy on some other endeavour.
>
> I had been writing, in the newspaper and elsewhere, so prosperously, that when my new success was achieved, I considered myself reasonably entitled to escape from the dreary debates. One joyful night, therefore, I noted down the music of the parliamentary bag-pipes for the last time ... though I still recognise the old drone in the newspapers, without any substantial variation (except, perhaps, that there is more of it) all the livelong session.   (48: 671)

The first point that I want to note about this passage is the narrator's reticence about his own work, and in particular his intention not to 'pursue the history of my own fictions'. He reiterates this point in very similar terms at the beginning of Chapter 61:

> In pursuance of my intention of referring to my own fictions only when their course should incidentally connect itself with the progress of my story, I do not enter on the aspirations, the delights, anxieties, and triumphs of my art. That I truly devoted myself to it with my strongest earnestness, and bestowed upon it every energy of my soul, I have already said. If the books have any worth, they will supply the rest. (61: 823)

This is one of many instances of the way in which 'The Personal History of David Copperfield' (to quote the book's full title) avoids the personal, and conceals even in the process of disclosing, or, to put it another way, discloses by concealment. The narrator of *David Copperfield* never fully discloses himself to any other character, to the reader, or even to himself, but rather he represents such self-disclosure as a rhetorical impossibility: 'That I suffered in secret, and that I suffered exquisitely, no one ever knew but I. How much I suffered, it is, as I have said already, utterly beyond my power to tell' (11: 157).

If, as post-Romantic literary critics were wont to suppose, the secret of the artist's (David's) sufferings is to be found in the art into which he has poured his soul, then the reader is not to know, since the fictions to which we are referred as telling their own story, do not exist.

The second point I want to note about the long passage quoted above is its representation of novel writing as both a profession and a vocation. David (and the novel?) conceives of novel writing as work that requires an apprenticeship in which the crafts of the trade are acquired, and as a form of intellectual labour which both requires and develops the bourgeois habits of punctuality, and earnest application. But authorship is also represented as a vocation to which only some are called: 'nature and accident had made me an author', writes David, and it is only his (self-) 'assurance' of this fact that enables him to continue with the career that he has chosen, but which (it is his inner conviction) has also chosen him. This is just one example of the way in which this novel masks the story of bourgeois self-making as the operation of providence.

Dickens's/David's description of a kind of work which is not *merely* work is located in a chapter entitled 'Domestic', a chapter which also describes how David and his child-wife Dora 'had given up the housekeeping as a bad job'. Increasingly, as he progresses from the role of parliamentary reporter to novel writer, the scene of David's writing (that is to say both its location and, if David's novels are like Dickens's, its subject) becomes the home. In this respect this earnest bourgeois man is like a middle-class woman; his work is the home and he works in the home. As Mary Poovey has pointed out, this linking of writing with domestic work (first, the visible domestic incompetence of Dora and, later on, the invisible domestic efficiency of Agnes) has the effect of conveying the impression 'that some kinds of work are less "degrading" and less alienating than others and that some labourers are so selfless and skilled that to them work is simultaneously an expression of self and a gift to others'.[22]

If one effect of the linking of writing and the domestic is to efface (if not entirely to erase) the connection between writing and labour, another is to feminize the writer, a process, which is the source of some anxiety to the narrator-protagonist and perhaps in the novel more generally. As the passage from 'Domestic' demonstrates, David is represented, on the one hand, as the type of the earnestly striving middle-class masculine subject, who is at once self-assertive and enterprising, self-conscious and self-effacing. On the other hand, he is a feminized Scheherazade, who owes his success, like the female narrator of the tales of the *Arabian Nights*, to his ability to divert and beguile his audience. One of the most interesting aspects of this novel's representation of the formation of the masculine subject who is its narrator-hero is its focus on both the instability of the category of masculinity and the way in which this category is formed in relation to, and often overlaps with, various models of femininity (and domesticity). Women – and the conceptualization of domesticity, maternality and sexuality to which they were habitually connected in this period – play a crucial part in David's formation as both a man and a writer. At the centre of the network of the types of femininity displayed in this novel is Clara Copperfield, David's mother. Clara is the embodiment of both perfect and fallen femininity for David. She is the centre of his world and the source of his memories or fantasies of union and completeness. A sensuous and beautiful woman, she is also (at least from David's perspective) a vain child who abandons her son for Murdstone and gives him up to the stern law of the (step)father. This maternal lack may be seen as one of the spurs to his creativity and ambition, and also as one of the reasons why he chooses Dora as his wife. The genteel, pretty, flighty, domestically incompetent and childlike Dora whom David first marries is another version of David's mother, and the spur to David's ambition for worldly success through his writing. Other models of femininity, equally formative of David's identity, are provided by the maternal (but childless) lower-class Peggoty, and the masculinized independent Aunt Trotwood, who provides David with a model of practical independence and resourcefulness which transgresses dominant conceptions of femininity. Moreover, Betsey Trotwood's financial failure has the important structural function of initiating David's progress to a culturally sanctioned model of manhood, when he takes up the 'traditional male burden of economic responsibility for his family ... [and] becomes earnest, rational and hardworking'.[23]

Transcending all of these models of femininity, and positioned by the narrative as the ultimate object of David's quest (along with, and indeed as part of, his quest for selfhood), is Agnes Wickfield/Copperfield. Agnes, who resurfaces in many different guises in Dickens's fiction, is a model of the omni-competent housekeeper with her jangling keys. She is also a devoted daughter who supports an undeserving father through her capable running of a school. In short, Agnes is the very model of the Angel in the House, the dutiful daughter whose 'destiny' is to be a wife and mother and, to paraphrase the closing words of David's narrative, to point him upward. David (and the novel) attributes to Agnes a foundational role in the construction of his bourgeois masculinity in earnestness and steady, plain, hard work:

> Some happy talent, and some fortunate opportunity, may form the two sides of the ladder on which some men mount, but the rounds of the ladder must be made of stuff to stand wear and tear; and there is no substitute for thorough-going, ardent, and sincere earnestness. (42: 591)

After setting out this credo, David notes: 'How much of the practice I have just reduced to precept, I owe to Agnes, I will not repeat here.' After Dora's death, when David is travelling in Europe, it is Agnes's letter that stimulates him to resume work on his novel, which he continues in the domestic tranquillity of his aunt's house at Dover, and it is the domestic angel Agnes who presides over the scene of writing with which the novel concludes. Agnes is thus David's muse, his mate, and his maker. If David does, in fact, turn out to be the hero of his own story, then it is Agnes who plays a significant part in making him that hero. She is his muse, but she is also monitor and guide. Indeed, perhaps it is Agnes – whose inner life is not narrated and whose passions, struggles and enterprises are only to be inferred from her role in David's narrative – who is the 'hero' of the novel.[24]

In this novel, ideas about gender are never very far removed from conceptions of class, and anxieties about class. For example, David's sense of Clara Copperfield's gendered and classed identity is closely associated with his own anxieties about gender and class. Before her marriage to David's father, Clara had been a nursery governess without friends and family, and entirely lacking in any experience of managing a genteel household. The death of David's father and Clara's marriage to Murdstone provide David with an experience of downward social mobility which shapes his ambition and the stories he tells about his past, present and future. David is also defined (and defines himself) in relation to classed conceptions of masculinity. If *David Copperfield* offers a portrait of the artist as a young man, it also offers a portrait of a classed and gendered masculine individual who is constructed and placed in relation to alternative embodiments of masculinity. Steerforth, the object of 'Daisy's' schoolboy adoration, represents, as Margaret Myers has argued, 'the worst aspects of indulged cultural manhood. Socially successful, revered by his male peers, he is sensual, amoral, and self-absorbed'.[25] As an indulged and self-indulgent, aristocratic dandy, Steerforth is simultaneously feminized and the embodiment of rapacious masculine sexuality and economic power. An object of David's social and, some would argue, sexual desire, and (perhaps) sexually desiring David, he also acts out David's desires for his surrogate sister Em'ly, seducing and betraying the lower-class girl, who is unmarriageable (and hence sexually unavailable) to the socially aspiring Copperfield. If Steerforth can be seen as David's *alter ego,* then the egregiously repulsive red-eyed Uriah Heep, the object of David's youthful loathing, can be seen as his dark double. Heep is a negative model of self-help, who helps himself to what belongs to others. His false accounting is a negative (indeed criminal) version of David's fiction making, and his creepy desire for Agnes a displaced version of David's unacknowledged (and possibly unacknowledgeable) sexual feelings for the woman who will eventually become the mother of his children.

David's formation as a middle-class masculine subject is accompanied by (indeed, perhaps one might even argue, the result of) the textual expulsion of a range of other class/gender models: the sexually self-indulgent, aristocratic Steerforth; the repressed, socially aspirant, lower-class Heep; the fallen sexual lower-class woman Em'ly; and the infantilized model of decorative feminine gentility, Dora. The conceptualization of middle-class masculinity offered by this and numerous other nineteenth-century novels involves a model of desire as something which is regulated by and has both its origin and its destination in the home, where, as Mary Poovey has argued, 'it is stabilised and its transgressive potential [is] neutralised in the safe harbour of marriage'.[26] However, in *David Copperfield* marriage is not simply a device of narrative closure – it is a subject of investigation. The pitfalls of marriage are suggested in the two marriages of David's mother, the first marriage of Betsey Trotwood, the illicit union of Steerforth and Em'ly, and David's youthful marriage to Dora. The marriages of Annie and Dr Strong, Traddles and Sophy, and of course David and Agnes provide more positive examples.

David Copperfield is also a novel about the family and about its hero's quest for a family. David repeatedly represents himself as an abandoned and beleaguered orphan. Even at the end of the novel, with Agnes at his side, he recalls his former self on the road to Dover, robbed, dusty and weary: 'Long miles of road then opened out before my mind; and, toiling on, I saw a ragged way-worn boy, forsaken and neglected, who should come to call even the heart now beating against mine, his own' (62: 843). *David Copperfield*, like *Oliver Twist*, is the story of an orphan's progress. However, unlike Oliver's, David's is not the eighteenth-century story of the discovery of his hitherto unknown family origins, but the mid-Victorian narrative of the hero's discovery or founding of his own family. In the process of his self-fashioning as husband and father, David encounters many different models of the family: the brief idyll of the feminine space of the single-parent family into which he is born; the harsh regulation of the patriarchal discipline of the family of the middle-class merchant Murdstone, with its master's belief in 'firmness', and 'control', and the need to 'correct' a boy of David's 'moping and droning' disposition', to 'bend it and break it', and force that disposition to 'conform to the ways of the working world' (10: 147); the pastoral idyll of the Peggoty household at Yarmouth which is destroyed by Steerforth, a member of an aristocratic family whose social legitimacy and lineage David desires, but which is fragmented, divided against itself and emotionally sterile; the vacuous gentility of the Spenlow family; the bourgeois striving of Traddles and Sophy towards their companionate marriage.

Yet another model of the family is offered in the comic grotesqueness of the Micawber clan. The Micawber family is a comic version of David's own perceived situation and also of the aristocratic Steerforths whom he wishes to emulate. Mr Micawber understands middle-class domestic economy, and the kind of personal and social regulation required for a proper middle-class existence, but because he lives in constant hope of recovering the social station, from which, like David, he feels that he and his wife have (supposedly) been displaced, he doesn't feel the need to practise it. With his numerous offspring, his prodigality with words, and always in debt, Micawber trusts to luck that something will turn up, rather than, as David is required by the plot to do, learning to discipline his desires, to measure his words (sometimes quite literally since when David becomes a writer he is paid by the word or page), and to rely on his own efforts.

David Copperfield continues the work of artistic and bourgeois self-fashioning that Dickens had begun in *Dombey and Son*, but it is also, as I have tried to suggest, a reflection on as well as an embodiment of this process. It is also fraught with hesitancies, uncertainties and evasions. In short, this novel whose narrative method is based on its narrator taking his readers into his confidence, also (consciously or unconsciously) invites its readers to deconstruct the multiple overlapping meanings of that word 'confidence'.

John Forster saw *David Copperfield* as a turning point in Dickens's career, partly because of the financial security that its success gave him. Certainly, the moment of *Copperfield* coincided with (and perhaps gave Dickens the confidence to embark on) an important new venture: Dickens's launching of a new periodical to be edited or 'conducted' by himself. This periodical was *Household Words,* a twopenny weekly miscellany which aimed to 'live in the household affections' of its readers, and to link the domestic to the public by bringing into 'innumerable homes, from the stirring world around us, the knowledge of many social wonders, good and evil'.[27] Before discussing Dickens's novels of the 1850s I will look briefly at the *Household Words* project and at some of Dickens's own writing for this periodical in order to suggest some of the numerous interconnections between Dickens's fiction and his journalism in the 1850s.

5

The Novelist as Journalist in Hard Times, 1850–7

I 'The spirit of the people and the time': *Household Words*

> To the wholesome training of severe newspaper-work, when I
> was a very young man, I constantly refer my first successes.
> Dickens, quoted in *Life*, I: 51

During the time in which he was engaged in writing about David
Copperfield's authorial self-fashioning, Dickens was also attempting
to bring to fruition a scheme which had long formed part of his
own authorial self-conception – the scheme to 'conduct' a periodical in which he 'could speak personally' to the readers of his
novels.[1] At the end of March 1850, some eight months before
Copperfield finished its run, the first number of Dickens's magazine
Household Words appeared. From this point on, as Peter Ackroyd
points out, Dickens was to engage for the rest of his life 'in laboured
and often difficult editorial work, day by day, week by week, correcting the articles of others, cutting and reshaping, entitling, col-
laborating with other writers, corresponding, dealing with printers
and distributors' (Ackroyd, 622). Of course, as I have emphasized in
earlier chapters, Dickens began his writing life as a journalist,
working for daily and weekly newspapers and periodical miscellanies of various kinds. He had maintained his contact with the newspaper and periodical press after the success of *Pickwick*, writing
reviews for *The Examiner*, between 1837 and 1843, and becoming
founding editor of the *Daily News* in 1846 (although he resigned
after only seventeen issues). His later work for *The Examiner*
(1848–9), after his friend John Forster took over the editorship of
this weekly, required him to address an enlightened middle-class

readership, and helped to form both the way he thought and the way he went on to write about contemporary society and its problems in *Household Words* and in his later fiction.

What kind of periodical did Dickens have in mind as the instrument through which he could speak personally to his readers? What kind of role did he envisage for its conductor? In October 1849 he wrote to Forster of his grand design:

> [M]y notion is a weekly journal, price either three-halfpence or twopence, matter in part original and in part selected [from work published elsewhere], and always having, if possible, a little good poetry. ... The original matter to be essays, reviews, letters, theatrical criticisms ... as amusing as possible, but all distinctly and boldly going to what *in one's own view ought to be the spirit of the people and the time*. ... Now to bind all this together, and to get a character established as it were which any of the writers may maintain without difficulty, I want to suppose a certain *SHADOW, which may go into any place ... and be in all homes, and all nooks and corners, and be supposed to be cognisant of everything ... a kind of semi-omniscient, omnipresent, intangible creature ... a cheerful, useful and always welcome Shadow.* ... I have an enormous difficulty in expressing what I mean, in this stage of the business; but I think the importance of the idea is, that ... it presents an odd, unsubstantial, whimsical new thing: a sort of previously unthought-of Power going about. That it will concentrate into one focus all that is done in the paper. That it sets up a creature which isn't the Spectator ... [or] anything of that kind: but in which people will be perfectly willing to believe, and which is just mysterious and quaint enough to have a sort of charm for their imagination, while it will represent commonsense and humanity.   (*DL*, V: 621–3, emphasis added)

Even though Dickens did not put all aspects of this grand but vague design into action when he finally came to set up his weekly miscellany, this letter throws very interesting light on the both the periodical project and on Dickens's work more generally in the 1850s. First, the letter shows Dickens's desire to create a uniformity of purpose, and a single voice for his journal: it is to be his mouthpiece and as such it is to articulate 'what in one's own view ought to be the spirit of the people and the time'. Thus, at this point in his career Dickens was setting himself up as one who could speak both to and for his age. What kind of voice did Dickens aspire to, and what was the source of its authority? Let us look for a moment at the figure of the 'Shadow', who looms large in Dickens's original scheme, but who does not appear in the journal. This Shadow has quite a close resemblance to Dickens's 'semi-omniscient' narrative persona in *Sketches by Boz*,[2] and it also glances back to the figure invoked by the narrator of *Dombey and Son*, the 'good spirit who would take the house-tops off, with a ... potent and benignant hand ... and show a Christian people what dark shapes issue from amidst their homes' (47: 623). The putative Shadow of *Household Words* was also to reappear in the narratorial perspective of *Bleak House* and other novels of the 1850s and 1860s whose narrators seek to go into the nooks and corners of society. The Shadow is also associated with Dickens's broader project in his journalism and his fiction in the 1850s to foster the imagination and fancy, the common sense and humanity of his readers.

Dickens wanted the distinctive quality of his periodical to be the personal relationship it established with its readers. As he puts it in 'A Preliminary Word', the opening editorial prospectus for the periodical:

> We aspire to live in the Household affections, and to be numbered among the Household thoughts, of our readers. We hope to be the comrade and friend of many thousands of people of both sexes, and of all ages and conditions, on whose faces we may never look. (*DJ*, II: 177)

An important and explicit aim of *Household Words* was to take into the heart of the home a knowledge of the modern world: 'the mightier inventions of this age' in 'the stirring world around us' at 'this summer-dawn of time' with its 'many social wonders, good and evil'. The Conductor of this miscellany announced his intention to eschew the 'mere utilitarian spirit' and 'iron binding of the mind to grim realities' which, it is implied, is to be found in other periodicals of the day. Instead, he and his journal will seek to develop the imagination and bring the social classes together. It was an early version of Matthew Arnold's project for 'culture', though not one that the classically educated Arnold would have endorsed. Dickens had his own version of the sweetness and light that Arnold was to advocate in *Culture and Anarchy* in 'that light of Fancy which is inherent in the human breast', which he sought to 'tenderly cherish' and foster by showing 'to all, that in all familiar things, even in those which are repellent on the surface, there is Romance enough, if we will find it out'. The 'light of Fancy' is Dickens's one thing needful, to teach the hardest workers at this whirling wheel of toil, that their lot is not necessarily a moody, brutal fact, excluded from the sympathies and graces of imagination; to bring the greater and the lesser in degree, together, upon that wide field, and mutually dispose them to a better acquaintance and a kinder understanding.

This project of individual and social enlightenment by means of the education of the Fancy was the 'one main object of our Household Words' *(DJ*, II: 177).

Dickens confronted Carlyle's (and anticipated Arnold's) characterization of the nineteenth century as an age of machinery, insisting instead (with more optimism than he displayed in some of his novels of the 1850s) that the 'mightier inventions of this age are not, to our thinking, all material, but have a kind of souls in their stupendous bodies'. Like Arnold, Dickens the conductor rejected the provincialism of 'presentism' and Anglo-centrism, when he affirmed that:

> Our Household Words will not be echoes of the present time alone, but of the past too. Neither will they treat of the hopes, the enterprises, triumphs, joys and sorrows, of this country only, but, in some degree, of those of every nation upon earth. For nothing can be a source of real interest in one of them, without concerning the rest. *(DJ*, II: 178)

Interestingly, the hand that was concurrently writing the writer David Copperfield claimed a special personal and autobiographical authority for carrying out the projected purpose of *Household Words*: the 'hand that writes these faltering lines, happily associated with *some* Household words before today, has known enough of such experiences [previously referred to] to enter in an earnest spirit upon this new task, and with an awakened sense of all it involves' *(DJ*, II: 177). The Conductor concludes his address to the reader (an address which, in effect, actively constructs the reader that he wants), by espousing a Copperfieldian rhetoric (touched with Agnes's upward vision), as he sets out to be the hero of his own periodical and invites his readers to join him on a journey onwards and upwards.

What sort of miscellany did this rhetorical fanfare launch? Ann Lohrli points out in the introduction to her checklist of articles and their authors that *Household Words* carried three main kinds of material: 'material of social import, informational articles, and material for entertainment'.[3] Throughout its nine-year run

Household Words had included articles on all manner of 'social evils', and lent its voice to what Dickens referred to as 'the general improvement of our social condition' (in letters soliciting contributions from Elizabeth Gaskell and Mary Howitt; see *DL*, VI: 22). *Household Words* brought the condition of London's homeless poor and slum-dwellers to the attention of its middle-class readers. It was a campaigning journal, which fought against illiteracy and championed the cause of education for the lower classes. It campaigned for improved working and living conditions for various categories of worker, concerned itself with matters of sanitation and public health, and advocated the reform of various outmoded laws and judicial practices. It attacked nepotism, incompetence and apathy in government. As Lohrli notes, none of the social issues on which *Household Words* campaigned were first brought to public attention in the pages of that journal, but its controversial and readable treatment was the means of bringing them into greater and wider prominence.

Dickens's mission to instruct and entertain was carried out in numerous informational articles on science, technology and natural history, and on the history, geography, economy and social institutions of Britain and other countries. There were biographical sketches and articles on travel, the arts and books (descriptions of their contents rather than reviews). Exhibitions and public events and spectacles at home and abroad also received attention. Entertainment with instruction (or vice versa) was also offered in the tales, short stories, poems and serialized novels that appeared in each weekly number, and in the special supplements containing poems and stories which appeared at Christmas.

The Conductor of *Household Words* was a very interventionist editor who sought to ensure that his initial vision of a periodical that would speak with one voice and in its (that is to say Dickens's) own distinctive style was maintained. This style was to be lively, fanciful, imaginative, picturesque, and quaint. Dickens preferred articles to open and close provocatively and have punning or otherwise clever titles, and he often provided these elements himself, so that many items in the journal were collaborative or composite pieces. In short, the whole thing was 'Dickensy' as Elizabeth Gaskell somewhat pejoratively remarked in a letter.[4] Many critics of the weekly felt that its characteristic modes were exaggeration and distortion. This criticism applied both to its relentless pursuit of the amusing and to its treatment of social questions. Reviewing a piece in the number for 22 October 1859, The *Press* complained that 'isolated blemishes in the social system are magnified through the hazy medium of exaggerated phrases to the dimensions of the entire system, and casual exceptions are converted into a universal rule and practice'.[5] Similar criticisms were also made of Dickens's great social novels of the 1850s, usually by those who did not think that society was in any great need of reform.

What of Dickens's own contributions to his periodical (rather than his additions and amendments to the work of others)? During the nine-year run of *Household Words* Dickens supplied his share of quaint, whimsical and fanciful pieces. Taking up the role of the Shadow who goes into the nooks and corners of society, Dickens also wrote some powerful pieces on the condition of modern England, such as 'A December Vision' (28 December 1850), 'Last Words of the Old Year' (4 January 1851), 'A Sleep to Startle Us' (13 February 1853), and 'A Nightly Scene in London' (26 January 1856), all of which read like trial runs for, reworkings of, or commentaries on the novels of the 1850s. Indeed, 'A December Vision' and 'Last Words of the Old Year' form a kind of bridge between the later novels and some of Dickens's earlier work, in their reiteration of the warnings contained in the Christmas Books about the failure of the institutions of modern society to deal adequately with the problems of the urban poor. 'A December Vision' represents England as a City of Destruction in which a visiting 'mighty Spirit' (another version of the Shadow) sees 'Thirty Thousand children, hunted, flogged, imprisoned, but not taught' (*DJ*, II: 307), and visits 'reeking and pernicious stews', which, like the slums of Tom-all-Alone's in *Bleak House*, spread contagion in 'particles of infection ... charged with heavy retribution on the general guilt' (*DJ*, II: 308). The legions of the unhoused and uneducated children of London are also at the centre of 'A Sleep to Startle Us', which deals with conditions in a 'Ragged Dormitory' (a free school for the poor), and of 'The Last Words of the Old Year'. In this latter piece, published in the year of the Great Exhibition, Dickens called for an alternative Exhibition: 'for the great display of England's sins and negligences, to be, by steady contemplation of all eyes, and steady union of all hearts, set right' (*DJ*, II: 313). Both 'A Sleep to Startle Us' and 'The Last Words of the Old Year' attack the incompetence and vested interests of public authorities – the 'Honourable Board of Commissioners of Sewers' in the latter, and, in the former, the 'preposterous Red Tape conditions' (*DJ*, III: 57) which prevented the Ragged Schools from being run in the best interests of their pupils. These are powerfully written essays which employ some of the rhetorical strategies of Dickens's late social fiction – for example, the powerful address to 'My Lords and Gentlemen' which concludes 'A Sleep to Startle Us', and which is taken up in the address to 'My Lords and Honourable Boards' in *Bleak House*.

Dickens's self-appointed role as a kind of moral special constable, policing the social and moral abuses of his society, was matched by his interest in the work of the police force. Four pieces which appeared between July 1850 and June 1851 – 'A Detective Police Party' (27 July 1850 and 10 August 1850), 'Three "Detective" Anecdotes' (14 September 1850), and 'On Duty with Inspector Field' (14 June 1851) – are evidence of Dickens's continuing concern with crime and its detection, and they reveal a fascination with the new detective police which was to surface in a number of his later novels, especially *Bleak House* (which began its monthly run in March 1852). 'On Duty with Inspector Field' is particularly interesting in the way it uses the police inspector's nightly beat as a way of taking the middle-class readers of *Household Words* on an armchair tour of those areas of the city which they would not usually enter, or from which they would normally avert their gaze. The essay conveys admiration for Field's power and for his control of the criminals whose activities he monitors, but it also conveys horror at the social conditions which breed crime. Field polices the boundaries between 'respectable' and 'criminal' society, but the essay leaves the reader with the distinct impression that by moving on the homeless and keeping the criminal population under surveillance, Field is merely keeping the lid on a powder keg created by rapid social change and social inequality. Again Dickens's rhetoric anticipates that of *Bleak House*:

> Thus we make our New Oxford Streets, and our other new streets, never heeding, never asking, where the wretches whom we clear out, crowd. With such scenes at our doors, with all the plagues of Egypt tied up with bits of cobweb in kennels so near our homes, we timorously make our Nuisance Bills and boards of Health, nonentities, and think to keep away the Wolves of Crime and Filth, by our ... gentlemanly handling of Red Tape. (*DJ*, II: 363)

The gentlemanly handling of Red Tape and its adverse social consequences was to be a major preoccupation of Dickens's novels in the 1850s, and it is to *Bleak House*, the first of those novels, that I will now turn.

II   Anatomizing Britain: *Bleak House*

Just two months after the last number of *David Copperfield* had appeared Dickens noted, in a letter to Mary Boyle, 'the first shadows of a new story hovering in a ghostly way about me (as they usually begin to do, when I have finished an old one)' (*DL*, VI: 297–8). Just over a year later, in March 1852, the first of the nineteen monthly parts of *Bleak House* was published. Like *David Copperfield*, *Bleak House*, at least in part, employs the form of autobiography. Esther Summerson, the novel's heroine, and one of its two narrators, self-effacingly tells – or, perhaps more accurately, attempts to reconstruct – the story of her own life. Like *Household Words*, Dickens's other big project of the early 1850s, *Bleak House* is a miscellany designed to entertain and instruct its readers, and also to shock them. Like the periodical, the novel consists of a variety of genres: it is a mystery story, a detective novel (and one of the first English novels to make use of the new detective police), a family romance, and a murderous melodrama. *Bleak House* is also a social problem novel, a 'Condition-of-England' novel which is concerned both to represent and to anatomize the signs of the times. It was, as John Butt and Kathleen Tillotson demonstrated in *Dickens at Work*, 'a fable for 1852'.[6] Perhaps the most topical of Dickens's novels, *Bleak House* does not simply *refer* to contemporary events in the manner of reportage; rather, it is organized around specific events and issues which had recently been reported and debated in the press, including its author's own *Household Words*: 'Red Tapism' and the iniquities of the Court of Chancery, slum conditions, sanitation reform, the education of the poor and orphaned, the operations of the detective police, Puseyite philanthropists, the Niger expedition, the home mission versus the overseas mission, and female emancipation, to name but a few. It is also thoroughly grounded in history. It draws on the author's personal history – Dickens's days as a legal and parliamentary reporter have obviously informed the representation of the various forms of 'wiglomeration'. It is also full of references to the history of oppression and rebellion from the days of the Pharaohs through to the Peasants' Revolt (Sir Leicester Dedlock is constantly invoking Wat Tyler, the peasants' leader, as a symbol of what will happen if the floodgates of change are opened), the English Civil War, the Gunpowder Plot, the Jacobite revolution and the industrial revolution.

If Dickens's concern in *Bleak House* was with the everyday social world, it was with the everyday world transformed into a strange unlikeness of itself. 'In Bleak House', he wrote at the end of his Preface to the one-volume edition of 1853, 'I have purposely dwelt upon the romantic side of familiar things' (*BH*, 6). These words announce another point of continuity between this novel and the *Household Words* project, and Dickens's objective that the periodical should cherish the 'light of Fancy' and 'show to all, that in all familiar things, even in those which are repellent on the surface, there is Romance enough, if we will find it out' (*DJ*, II: 177). This emphasis on the Romance of the familiar, on Fancy and Imagination, on the sympathies and the nurturing of them, can be seen as part of a wider project of rethinking and reworking the relationship between romance and realism, and developing an ethics and aesthetics for fiction at mid-century. They anticipate by a few years George Eliot's advocacy of a form of novelistic art that would educate the sympathies, and they echo Elizabeth Gaskell's location of her own mixed-genre 'Condition-of-England' novel, *Mary Barton,* in her perception of 'how deep might be the romance in the lives of those who elbowed me daily in the streets of the town in which I resided'.[7]

When Dickens dwells on the romantic side of familiar things in *Bleak House*, the effect is to defamiliarize and even to destabilize them. This particular romance of the familiar begins, not as romances often do, 'once upon a time', but here, now and in England, as Dickens places his readers in a world which is vividly and uncannily both real and fantastical:

> LONDON. Michaelmas Term lately over, and the Lord Chancellor sitting in Lincoln's Inn Hall. Implacable November weather. As much mud in the streets, as if the waters had but lately retired from the face of the earth, and it would not be wonderful to meet a Megalosaurus, forty feet long or so, waddling like an elephantine lizard up Holborn Hill. Smoke lowering down from chimney-pots, making a soft black drizzle, with flakes of soot in it as big as full-grown snow-flakes – gone into mourning, one might imagine, for the death of the sun. (*BH*, 1: 11)

Here is London in the year after the Great Exhibition, that great expression of London's sense of itself as the centre of a growing empire, represented in highly metaphorical language as if it were just emerging at the dawn of creation, or as if it were declining with the entropic death of the sun. As the opening paragraph continues the language of the new geology and fiscal metaphors combine in an energetic phantasmagoria to represent London – one of the major capitals of Capital – as the city of modernity, signifying urban chaos and atomization:

> Dogs, undistinguishable in mire. Horses, scarcely better; splashed to their very blinkers. Foot passengers, jostling one another's umbrellas in a general infection of ill-temper, and losing their foothold at street corners, where tens of thousands of other foot passengers have been slipping and sliding since the day broke (if this day ever broke), adding new deposits to the crust upon crust of mud, sticking at those points tenaciously to the pavement, and accumulating at compound interest.   (1:11)

And finally, in this densely metaphoric opening, there is the emergence of the dominant figure of the fog, as Dickens uses the London 'pea-souper' as a common element that both separates and connects disparate individuals and different social spheres, and as a metaphor for the obfuscating operations of the Court of Chancery:

> The raw afternoon is rawest, and the dense fog is densest, and the muddy streets are muddiest, near that leaden-headed old obstruction, appropriate ornament for the threshold of a leaden-headed old corporation: Temple Bar. And hard by Temple Bar, in Lincoln's Inn Hall, at the very heart of the fog, sits the Lord High Chancellor in his High Court of Chancery.   (1:12)

Thus the novel launches into the sustained critique of the Court of Chancery which is at the centre of its attack on the asinine, self-serving, nepotistic, moribund and deadlocked social institutions – the law, parliament, the aristocracy, Evangelical religion – that serve as both symptom and symbol of the condition of mid-Victorian England: the 'do-nothing dilettantism' so fiercely criticized by Thomas Carlyle in the 1840s.[8]

Bleak House conducts its social critique not simply through its defamiliarization of the world of habit and the taken-for-granted social world in highly metaphorical passages such as the one just quoted, but also through the way in which its two narrators variously direct the reader's gaze and make us look at and think and feel about aspects of everyday social life that we might prefer not to think about or respond to. *Bleak House* represents an atomized society, a society in which human beings are isolated, self-divided and alienated from one another. At the same time it seeks to insist, not least through the operations of its labyrinthine plot, on the interconnectedness of society and the inescapability of the consequences of social action or inaction. As the novel develops, so does its Carlylean sense that 'if something be not done' – about the condition of England – 'then something will *do* itself and in a fashion that will please nobody'.[9] Like other contemporary social commentators, Dickens has recourse to the imagery of disease and contagion to figure the condition of the social and political body. Chapter 16, 'Tom-All-Alone's', is a very good example of this. This chapter offers an apocalyptic vision of urban degradation in its representation of the crazy houses in the back streets, houses and streets which are 'avoided by all decent people'. These houses (which are, of course, involved in a Chancery suit), are described as having been colonized by bold vagrants and, like a rotting corpse, they have bred a 'swarm of misery' in 'maggot numbers', spreading fever and 'sowing more evil … than Lord Coodle, and Sir Thomas Doodle … and all the fine gentlemen down to Zoodle, shall set right in five hundred years – though born expressly to do it' (16: 236). The contemporary fear of contagion evoked in this chapter echoes Carlyle's story of the Irish widow (in *Past and Present*), who was 'reduced to prove her sisterhood' with those who sought to ignore or deny her membership of the brotherhood of man, 'by dying of typhus-fever and infecting seventeen persons – saying in such an undeniable way, "You *see*, I was your sister!"'[10] It is this chapter which introduces Jo, the slum-dwelling crossing sweeper, who performs a similar function to Carlyle's Irish widow and acts as a key figure in the novel's social critique and in the way in which it works upon the reader's sympathies.

Dickens's presentation of Jo also indicates some of the problems of the rhetoric of sympathy which he developed in this novel. The third-person narrator attempts to obtain the reader's sympathy by making us imagine what it is to be like Jo, but the means by which he does so paradoxically runs the risk of reinserting the orphan and vagrant into a discourse of the poor as 'other'. An illiterate in a novel which is about the reading and the interpretation of documents, Jo is represented in this chapter as a dumb animal, a creature possessed of as little understanding as the sheepdog who stands beside him listening to a passing band. The othering of Jo is perhaps mitigated by the narrator's insistence on 'connexion':

> What connexion can there be, between the place in Lincolnshire, the house in town, the Mercury in powder, and the whereabouts of Jo the outlaw with the broom, who had that distant ray of light upon him when he swept the churchyard step? What connexion can there have been between many people in the innumerable histories of this world, who, from opposite sides of great gulfs, have, nevertheless, been very curiously brought together?   (16: 235)

Here, as so often in this novel, the impersonal third-person narrator addresses the reader directly, using a preacherly mode of address and a series of rhetorical questions which are, in effect, answered by the novel's plot. In this case, the plot is structured so as to insist on the connections between the outlaw with the broom and other classes and locations, and, in particular, to insist on the connection between the outlaw with the broom and the decaying aristocracy, isolated and apparently insulated from the world of Tom-All-Alones by their grand houses, their flunkies, intermediaries, and the other appurtenances of power.

Like virtually all of Dickens's novels (indeed, like virtually every other Victorian novel), *Bleak House* has a complex plot, or rather it has multiple plots, which snake in and out of each other, linking together in various (often surreptitious) ways. At the centre of all of the plots is the expensive and complicated Chancery case of Jarndyce and Jarndyce. John Jarndyce, who refuses to involve himself in the legal proceedings, brings together at his home, Bleak House, Richard Carstone and Ada Clare – the two orphaned wards in Jarndyce – and Esther Summerson, supposedly an orphan, who has been brought up to feel guilty about her very existence. Esther, who acts as sort of companion to Ada and housekeeper for them all, watches Richard and Ada fall in love, and observes the process by which the Chancery suit and his 'expectations' of what he might obtain from its resolution combine to erode Richard's power to commit himself to work and a life in the present, and result in his destruction. (As I noted on page 83, Richard is one of a long line of Dickens's studies of the malign effects in young men of the middle and upper classes of the psychology of expectations.) Esther's story culminates in her discovery of her parentage, and in her marriage to a hardworking man of a reforming persuasion.

The other main plot-line centres on the aristocratic Sir Leicester Dedlock and his wife (inhabitants of the world of fashion), and ripples out from the Lawyer Tulkinghorn's observation of Lady Dedlock's discomfiture when she apparently recognizes the handwriting in a legal document written by a down-at-heel law writer, Nemo. Nemo and Jo, the destitute crossing sweeper whom he befriends, prove to be links which bind together the main plots and various of the numerous sub-plots, not least through the spreading of the smallpox which kills one character and, for a time, disfigures another.

As usual in Dickens's novels there is an enormous cast of colourful, comic, satiric, grotesque, and downright repulsive characters: representatives of the law, the political establishment, evangelical religion, telescopic philanthropy (Mrs Jellyby, who neglects her family and social problems close to home, while writing pamphlets and organizing schemes for 'educating the natives of Borrioboola-Gha'), hangers-on of the aristocracy, parasites such as Harold Skimpole and Mr Turveydrop, as well as representatives of a new world, such as the doctor Alan Woodcourt, and the ironmaster Rouncewell. To add to the complexity of plot, many of the characters and sub-plots are shrouded in mystery, like the fog which hangs over the opening pages. Several characters are not who or what they seem to be, and the mysteries of the histories and/or parentage of several of them have to be cleared up during the course of the novel. Several characters have guilty secrets (for example, Lady Dedlock, who anticipates the 'woman-with-a-secret' of the sensation novel), or they feel they have guilty secrets (Esther), or alternatively they spend their lives in a state of inexplicable guilty confusion, like Mr Snagsby, who feels that 'something is wrong, somewhere; but what something, what may come of it, to whom, when, and from which unthought-of ... quarter, is the puzzle of his life' (25: 374). There is also a violent murder which Inspector Bucket, a member of the new detective police, is called in to solve.

In *Bleak House* the complexly interconnected multiple plot is, so to speak, the novel's theme or subject. *Bleak House* has an added dimension of narrative complication: it is a double or split narrative. In his attempt to represent a whole society as an interconnected web Dickens makes use of two narrators – an impersonal (though sometimes quite emotional) third-person narrator, narrating in the present tense, and a first-person narrator – the self-

effacing, saintly, and often coy and evasive, Esther Summerson –
who is also the novel's heroine. Esther narrates her story retrospectively, and, it would seem, reluctantly, and also in a manner
which questions her own narrative authority:

> I have a great deal of difficulty in beginning to write my portion of
> these pages, for I know I am not clever. I always knew that, I can
> remember, when I was a very little girl indeed I used to say to my doll,
> when we were alone together, 'Now Dolly, I am not clever, you know
> very well, and you must be patient with me, like a dear!'   (3: 24)

Dismissed by many early readers as merely 'weak and twaddling',
as Charlotte Brontë put it in a letter to her publisher George
Smith,[11] Esther's narrative and its place in the double narrative has
been one of the main interests of much recent writing on *Bleak
House*. Indeed, the novel is now more likely to be read as a
comment on the nineteenth-century construction of a (feminine)
gendered self rather than merely a reproduction of it. It is, then,
less likely to be read as a 'weak and twaddling' representation of
the angel in the house, than as a psychologically acute representation of a young woman damaged and self-alienated by a loveless
childhood and by the sense of personal and social guilt inculcated
by her 'godmother' (actually her aunt), who brings her up to
regard herself as a double disgrace: 'Your mother, Esther, is your
disgrace, and you were hers' (3: 26). Esther's coyness may, on
occasions, make her an unreliable or evasive narrator, but it is also
an integral part of a self-consciously constructed narrative of self-
fashioning, in which the female narrator constructs the story of her
life as the good girl's story. This is a narrative which seeks to
'repair the fault I had been born with (of which I confusedly felt
guilty and yet innocent)' (3: 27). It is a narrative of industrious-
ness, contentedness, and kind-heartedness, aimed at winning some
love for herself.

The device of the double narrative mediated by such very different narrators is an interesting one. It requires readers constantly to
shift their perspectives and to view the same events and situations
through different value systems. This is a process which, as
Virginia Blain has suggested, 'sets up a submerged dialectic'
between masculine and feminine viewpoints.[12] The third-person
narrator adopts the pose of an authoritative social commentator,
who indicts Chancery and the system. He is rather like the
shadowy super-reporter persona whom Dickens self-consciously

sought to develop in *Household Words,* the freely-moving *flâneur,* who 'may go into any place ... and be in all homes, and all nooks and corners, and be supposed to be cognisant of everything, and go everywhere ... a kind of semi-omniscient, omnipresent, intangible creature' (*Life*, I: 395). Esther, on the other hand, is a limited narrator, both in the technical sense that her knowledge of the action is restricted to those aspects of it which she actually experiences or learns about within the conventions of realism, and in the sense that she herself insists on, when she repeatedly describes herself as 'not clever'. The limitations of Esther's knowledge and understanding are in large part the limitations of the way in which middle-class femininity was constructed in the nineteenth century. The apparent limitation of Esther's perspective is also a device for the education of the reader. One example of this is the scene in which Esther reluctantly accompanies Mrs Pardiggle on her charitable visit to the brickmakers, and confides to the reader her feeling of being 'painfully sensible that between us and these people there was an iron barrier, which could not be removed' by Mrs Pardiggle's charity, before going on to confess the extent and limitations of her knowledge of social questions: 'By whom, or how it could be removed, we did not know; but we knew that' (8: 122).

Knowledge and problems of knowledge are at the centre of this text and of many twentieth-century readings of it. For Raymond Williams *Bleak House* was a representation of a world 'increasingly dominated by processes that could only be grasped statistically or analytically – a community unknowable in terms of manifest experience'.[13] For J. Hillis Miller it was a document about the interpretation of documents, a novel whose characters and readers alike are faced with problems of interpretation, of making connections, and of solving mysteries.[14] *Bleak House* makes detectives of most of its characters and all of its readers. It is for this reason, as well as its inclusion of Inspector Bucket on the trail of Tulkinghorn's murderer, that *Bleak House* might be seen as an early example of the English detective novel, the modern form of the quest narrative. Just as Esther's narrative is a quest for her own identity and for her parentage; so, too, the third-person narrative is a series of interconnected quests (and false quests) for identity, as others seek out the identity of Esther and her connection to Lady Dedlock (Guppy); the identity of Nemo and his connection to Lady Dedlock (Tulkinghorn); the identity of Tulkinghorn's killer and the disguised Lady Dedlock (Bucket); the identity of Jo and his connection to Mr Snagsby (Mrs Snagsby), and so on.

At the heart of each of these quest narratives, and of the novel as a whole, is that universal suspicion which fiction reviewers in the 1860s attributed to writers of sensation novels (of which *Bleak House* is an early example), those novels of crime and mystery that sought to persuade their readers that each of their neighbours was concealing some dreadful secret in his (or, more usually, her) bosom. This universal suspicion was also, in the view of Walter Benjamin, one of the defining characteristics of the detective novel, a fictional form which he saw as being produced by, and articulating the conditions of, urban modernity. Such fiction, Benjamin argued, describes 'big-city dwellers ... the best as well as the most wretched', as carrying around 'a secret which would make him hateful to all others if it became known'. Moreover, according to Benjamin, in modern times ('times of terror'), everyone is 'something of a con-spirator', and 'will be in a situation where he has to play detective'.[15] This model of a form of detective fiction in which everyone is either or both a guilty party and a detective or spy seems particularly apt for an analysis of *Bleak House*. The genre of detective fiction also provides another perspective on the double narrative. Tzvetan Todorov has argued that the detective story is usually a double nar-rative: it is the story of the crime (in the past tense) and the present-tense story of its detection.[16] The gradual convergence of the two narratives of *Bleak House* can be read as conforming to this pattern, except, perhaps, that the reader of this novel is not quite sure what the real crime is, and, like Esther, is left feeling innocent yet guilty.

As I have shown in earlier chapters, from the very beginning of his career as a writer Dickens was fascinated by the law and crime. In the 1850s he was increasingly interested in the police, and espe-cially the new detective police force, which was established just ten years before the appearance of *Bleak House*. Starting with 'A Detective Police Party' (27 July and 10 August 1850), he wrote several admiring sketches of and interviews with members of the detective force for *Household Words*. Several recent critics (taking their lead from D. A. Miller) have suggested that *Bleak House* is not just a response to the rise of the new Detective Force, but that it is concerned with more subtle and pervasive forms of policing – with the processes of (self-)surveillance, (self-)control and (self-) management that are characteristic of modern bourgeois society, and which produce the modern bourgeois subject. In his influential Foucauldian reading, Miller argues that despite its ostensible attack on bureaucracy, nepotism and corruption, the complexly plotted form and even the length of this novel mimic the proliferating forms of social control and discipline that were developing in the nineteenth century. In short, it 'trains' its readers 'in the sensibility for inhabiting the new bureaucratic and administrative structures'. Novel reading in this account is itself a kind of 'bleak house': the form and duration of the novel 'presents itself as a kind of home', but one which more closely resembles 'the social-institutional world at large', than 'comfortable domestic quarters'.[17]

Miller's reading is persuasive, even to the extent that it attempts to account for the novel's reticence about appearing 'an agency of the police', as seen in its 'reservations about the nature and effects' of policing power. However, rather than seeing the novel's qualification of the approval it accords to the Detective Police as a shifty attempt to cover its own tracks, I would suggest that in its representation of Esther (with her 'noticing way'), on the one hand, and the inquiring Vholes and Tulkinghorn on the other, it displays a degree of self-consciousness about the surveillance society and the processes by which the products of this society internalize both self-surveillance and spying on others. Moreover, like Dickens's pieces on the Detective Force in *Household Words*, *Bleak House* calls attention to the way in which the police work by co-opting ordinary citizens as spies and informers, in this case (when Bucket co-opts Skimpole with a bribe) with deadly consequences for Jo.

Perhaps the greatest challenge to the 'disciplinary' reading of this novel, however, is provided by its own indiscipline: the loose, baggy, capaciousness of the big serial novel, its constantly changing cast of characters, the energy of its language, its failure to tie up all the loose ends. This is, after all, a novel which concludes with a dash, as its first-person narrator concludes her narrative with the inconclusive '– even supposing –'. *Bleak House* begins fantastically and ends fancifully. Moreover, as a novel with two narrators it begins and ends twice. In between, the power of Dickens's fancy and fantasy conjures into being a host of different and disparate voices. *Bleak House*, like Dickens's fiction more generally, exemplifies the Russian critic Mikhail Bakhtin's view of the novel as a multi-voiced or heteroglossic and dialogic (double-voiced) form which puts into play different voices and contending discourses through the idiolects of different characters, through irony and parody, and by means of dialogue with other social and fictional discourses. Bakhtin saw language as itself heteroglossic and dialogic: at any one historical moment comprising 'the mutual interanimation'[18] of different class, gender, professional, theological or epistemological discourses. However, when heteroglossia enters the novel, Bakhtin argued:

> it becomes subject to an artistic reworking. The social and historical voices populating language, all its words and all its forms ... are organized into a structured stylistic system that expresses the differentiated socio-ideological position of the author amid the heteroglossia of his epoch.[19]

This process of differentiation and its accompanying tendency to undermine the truth claims of the dominant discourses of the author's epoch, is potentially subversive. At its most subversive novelistic dialogism becomes 'an extended parody of the discourses of power', which undermines the authority of these discourses 'by fusing them with a persistently opposing point of view',[20] and offers readers another way (or other ways) of viewing the way things are. Doing the novel in different voices is thus not simply a way of 'Doing discipline in different voices' (as Miller argues) but rather of interrupting the disciplinary discourses of (among others) providential religion and the law to reveal an inharmonious and unjust society. Discipline and the critique of modern disciplinary procedures are also at the centre of Dickens's next novel, *Hard Times*, which appeared weekly in *Household Words* between 1 April and 12 August 1854.

III Setting the muddle to rights? *Hard Times*

> People must be amuthed ... they can't be alwayth a working, nor yet they can't be alwayth a learning.
>
> Dickens, *Hard Times*, 1: 6, 47

Hard Times is concerned, among other things, with the production of the modern disciplinary subject, with the relations between discipline and fancy, and with the adverse consequences of the over-disciplining of fancy. Uncharacteristically short, *Hard Times* is also untypical of Dickens's work in its setting in the industrial north of England, and its apparently obvious thesis – its opposition of system and fact on the one hand, and life and fancy on the other (or Gradgrindery versus Sleary's Circus). *Hard Times* became one of Dickens's most widely read novels in the second half of the twentieth-century, not least because it is relatively short and has an apparently simple message. However, *Hard Times* has had a chequered critical history, and has been regarded by many critics as Dickens's least successful novel: a novel 'in the grip of an idea' with a 'bleakly deterministic view of the hopelessness of the human condition'.[21] It was precisely what he took to be the strength and clarity of the novel as 'moral fable' that led F. R. Leavis to claim *Hard Times* as a 'masterpiece', 'a completely serious, and in its originality, a triumphantly successful, work of art'.[22] Most recent criticism, however, has focused on the novel's inconsistencies, conflicts and contradictions, and what they reveal of the anxieties of mid-Victorian Britain about class, gender, the family, divorce, work, education, industrialism and the factory system, labour relations, the nature of society and the relationship between the individual and society.

Hard Times has a triple plot. There is a melodramatic plot of family disintegration (and partial recovery), focusing on the Gradgrinds and linking them to Bounderby, a self-proclaimed, self-made man and factory-owner (who is apparently without a family), and also to the alternative family of Sleary's Circus. Bounderby also figures prominently in the novel's industrial plot which centres on a strike. Finally, there is a sensational plot of robbery, betrayal and attempted seduction, Harthouse's attempt to manoeuvre the married Louisa into eloping with him being one of several examples of Dickens's use of the quasi-adultery plot in his novels of the late 1840s and 1850s. Like *Bleak House*, *Hard Times* is concerned with contemporary events; in this case, the eight-month Preston Strike of 1853–4, on which Dickens had reported for *Household Words*. *Hard Times* also continues the mode of satirizing British parliamentary and governmental institutions begun with the ridiculing of Boodle, Coodle, Doodle and Foodle etc. in *Bleak House* and developed further in the attack on the Circumlocution Office in *Little Dorrit*. In *Hard Times*, as in *Bleak House*, Parliament is represented as a self-interested talking shop. It is the 'little noisy and rather dirty machinery, in a by-corner' into which Gradgrind is 'hustled' by the passage of time, to become one of the respected members for ounce weights and measures, one of the representatives of the multiplication table, one of the deaf honourable gentlemen, dumb honourable gentlemen, blind honourable gentlemen, lame honourable gentlemen, dead honourable gentlemen to every other consideration.   (1: 14, 96)

Hard Times is perhaps best known, even to those who have never actually read it, for its critique of utilitarian, instrumental forms of education that attempt to fill pupils with facts, like the little cabinets in which the Gradgrind children arrange and label their specimens of 'the various departments of science' (1: 3, 17). The novel is 'inscribed' to Thomas Carlyle, and it develops the attack on the 'age of machinery' that Carlyle mounted in 'Signs of the Times' (1829), and continued in his critique of statistics in *Chartism* (1840). The chief exponents of the mechanical doctrine of facts are the schoolteacher, Mr M'Choakumchild, and Thomas Gradgrind, who uses his children Louisa and Tom, as well as the working-class children of Coketown, as experimental animals on which to test his educational theories. The novel opens with Gradgrind's recital of his creed of facts as the one thing needful for the education of children:

> Herein lay the spring of the mechanical art and mystery of educating the reason without stooping to the cultivation of the sentiments and affection. Never wonder. By means of addition, subtraction, multiplication and division, settle everything somehow, and never wonder. 'Bring to me,' says M'Choakumchild, 'yonder baby just able to walk, and I will engage that it will never wonder.' (1: 8, 54)

The awful consequences of this educational philosophy, and its embargo on wonder and fancy, are seen in the blighted life of Louisa Gradgrind, who, after carefully considering the facts of the case (and in order to assist her brother), embarks on a loveless marriage with a man whom she finds repulsive. One of the novel's own pedagogic strategies is to educate both Louisa and the reader by making them increasingly aware of a profound absence in Louisa's experience and education, which is associated with a complete lack of knowledge of 'fancies ... aspirations and affections', of a 'child's heart' and a 'child's dream' (1: 15, 104). The consequences of Gradgrindery are seen, too, in the calculating self-interest of Louisa's brother Tom, and of his working-class counterpart Bitzer,

who is the novel's representation of the characteristic product of
the instrumental education for the lower classes introduced by
reformers such as James Kay-Shuttleworth. (Dickens took up this
theme again in his portrayal of Bradley Headstone, Charley Hexam
and Miss Peacher in *Our Mutual Friend.*) The pale, cold-eyed Bitzer
learns his lessons of fact so well that he grows up into

> An extremely clear-headed, cautious, prudent young man, who was
> safe to rise in the world. His mind was so exactly regulated, that ...
> [a]ll his proceedings were the result of the nicest and coldest calcu-
> lation. ... Having satisfied himself, on his father's death, that his
> mother had a right of settlement in Coketown, this excellent young
> economist had asserted that right for her with such a steadfast
> adherence to the principle of the case, that she had been shut up in
> the workhouse ever since. It must be admitted that he allowed her
> half a pound of tea a year, which was weak in him: first, because all
> gifts have an inevitable tendency to pauperize the recipient, and sec-
> ondly, because his only reasonable transaction in that commodity
> would have been to buy it for as little as he could possibly give, and
> sell it for as much as he could possibly get; it having been clearly
> ascertained by philosophers that in this is comprised the whole duty
> of man.   (2: 1, 120)

This blistering portrait of Bitzer is not simply an attack on a mech-
anistic theory of education, but it also continues Carlyle's attack
(in the sixth chapter of *Chartism*) on a society in which the 'cash
nexus' has become the basis of human relations.

Significantly, it is Sissy Jupe ('Girl number twenty'), the child
who fails to learn Gradgrind's lessons of facts, economics and statistics, who undermines Gradrind's faith in his creed by making
him conscious of 'something in [her] ... which could hardly be set
forth in a tabular form' (1: 14, 95), and who becomes the means
by which he and his family are (at least in part) rescued from the
worst consequences of those lessons. Sissy Jupe's perpetual state
of confusion about the questions her teachers ask of her and the
answers they supply when her own answers fail to satisfy them is
also used to unsettle the reader's too ready acceptance of the
orthodoxies of liberal economic theory. Sissy's responses to
M'Choakumchild's questions (in 1: 9) about what is demonstrated
by his figures and statistics on National Prosperity, and the proportion of the population starved to death in the streets, are those of a
reasonable human being rather than a merely (economically) rational one. When he represents Sissy as affirming that she is unable to

answer M'Choakumchild's question about whether someone living
in a nation in which 'there are fifty millions of money' must be in a
prosperous state, unless she knows 'who had got the money, and
whether any of it was mine', and when he represents her as
remarking on the 'proportion' involved in the fact that only
twenty-five in a million inhabitants of an hypothetical town starve
in the streets with the words that ' it must be just as hard upon
those who were starved, whether the others were a million, or a
million million' (1: 9, 62–3), Dickens is directing his readers'
attention to the ways in which 'facts' and statistics mask personal
and social realities even as they claim to elucidate them.

Sissy's humanely commonsensical and literal-minded failure to
share M'Choakumchild's statistical point of view is another aspect
of the Carlylean impulse of *Hard Times* – the attack on the collection and aggregation of facts and statistics that enable Gradgrind
and his kind, in Dickens's period and our own, to 'prove that the
Good Samaritan was a bad economist'(2: 12, 215). The novel's critique of statistics, like its critique of education, is part of its representation and exploration of the atomization of capitalist,
industrial society and of the production of the modern disciplinary
subject. These aspects of the novel's project can also be seen in its
representation of the family and in its use of the family–society
metaphor. In this novel, as in much reformist discourse of the mid-
nineteenth-century, social relations are compared to family relations, but in this case the effect is sometimes to reveal (more or less
unconsciously), and sometimes consciously to expose the contradictions inherent in this discourse and in the use of the
family–society metaphor. As Catherine Gallagher has demonstrated in *The Industrial Reformation of English Fiction* (1985),
paternalistic reformist discourse and liberal reformist novels, such
as Elizabeth Gaskell's *North and South* (the Manchester novel
which succeeded Dickens's Preston novel as the *Household Words*
serial in September 1854), seem to yearn for a form of social unity
that would result from the extension of familial bonds and co-
operative, domestic values from the private into the public
domain: in short, modern, industrial, capitalist society should be
more like an harmonious family. Dickens's novel, however, not
only demonstrates that modern, individualist, industrial capitalist
society is (or is like) a dysfunctional family which is in need of
reform, but it also suggests that capitalist society typically produces

dysfunctional families like those of Bitzer, Thomas Gradgrind and Josiah Bounderby.

Hard Times represents the working class as occupying the same position in the social family as children do in the nuclear family; both the working class and children are oppressed and/or neglected by the ruling class or parents. Thus Bitzer and Stephen Blackpool, on the one hand, and Tom and Louisa Gradgrind, on the other, are oppressed, deformed and/or neglected by Thomas Gradgrind, Josiah Bounderby, and by the wider social forces which they represent. Dickens does not entirely avoid the danger inherent in representing the working classes in terms of this familial model – that of merely infantilizing them. This can be seen in the representation of Stephen Blackpool's bewilderment at the 'muddle' of the society in which he lives:

> Look round town – so rich as 'tis ... Look how we live, and where we live, an in what numbers, an by what chances, an wi' what sameness; and ... how the mills is awlus a goin, and how they never works us no nigher to ony dis'ant object – ceptin awlus, Death. Look how you considers of us, an writes of us ... and goes up wo' your deputations to Secretaries o' State 'bout us, and how yo' are awlus right, and how we are awlus wrong, and never had no reason in us sin' ever we were born ... Who can look on't, sir, and fairly tell a man 'tis not a muddle?   (2: 5, 53)

Passages such as this, to some extent, work like Sissy's responses to M'Choakumchild's questions: their function is to make the reader question social orthodoxies. However, other aspects of Stephen's bewilderment – such as his contention that it is 'for them as is put ower me' to set the muddle to rights – tend to work to reinscribe him in the status quo.

Stephen is not simply used as an illustration of the way society may be compared to a dysfunctional family. He is also – as the husband of an alcoholic woman whom he is unable to divorce – a member of one of the dysfunctional families produced, or in this case, perpetuated by the social muddle that he is unable to solve. Like some of his contemporaries, Dickens was sometimes concerned to make the case for reforming society by extending family values into the public sphere, but in novels, from *Dombey and Son* to *Our Mutual Friend*, he demonstrated that the family was also in urgent need of reform, and that familial bonds and affections, and domestic values more generally must be protected from the incursions of the individualistic, economic, rational values of a modern industrial society. The history of the degeneration and ultimate rescue or redemption of the Gradgrind family as a result of Sissy Jupe's influence and actions, and Gradgrind's enforced education about the destructive nature of his social and educational philosophy by means of his daughter's trials, and the self-interested plotting of his son and the heartless Bitzer (see 3: 8) is just such a family reform narrative. Ironically, the reform of Gradgrind, Lousia and Tom – the surviving members of the alienated and atomized Gradgrind family – coincides with familial dispersal and disintegration. A penitent Tom dies a lonely death thousands of miles away from his father and sister. Louisa, who is saved by her father's relinquishing her to Sissy's good offices, is first separated from her husband, and then lives out her life as his disinherited and childless widow. Catherine Gallagher sees this pattern as conveying a kind of 'hopelessness about family relationships', arguing that 'even the reformed Gradgrinds are powerless to change Coketown', and that their 'fragile and ambiguous' family cohesion is an inadequate source of 'inspiration for social cohesion'.[23] However, the novel offers other models of the family which might be thought to offer greater 'inspiration for social cohesion'. For example, there is the raffish, even disreputable, extended family of the circus, which, under the direction of Sleary – 'a stout modern statue with a moneybox at its elbow' – somehow manages to combine materialism with fancy and heart (as does Dickens in his self-conception of his role as popular entertainer). And, of course, there is Sissy's putative family and its role in Louisa's refashioning, which is conjured up in the vision of futurity which the narrator sees in the fire into which Louisa looks:

> Happy Sissy's happy children loving her ... she grown learned in childish lore ... trying hard to know her humbler fellow-creatures, and to beautify their lives of machinery and reality with those imaginative graces and delights, without which the heart of infancy will wither up ... and the plainest national prosperity figures can show, will be the Writing on the Wall.   (3: 9, 297–8)

Hard Times thus concludes with an affirmation of the domestic ideal, but it does so in a way that foregrounds the fact that is an *ideal*, and that it will only be made real by imagination and a collective act of human will: 'Dear reader! It rests with you and me, *whether*, in our two fields of action similar things shall be or not'

(3: 9, 298). The domestic ideal (personified by its eponymous heroine) and imaginative human agency are at the centre of one of the darkest of Dickens's novels, *Little Dorrit*. They are also at the centre of its contradictions, as I shall explore in the next section.

IV 'The inquest into contemporary civilization': *Little Dorrit*

> 'Society,' said Mrs Merdle ... 'is so difficult to explain to young persons (indeed is so difficult to explain to most persons) ... I wish Society was not so arbitrary, I wish it was not so exacting. ... But ... we must take it as we find it. We know it is hollow and conventional and worldly and very shocking, but unless we are Savages in the Tropical seas ... we must consult it. It is the common lot.'
>
> Dickens, *Little Dorrit*, I: 20, 237

Like *Bleak House,* Dickens's other major novel of the 1850s, *Little Dorrit* (which appeared in nineteen monthly parts between 1 December 1855 and 1 June 1857), is a massive and complexly plotted work, whose narrative is played out in the shadow of decaying properties, and which paints a bleak picture of English social life and institutions. Like *Bleak House, Little Dorrit* is a social novel which is also a prototypical sensation novel, in this case with a plot structured around a woman with a secret (Mrs Clennam), a mad mother (Arthur's real mother), a bigamous marriage, and a concealed codicil to a will. Dickens's working title for this novel was 'Nobody's Fault', and one of its originating ideas (as indicated in his working notes for the novel) was 'the man who comfortably charges everything on Providence'.[24] Dickens's abandonment of his original title was apt, since his novel seems to suggest that the current state of society is nobody's fault only because it is everybody's fault, and thus it must be somebody's fault, and perhaps the fault of some more than others – namely those, like the Boodles and Coodles of *Bleak House,* who cannot put it right, though expressly born to do so.

In his Preface to the first one-volume edition (May 1857), Dickens claimed that no novel of his had ever had more readers than *Little Dorrit*. However, this novel deeply divided critical opinion from the outset. *Blackwood's* described it as 'a wilderness', 'destitute of well-considered plot' (1857, *CH*, 360), and *Fraser's* thought it 'decidedly the worst' of Dickens's novels, and further evidence of his 'habit of repeating himself to a degree which becomes wearisome' (*CH*, 350). James Fitzjames Stephen, a member of an influential family who was stung by *Little Dorrit's* attack on the Barnacles and the Circumlocution Office, waged war on the novel in a series of reviews (often under the cover of anonymity) in the *Edinburgh* and *Saturday Review* and elsewhere. Looking back on Dickens's career in 1882, A. W. Ward voiced what had by then become a common view (shared by Dickens's biographer, Forster): that *Little Dorrit* showed a sharp decline of Dickens's power in the mid-1850s (1857, *CH*, 356). However, by 1898 Gissing was claiming that *Little Dorrit* contained some of Dickens's finest work,[25] and in 1937 George Bernard Shaw asserted that '*Little Dorrit* is a more seditious book than *Das Kapital*'.[26] It was a Marxisant critic, T. A. Jackson, also writing in 1937, who set the tone for some of the most influential mid-twentieth-century readings of *Little Dorrit*, in his discussion of the pervasiveness of images and states of imprisonment in what he described as both the most pessimistic and 'near to being the most revolutionary' of all of Dickens's novels.[27] Edmund Wilson's 'Dickens: The Two Scrooges',[28] Lionel Trilling's introduction to the Oxford Illustrated Edition of *Little Dorrit* (1953), and J. Hillis Miller's discussion of the novel in *Charles Dickens: The World of His Novels* (1958) all took up Jackson's suggestion that the novel should be read as an allegory of whose meaning its creator was only partly conscious, in which imprisonment – in the form of physical confinement, or psychological, spiritual (or theological), or material incarceration – is the universal mode of being: 'Only when the riches have been annihilated and the theology has crashed into ruin,' Jackson wrote, 'are the long-tormented prisoners set free to make what they can of what is left of their lives, and of such slender resources as have been left to them.'[29]

Of course, as I have noted earlier in this study, Dickens had a continuing fascination with prisons, from his depiction of Newgate in *Sketches by Boz* and *Barnaby Rudge*, through the Fleet in *Pickwick Papers* and the condemned cell in which Fagin spends his last night in *Oliver Twist*, to the Bastille in *A Tale of Two Cities*. However, it is generally acknowledged that *Little Dorrit* is his most searching exploration of the state of imprisonment, as experience, metaphor and symbol. For Foucauldian critics, Dickens's representation of prisons and imprisonment in *Little Dorrit* is yet another example of the ubiquitous operations of discipline and the carceral in nineteenth-century culture. As Lionel Trilling (writing before the height of Foucauldian fashion) observed, the prison is 'the practical instrument for the negation of man's will which the will of society has contrived. As such, the prison haunted the mind of the nine-teenth century, which may be said to have had its birth at the fall of the Bastille' (Ford, 282). Certainly *Little Dorrit* is haunted by the image of the prison, whether it be in the verbal representation of the actual prison in which it opens (Marseilles) or in which much of its action is set (the Marshalsea); the metaphorical self-imprisonment of the fraudulent financier Mr Merdle who is per-petually clutching his wrists as if taking himself into custody; Mrs Clennam's imprisonment in her dark house and her Calvinistic religion; Arthur Clennam's imprisonment in his guilt; or the invisible prisons of Society and the Circumlocution Office.

In this novel Dickens's habitual terrain of London has itself become a prison. Carceral London is represented with particular intensity in the chapter ironically titled 'Home' which describes Clennam's return, after twenty years' absence in China, to the imprisonment of a London Sunday:

> Everything was bolted and barred that could by possibility furnish relief to an overworked people ...
> Ten thousand responsible houses surrounded him, frowning... heavily on the streets they composed. ... Miles of close wells and pits of houses, where the inhabitants gasped for air. ... Through the heart of the town a deadly sewer ebbed and flowed, in the place of a fine fresh river ...
> He sat in the same place as the day died, looking at the dull houses opposite, and thinking, if the disembodied spirits of former inhabitants were ever conscious of them, how they must pity them-selves for their old places of imprisonment.   (1: 3, 41 and 43)

The city to which Clennam has returned is a haunted city – a city haunted by both his own and its own past. Clennam's reflections on this haunted city register the novel's peculiar preoccupation with change, and particularly its sensitivity to changes in the topography of the city and their impact on the individual's sense of the order of things, a sensitivity I noted in my discussion of the *Sketches by Boz*. The sense of imprisonment created in the passage quoted above is, in part, the product of Dickens's Christian theol-ogy; it is an imprisonment in 'this lower world', cut off from heaven by the barrier of the sun (2: 30, 729). However, the passage also suggests that the death-in-life of an English

Sabbatarian Sunday, and the cramped and fetid conditions of the city dwellers, are specifically prisons of mankind's making.

If the prison is one of the dominant metaphors and subjects of *Little Dorrit,* the other is the family. Dickens, who has been revered and reviled in equal measure for his idealized representations of the family, peoples this novel (as he does so many of his works) with unhappy families. *Little Dorrit* engages in a thoroughgoing critique of false or outmoded models of the family, and more especially of the paternalistic, patriarchal or tribal models of social organization on which they are based and which they reproduce. Mr Dorrit, a failed business man and a self-deluded, selfish, and wholly inadequate father to his children, is installed by an invented tradition as the 'Father of the Marshalsea'. The title is conferred upon him by the dying turnkey, a 'tradition afterwards handed down from generation to generation' (1: 6, 75). The Father of the Marshalsea sustains his fictional role through rhetorical forms and social practices (punctiliously exacted ceremonies), much in the way that the Barnacles and Stiltstalkings maintain their role as the Fathers of the Nation: he preserves a distinction between the 'Pump and Poor' sides of the College-yard, equips himself with a feudal retainer in the shape of 'old Nandy', holds levèes for newcomers to the prison and receives gifts from departing collegians 'as tributes from admirers, to a public character' (1: 6, 175).

Dorrit's more pernicious counterpart as fictional patriarch is Casby, the landlord of Bleeding House Yard, described by Lionel Trilling as 'a parody of all Dickens's benevolent old gentlemen from Mr Pickwick ... to John Jarndyce' (Ford, 288). Casby owes his title of 'The Last of the Patriarchs' and his post as the town agent of Lord Decimus Tite Barnacle merely to his appearance, to 'his looking so supremely benignant that nobody could suppose the property screwed or jobbed under such a man' (1: 13, 151). In an economical and humorous analysis of the operations of power, Dickens demonstrates how Casby preserves the fiction of his paternalistic benevolence by employing Pancks as the steam engine to grind the rents out of the tenants of Bleeding House Yard. Pancks is to Casby what Casby is to the Barnacles: their function is to mask the operations of power. Just as Mr Dorrit grew to believe in the fiction of his right to the title of the Father of the Marshalsea, the Barnacles 'considered themselves in a general way as having vested rights' (1: 10) in the administering of the Circumlocution

Office. Dickens's creation of this family and the office to which (like its nautical namesake) it has attached itself continues the Carlylean attack on the 'do-nothing dilettantism' of the ruling class, begun in the Boodles and Coodles of *Bleak House*, which was published in the same year as the Northcote–Trevelyan Report outlining the failings of the Civil Service. The findings of this report were confirmed by the administrative incompetence which surrounded the fighting of Crimean War (1854), and Dickens lent his voice to the campaign for reform through articles in *Household Words*, public speeches, and (uncharacteristically for the non-joiner) by joining the Administrative Reform Society in 1855. The tenth chapter of *Little Dorrit*, 'Containing the Whole Science of Government', is not only his most effective contribution to this mid-nineteenth-century campaign, but it is also a brilliant indictment of hereditary power and government by place-men whenever and wherever it occurs:

> The Circumlocution Office was (as everybody knows without being told) the most important Department under government ...
> Whatever was required to be done, the Circumlocution Office was beforehand with all the public departments in the art of perceiving – HOW NOT TO DO IT.   (1: 10, 110)

The paragraphs following on from the above extract provide an excellent example of the operations of heteroglossia which Bakhtin outlined in 'Discourse in the Novel'. Bakhtin noted the heteroglossic capacity of the novel as a genre for exposing the superficiality and hypocrisy of social mores by means of a 'comic-parodic reprocessing' of such examples of contemporary language as 'the forms of parliamentary eloquence, ... [and] particular forms of parliamentary protocol', and also by means of the objectification of a form of speech which represents (and, at the same time, exposes) the 'the *going point of view* and the going *value*'.[30] This process of comic-parodic reprocessing can be observed in Dickens's representation of the 'very high' and 'very large' family of the Barnacles, 'dispersed all over the public offices', and holding 'all sorts of public places', to the extent that:

> Either the nation was under a load of obligation to the Barnacles, or the Barnacles were under a load of obligation to the nation. It was not quite unanimously settled which; the Barnacles having their opinion, the nation theirs.   (1: 10, 113)

By means of his representation of the 'Shoal of Barnacles' which extends itself into every corner of the Empire, and, through influence and intermarriage, permeates the whole of Society, Dickens satirizes the way in which this class or interest group has identified the nation as a family – the Barnacle family – and has appropriated to itself the interests of the nation. Thus at a dinner given by Mrs Gowan:

> It was agreed that the country (another word for the Barnacles and Stiltstalkings) wanted preserving, but how it came to want preserving was not so clear. It was only clear that the question was all about John Barnacle, Augustus Stiltstalking, William Barnacle and Tudor Stiltstalking, Tom, Dick, or Harry Barnacle or Stiltstalking, because there was nobody else but mob.   (1: 26, 306)

The other main topical satire in *Little Dorrit* is found in the spectacular rise and fall of Mr Merdle, which is based on the case of John Sadlier, the financier whose suicide in February 1856 led to sensational revelations of fraud and forgery. An analysis of the language in which Dickens represents Merdle is central to Bakhtin's examination of what he describes as the use of 'the concealed speech of another' to unmask the hypocrisy of society. This concealed speech – a ventriloquized language of self-satisfied maxims and platitudes (to be satirized with more direct force in Mr Podsnap in *Our Mutual Friend*) – is indicated in the italicized words in the following quotation which Bakhtin quotes in his discussion of heteroglossia:

> Mr Merdle came home *from his daily occupation of causing the British name to be more and more respected in all parts of the civilized globe capable of the appreciation of worldwide commercial enterprise and gigantic combinations of skill and capital.* For though nobody knew with the least precision what Mr Merdle's business was, except that it was to coin money, these were the terms in which everybody defined it on all ceremonious occasions.
> (1: 33,382, emphasis added)

Or, more sharply:

> O, what a wonderful man this Merdle, what a great man, what a master man, how blessedly and enviable endowed – in one word, what a rich man!   (2: 12, 540)

Merdle the fraudster forges his own life, but in 'Mr Merdle's Complaint' (1: 21), and particularly in the representation of the voice of society through the use of the concealed speech of another, the narrator focuses the reader's attention on the role played by Society as co-constructors of the fiction of the great man. The Merdle family is also a forgery, a construction, bought ready-made, solely for the purpose of 'Moving in Society'. It is a grotesque distortion of the family of the domestic ideal, just as Mrs Merdle is a distortion of the womanly ideal, with her 'extensive bosom, which required so much room to be unfeeling enough in ... not a bosom to repose upon, but ... a capital bosom to hang jewels upon' (1: 21, 244). Mrs Merdle's extensive bosom is also one in which to nurse the fiction that Mrs Gowan must genteelly resist before accepting the marriage of her impecunious but well connected son Henry to Pet Meagles, the pampered daughter of well-off but low-born parents. Mrs Merdle 'knew what Society's mothers were, and what Society's daughters were, and what Society's matrimonial market was, and how prices ruled in it, and what scheming and counter-scheming took place for the high buyers, and what bargaining and huckstering went on' (1: 33, 381–2).

Like most of Dickens's novels, and all of them from *Dombey and Son* onwards, *Little Dorrit* is concerned with the commodification of all human relations, and particularly with the 'bargaining and huckstering' of women. Like *Dombey*, *Little Dorrit* also focuses on the way in which women are circulated as property and, more particularly, it explores the social and psychological effects of this process. In Mrs Merdle, for example, Dickens combines 'Cleopatra' Skewton's attitudinizing with her daughter Edith's role as a bought object, purchased for the display of her husband's status and wealth. The most stark commentary on the (self-) objectification of women, however, is to be found in the representation of Miss Wade and particularly in her curious interpolated narrative, 'The History of a Self Tormentor' (2: 21). Miss Wade is the monster which results from the Frankensteinian experiment in which Dickens develops the self-lacerating masochism of an Edith Dombey and combines it with a 'perversion' (to use a word Mr Meagles uses of Miss Wade) of the self-effacing orphan Esther Summerson's desire for love. 'The History of a Self Tormentor' is (as Hilary Schor points out) a Browningesque monologue by the independently minded daughter of a somebody who interprets every sign of love and kindness as condescension or a potential trap. It is an entirely self-contained utterance, which has no obvious plot function, is accompanied by no narratorial glossing, and gives no sense of the reaction of its addressee (Arthur Clennam).[31] Miss Wade's narrative, like Dickens's story of Amy Dorrit, is simultaneously a narrative of daughterly dispossession and of self-possession. It is also, like Mrs Clennam's story, a 'disturbance in the narrative field', one of several examples of the way in which this novel is constantly interrupted so that women can tell their own stories.[32]

Mrs Clennam is another self-tormentor and (like Miss Wade) a tormentor of others: 'stern of face and unrelenting of heart' and 'bound like her own construction of [the bible] ... in the hardest, barest and straitest boards' (1: 3, 42). Her dark, decaying house, 'leaning on some half dozen gigantic crutches' is less hospitable than the Marshalsea, and a perversion of the idea of 'Home' (the title of the chapter in which it is described), just as she is an inversion or perversion of the concept of motherhood which is at the heart of the Victorian domestic ideal. Of course, mid-Victorian conceptualizations of motherhood are complex and contradictory. Mrs Clennam's disciplining of the young Arthur with a 'restraining and correcting hand' designed to prevent the sins of the fathers being perpetuated into the next generation is, in one sense, merely an exaggerated or grotesque version of a model of mothering that would have been accepted by many of Dickens's readers. Similarly, a comic parody of the conduct-book mother eulogized by such writers as Sarah Stickney Ellis – author of books on and for the mothers, daughters and wives of England – can be found in Mrs General (employed by the newly enriched Mr Dorrit to act as a companion to his daughters), who sets herself up to ' "form the mind" and eke the manners of some young lady of distinction', or 'harness the proprieties to the carriage of some rich young heiress ... and become at once the driver and the guard of such a vehicle through the social mazes' (2: 2, 432).

For many readers, the novel's eponymous heroine is its embodiment of the womanly ideal: innocent, angelic, self-effacing, self-sacrificing, maternal. However, the novel's representation of Little Dorrit reveals as much about the contradictions of that ideal as it does about the saving power with which it is invested. Patricia Ingham has suggested that these contradictions are evident in a discrepancy between narration and plot, arguing that, whereas the narrator 'insists on a conventionally eulogistic reading' of Amy, at the level of plot she is 'ultimately a contradictory and disruptive figure who sustains nothing more than a sadly dysfunctional family'.[33] I would suggest that the contradictions of the feminine ideal are evident both in the narration and the pattern of relationships and events in which this novel locates its heroine. Her child-like self-sacrificing, self-effacing femininity – 'worldly wise in hard and poor necessities, ... innocent in all things else' (1: 7, 86) – places her at the centre of the novel's redemptive plot. However, the narrator also insists on the negative effects of these 'womanly' qualities, by exposing her complicity in constructing and maintaining her father's selfish delusions. By means of her collusion in his fictions of gentility and her concealment of the harsh truths of her own and her siblings' lives from him, Little Dorrit 'varnishes' the cracked surfaces of life just as thoroughly as Mrs General does.

Like so many of Dickens's heroines, Amy Dorrit is placed in a family whose relationships have become inverted or distorted. The child of the Marshalsea is a dutiful daughter, a mother to her motherless siblings, and a mother/wife to her widowed father. The narrative of her redemption of Arthur Clennam is one in which she recapitulates each of these roles. She is, by turns (and sometimes simultaneously), a child, mother and wife to the motherless and falsely mothered Clennam. Little Dorrit restores to Arthur the childhood he never had and the youth prematurely destroyed. After having first learned to cease addressing her as his child and to stop speaking of himself 'as one who was turning old' (2: 27, 699), Clennam's rebirth is continued in one of the many scenes of reading in nineteenth-century fiction in which a male character is emotionally educated by a woman. This particular scene of reading occurs during Arthur's own imprisonment in the Marshalsea, and the educative effect is produced not by Amy's text but by the texture of her voice, in which Arthur hears:

> all that great Nature was doing ... all the soothing songs she sings to man. At no Mother's knee but hers had he ever dwelt in his youth on hopeful promises, on playful fancies, on the harvests of tenderness and humility that lie hidden in the early-fostered seeds of the imagination. ... But in the tones of the voice that read to him, there were memories of an old feeling of such things, and echoes of every merciful and loving whisper that had ever stolen to him in his life. (2: 34, 776)

Despite the determining conditions of her life, Amy Dorrit is thus, at least in part, essentialized and aligned with 'Mother Nature', as the final destination of this narrative is a return to or remaking of the natural family (as distinct from the distorted families of Society that pervade the novel). In this respect *Little Dorrit* could be said to retreat into the privacy of the domestic ideal, 'a modest life of usefulness and happiness' (2: 34, 787), and thus – as Catherine Gallagher argues of its predecessor, *Hard Times* – to reproduce the paradoxes of the social paternalism and the domestic ideology that inform it. However, in doing so the later novel more openly acknowledges the limitations of both social paternalism and the domestic ideal. Daniel Doyce, the inventor who spends years navigating the Kafkaesque labyrinth of the Circumlocution Office in his efforts 'to turn his ingenuity [as an inventor] to his country's service' (1:10, 124), the Plornishes, who maintain an iconic 'Happy Cottage' in Bleeding Heart Yard, the Meagleses, devoted parents who are distanced from their beloved daughter and disowned by their gentlemanly son-in-law, and Arthur and Amy are all survivors, but the social conditions that they have survived persist. *Little Dorrit* takes its hero and heroine to the conventional destination of marriage, but it makes it abundantly clear that this is a private blessing rather than a public solution. 'Inseparable and blest', Amy and Arthur Clennam descend from the steps of the church in which they marry, but they step down into the lower world of city streets which are ignorant of their private state, streets in which they must walk in both 'sunshine and shadow', and in which 'the noisy and the eager, and the arrogant and the forward and the vain fretted, and chafed, and made their usual uproar' (2: 34, 787).

6

These Times of Ours, 1858–70

I Trading places: *All the Year Round*

Dickens's career as a novelist and journalist took another turn with the collapse of his marriage in 1858, when he severed his long-standing connection with Bradbury and Evans. This firm had printed all of Dickens's books from *Pickwick* onwards, and had published all of his novels from the mid-1840s. They were also the publishers of his periodical *Household Words*. The break came when Bradbury and Evans refused to reprint in *Punch* (another of their periodical titles) the extraordinary public announcement of his innocence of marital wrongdoing which Dickens had issued in *Household Words* on 12 June 1858, in an attempt to silence harmful rumours about his personal circumstances, including suggestions that he had left his wife for his sister-in-law, Georgina Hogarth. *All the Year Round* was launched as the successor to *Household Words* in April 1859, carrying much the same weekly mix of entertainment, instruction and topical journalism as before. The announcement of the new periodical affirmed its editor's continuing commitment to 'that fusion of the graces of the imagination with the realities of life, which is vital to the welfare of any community'. The most important change was the new magazine's commitment to reserving 'the first place in these pages for a continuous original work of fiction ... [which] it is our hope and aim ... may become a part of English Literature'.[1] *All the Year Round* certainly succeeded in this latter aim: Wilkie Collins's *The Woman in White* and *The Moonstone*, as well as Dickens's own *A Tale of Two Cities* and *Great Expectations* were among the lead serials in its first ten years.

Dickens wrote less for *All the Year Round* than he had for *Household Words*, particularly after 1863 when he became more and more involved in his programme of public readings from his novels. His most notable contributions to the new weekly (apart from the novels already mentioned) were a series of sketches by the 'Uncommercial Traveller'. This new journalistic persona had its origins in a speech that Dickens gave at a dinner for the Commercial Travellers' Schools late in 1859, in which he pondered what kinds of play he could make on the word 'traveller', and considered 'whether any fanciful analogy could be drawn between those travellers who diffuse the luxuries and necessities of existence', and other travellers, literal or figurative. Of course, this most successful of writers was himself something of a commercial traveller in the fancy goods line (or, as he might have put it, the line of good fancy), and he was becoming more so as he toured the country giving readings from his novels. In his first sketch as the 'Uncommercial' Dickens merged the figurative and literal meanings on which he had pondered in his 1859 speech:

> I am a town traveller and a country traveller, and am always on the road. Figuratively speaking, I travel for the great house of Human Interest Brothers, and have rather a large connection in the fancy goods way. Literally speaking, I am always wandering here and there ... seeing many little things, and some great things, which because they interest me, I think may interest others. ('His General Line of Business', *UCT*, 1–2)

The concerns of the 'Uncommercial' overlap considerably with Dickens's fiction in the early 1860s, but this new journalistic persona also looks back to the urban street walker of the *Sketches by Boz*, and the night-time wanderer of the city streets who is at the centre of several of his pieces for *Household Words*. Like *Great Expectations* (which was appearing at the same time as some of these pieces), one of the early Uncommercial Traveller essays returns to the scenes of Dickens's boyhood and is much preoccupied with the contrast between past and present. 'Dullborough Town' (*All the Year Round*, 30 June 1860) stages a fictional revisiting of the town in which the Uncommercial grew up, and charts the Traveller's discovery not only that the past is a foreign country, but also that his own history has worked its own processes of estrangement. 'Dullborough Town' is, in part, an urbane social essay on the manifestations of modernity and the increasingly commonplace nineteenth-century experience of the social and geographical deracination that resulted from education, and the movement from the country to the city. The Traveller recalls the departing (and departed) child as leaving a green and flowery Dullborough on a coach, 'melodiously called Timpson's Blue-Eyed Maid', but the returning man has been deposited by a locomotive engine belonging to S.E.R., 'called severely No. 97, ... and ... spitting ashes and hot water over the blighted ground' (*SJ*, 64–5). In the intervening years, Timpson's little coach office and several of the surrounding buildings have been replaced by a 'great establishment' out of which Pickford's wagons constantly rattle. The Theatre, whose Shakespearean productions had enchanted the Traveller's childhood, has been taken over by a dealer in wine and bottled beer, and present-day youth must make do with a Panorama which is advertised as 'pleasingly instructive', a phrase which the Traveller describes as a terrible expression with whose 'fatal meaning and leaden import' he expects his readers to be all too familiar (*SJ*, 68). Indeed, folded into 'Dullborough Town' is another mini essay on the amusements of the people, or the alleged modern tendency (despised by the Traveller) towards 'putting the natural demand for amusement out of sight' (*SJ*, 70).

'Dullborough Town' (like *Great Expectations*) is also about the psychology of change and of social and geographical deracination; it is much preoccupied with the Traveller's response to the ways in which Dullborough has stayed the same in the midst of change, and, more particularly with the ways in which the town and its inhabitants have gone on without its errant son. At the centre of the piece are two meetings by means of which the Traveller (and hence the reader) is made to reassess the changes in himself and his own response to both change and stasis. The first is the meeting with the phlegmatic greengrocer, who greets the Traveller's announcement that he had left the town when a child with 'a sarcastic kind of complacency', inquiring whether the Traveller found that the town had 'got on tolerably well' without him. The second meeting, with his boyhood friend, Joe Specks, who has become a successful doctor and married the girl whom they had both admired (now transformed into a fat matron), illuminates the Traveller's response to the greengrocer and reconciles him to the processes of change and the nature of his estrangement:

> Ah! Who was I that I should quarrel with the town for being changed to me, when I myself had come back so changed to it! All

> my early readings and early imaginations dated from this place, and
> I took them away so full of innocent construction and guileless
> belief, and I brought them back so worn and torn, so much the
> wiser and so much the worse!   (*SJ*, 72)

This self-reflexive retrospection on innocence and experience
resurfaces in *Great Expectations,* the companion piece to
'Dullborough Town'.

Some of the London scenes of *Great Expectations* are echoed in
the restless energy and hallucinatory imaginings of 'Night Walks'
(21 July 1860), one of the most vivid of the 'Uncommercial'
pieces. The hallucinatory peregrinations of 'Night Walks' also
anticipate the dark wanderings of Bradley Headstone and Eugene
Wrayburn in *Our Mutual Friend,* and the seedy underworld and
blurring of the boundaries of consciousness and unconsciousness,
madness and sanity in the dark imaginings of *The Mystery of
Edwin Drood.* Like many of the 'Uncommercial' sketches, 'Night
Walks' reworks earlier sketches, or takes up where they left off.
'Night Walks' revisits the territory explored in the *Household
Words* piece, 'Lying Awake' (30 October 1852), recalling the time
'Some years ago, [when] a temporary inability to sleep, referable to
a distressing impression, caused me to walk about the streets all
night, for a series of several nights' (*SJ*, 73). However, whereas
'Lying Awake' offered the roaming (and very literary) night-time
thoughts of the insomniac, 'Night Walks' recounts the nocturnal
wanderings of the sleepless social commentator who gives his
readers a glimpse of a London that most of them rarely see. In
'Night Walks' the 'Uncommercial' (and by proxy his reader) com-
pletes his 'education in a fair amateur experience of houselessness',
roaming the streets of London, and observing and providing an
inventory of their misery and squalor. At the centre of the essay is
the Traveller's visit to the Bethlehem Hospital (Bedlam). Whereas
daytime visits to Bedlam (a popular pastime among the middle
classes) served to reinforce the sense of the 'otherness' of its
inmates, this nocturnal visit produces a reverie on the night-time
equality of the sane and the insane 'as the sane lie a dreaming' and
thus temporarily share the deluded condition of the mad; a condition which the Traveller confesses that he himself shares. But of
course, the madmen and madwomen confined in Bedlam are not
the equals of either Dickens's persona, or Dickens the author, who
roam the streets at will, and sell the stories of their wanderings
and their dreams to the press, or transform their imaginings about

tortured psyches and madmen into the stuff of fiction – for example, in the portrait of Dr Manette in *A Tale of Two Cities*, or John Jasper in *The Mystery of Edwin Drood*. These late sketches mix the commercial and the uncommercial, as they market human interest, and merge public and private concerns. They both reveal and conceal the processes by which Dickens mined the streets of London, his childhood experiences and his own hallucinatory ways of seeing in the making of fiction.

II   Making history: *A Tale of Two Cities*

The serial with which Dickens launched his new weekly was *A Tale of Two Cities* (also published simultaneously in monthly numbers with illustrations by Hablot Browne). Like *Barnaby Rudge*, which also deals with historical events, rioting mobs, and the storming of a prison, *A Tale of Two Cities* was not greatly admired by critics in the nineteenth, or, for the most part, in the twentieth century. However, this melodramatic interweaving of a powerful love story and the dramas of family history with the drama of one of the major events of eighteenth-century European history has been enduringly popular with readers. Its wide audience appeal also owes a great deal to a very successful nineteenth-century stage version – *The Only Way* – and to popular film adaptations in 1935 and 1958, the first starring Ronald Colman and the second Dirk Bogarde as Carton, the English cynic who sacrifices his life to save that of the Frenchman (the aristocrat, Charles Darnay) whose wife (the daughter of a former Bastille prisoner), he loves. The *Tale* has also been the subject of some interesting critical discussion since the 1980s, perhaps stimulated by Avrom Fleishman's analysis in *The English Historical Novel* (1971).[2]

Why did the novelist who had established himself as the leading chronicler and anatomizer of contemporary English (and especially London) life turn at this point in his career towards Paris and the past? Some commentators have answered this question by invoking biography, and locating the genesis of the *Tale* in Dickens's intimate acquaintance with and long-standing love for France and particularly its capital city, and also in the revolution in his own life which resulted from his ending of his marriage and his infatuation with the young actress Ellen Ternan. Others have pointed to the central place that the French Revolution occupied in the nineteenth-century cultural imaginary. Others still have noted that although Dickens situates the action of this novel in a different time and, for the most part, in a different place, its preoccupations remain the same as those of his other novels of the 1850s: the historical process, change, the nature of society, the individual, the family.

Certainly, it is possible to see a kind of biographical imperative for this novel in the oddly confessional Preface which Dickens wrote for its first edition in volume form, in which he insisted on an identification between himself and his text. This Preface obliquely acknowledges the indebtedness of Dickens's plot to *The Frozen Deep*, a play by Wilkie Collins which also includes the death of a young man who sacrifices his own life for that of his friend. Dickens had taken a leading role in a production of the play, and it was through his involvement in this production that he had met Ellen Ternan. The Preface to the first edition also records that having conceived of 'the main idea of this story', a 'strong desire was upon me ... to *embody it in my own person* ... [and] throughout its execution, it has had *complete possession of me*' (*TTC*, 397; emphasis added). It also indicates that Dickens saw his novel as fulfilling an obligation to contribute to his culture's understanding of the French Revolution: 'It has been one of my hopes to *add something to the popular and picturesque means of understanding that terrible time*' (*TTC*, 397–8, emphasis added). This curious use of 'picturesque' echoes an earlier letter to Forster, in which the term seems to denote a foregrounding of incident: 'I set myself the little task of making a *picturesque* story, rising in every chapter with characters true to nature, but whom the story itself should express, more than they should express themselves by dialogue ... In other words, ... a story of incident' (*DL*, IX: 112). Dickens claims both a subjective and an objective truth for this story of incident. He has, he writes in the Preface, 'verified what is done and suffered in these pages' both in his own experience ('I have certainly done and suffered it all myself'), and in the experience of those who witnessed the events in France: 'Whenever any reference ... is made here to the condition of the French people before or during the Revolution, it is truly made, on the faith of the most trustworthy witnesses' (*TTC*, 397).

Dickens's grounding of his tale both in his own history and experience, and in the doings and sufferings of those undergoing the history which is his subject, may account for that ambivalence towards the Revolution which has preoccupied many critics of this novel. For example, in his introduction to the 1970 Penguin edition, George Woodcock attributed the energy of the scenes of Revolutionary violence to Dickens's *ressentiment* against a society which he felt had betrayed his youthful self. Others have located Dickens's ambivalence to the Revolution not simply in class politics, but rather in that point at which the politics of class and gender intersect or become mutually constitutive. Thus Catherine Gallagher has suggested that Dickens's depiction of the Revolutionists' invasion of the private sphere serves as a means of masking the nature of his own novelistic invasion of the domestic sphere and thus of making it seem comparatively benign.[3] What is needed, Dickens's *Tale* implies, is the good novelistic spirit who will raise the rooftops for humankind's edification, as in *Dombey and Son,* rather than revolutionaries bent on destroying the houses and the lives who inhabit them. John Rignall, on the other hand, has linked what he sees as this novel's 'direct, unmediated expression' of 'violent fears and violent reactions' to an eschatological theory of history and a vision of the historical process as a catastrophic continuum, 'the single catastrophe piling wreckage upon wreckage'.[4] The only terms in which Dickens can envisage liberation from this nightmare, Rignall argues, are 'eschatological': 'the Christ-like intervention of a self-sacrificing individual' (Carton), which offers 'a vision of a better world which seems to lie beyond time and history'.[5] I want to suggest that we should read Dickens's ambivalence towards the Revolution in this historical novel in the light of the 'inquest into contemporary civilisation' which he conducted in his other novels of the 1850s. It is an inquest into a class-divided society, which was, as seen by Dickens, still bedevilled by the 'do-nothing dilettantism' berated by Carlyle in the 1830s and 1840s. *A Tale of Two Cities* is an historical novel, but it is also a 'condition-of-England' novel which is informed by Carlyle's monitory study of the French Revolution (1837), and which also engages with some of the problems of social anarchy which were to preoccupy Matthew Arnold in the 1860s.

This political reading of the tale is supported by Cates Baldridge, who locates its central ambivalence in the tension between 'the narrator's middle-class horror at the collectivist Revolutionary ideology', and the novel's sensitive explorations of 'the liberating possibilities' offered by an ideology that is not simply centred on 'the autonomous self'. Dickens was attracted to such an ideology, Baldridge suggests, because of his 'deep dissatisfaction' with 'the social relations fostered by his own acquisitive and aggressively individualist society'[6] – a dissatisfaction which had become increasingly evident in his novels of the 1850s, as I argued in the last chapter. Dickens's novel is, of course a tale of *two* cities, and Dickens's ambivalence about his subject can also be seen in his representation of London as well as Paris. Revolutionary Paris is the city of the spectacle, a public theatre on whose stage the drama of history is enacted before a participatory mass audience. In contrast, London is a quiet, polite and private city, whose citizens – from the gentlemanly Mr Lorry to the comic-grotesque Resurrection Man, Jerry Cruncher – pursue their avocations conscientiously and in an orderly manner. But, as Dickens's discarded working title 'Buried Alive' reminds us, London is also the secretive, imprisoning city of *Little Dorrit*. Something of Arthur Clennam's disenchanted homecoming to the streets of London is repeated in the much discussed 'anomalous' or 'digressive' first-person narration which abruptly opens the 'Night Shadows' chapter:

> A wonderful fact to reflect upon, that every human creature is constituted to be that profound secret and mystery to every other. A solemn consideration, when I enter a great city by night, that every one of those darkly clustered houses encloses its own secret; that every room in every one of them encloses its own secret; that every beating heart in the hundreds of thousands of breasts there, is, in some of its imaginings, a secret to the heart nearest it! Something of the awfulness, even of Death itself, is referable to this ... it is the inexorable consolation and perpetuation of the secret that was always in that individuality. ... In any of the burial places of this city through which I pass, is there a sleeper more inscrutable than its busy inhabitants are, in their utmost personality, to me, or than I am to them?   (1: 3, 14–15)

Like much of *Little Dorrit*, this passage represents modern urban existence as a 'kind of living entombment', and it functions both as complaint about (or lament upon) the self-enclosed and self-referential nature of such an existence and as an expression of longing for the secrets of the heart, the 'buried treasure' (1: 3, 15) of more communal forms of human knowledge and being.

Dickens's *Tale* rejects the particular kind of collectivism espoused by Madame Defarge and her ilk – with their insistence on making individuals (such as Darnay) responsible for the guilt of their ancestors, class or 'race' (as she puts it), whatever their own actions have been. Instead, it offers a vision of other-directed individualism as the 'one thing needful' (as Arnold put it), or at least one of the necessary conditions for escaping the solipsism of modern urban life and transcending or transforming the anarchy of nineteenth-century modernity. As usual, one of the main embodiments of this vision is a woman – in this case Lucie Manette with her inspiring and saving power of love. The other vehicle of this vision is the novel's charting of Sydney Carton's journey from cynical self-enclosure to freely chosen self-sacrifice. In the 'rust and repose', the 'waste forces within him, and ... desert all around' that typify Carton at the beginning of the novel, Dickens represents the alienated other side of the 'driving and riving, and shouldering and pressing' (2: 5, 94) that characterize both the modern world of competitive individualism, and also, curiously, the revolutionary mob. If Carton's life is an entrapment in an alienated self, then his freely chosen death is offered (as Baldridge notes) as a transcendence of self in other-directed action. Dickens perhaps acknowledges that this is a utopian vision when he places Carton's reflections on his own actions outside of time and history. The most quoted words in the most quoted speech that Dickens ever wrote were, of course, never actually uttered: 'It is a far, far better thing that I do ...' are words that Carton *might* have spoken, the narrator muses, had he been given the opportunity requested by Madame Roland, an earlier victim of the Guillotine.

A Tale of Two Cities is, like most of Dickens's novels, full of sharp contrasts and contradictions. Nowhere are these more evident than in the opening rhetorical flourish on 'The Period', which foregrounds the contrasts between London and Paris in the Revolutionary period, and alludes to different ways of viewing the events of the Revolution. It also embodies the contradictions of the mid-nineteenth century:

> It was the best of times, it was the worst of times, it was the age of wisdom, it was the age of foolishness, it was the epoch of belief, it was the epoch of incredulity, it was the season of Light, it was the season of Darkness, it was the spring of hope, it was the winter of despair, we had everything before us, we had nothing before us, we were all going direct to Heaven, we were all going direct the other way – in short the period was so far like the present period that some of its noisiest authorities insisted on its being received, for good or for evil, in the superlative degree of comparison only. (1: 1, 5)

This passage could stand as an epigraph for any of the novels discussed in this chapter, or indeed for virtually all of Dickens's novels from *Dombey and Son* onwards.

III Lost illusions: *Great Expectations*

The turn to history and to the personal past is continued in *Great Expectations*, which is set in the 1820s – the period of Dickens's childhood. Among other things, this novel explores the processes of history and the links between past and present, as the reader is required repeatedly to 'pause' and 'think' about 'the long chain of iron or gold, of thorns or flowers, that would never have bound you, but for the formation of the first link on one memorable day' (*GE*, 1: 9, 71). However, although it is set in the past the major concerns of this novel are as up-to-date as those of Dickens's other novels of modern life, *Bleak House, Little Dorrit* and *Our Mutual Friend*.

The form of this tale of the 'progress' of a fabulist and 'self-swindler' is autobiographical, and during its genesis Dickens reread his earlier autobiographical novel, *David Copperfield*, 'to be quite sure I had fallen into no unconscious repetitions' (*Life*, 2: 285). Dickens also confessed to being extraordinarily 'affected' by this rereading, and one aspect of this can, perhaps, be seen in the nostalgic and restrospective tone which characterizes much of the novel. This elegiac quality derives, in part, from the novel's focus on childhood and adolescence, and especially from its representation of the child's sense of guilt, oppression and perplexity, and the adolescent's confusions, longings and fantasies. It is also associated with the way in which *Great Expectations* combines a tale of *Bildung* with a tale of lost illusions.

Great Expectations, like *David Copperfield*, is a *Bildungsroman*, a novel of growth and development, which, in this case, charts its hero's route from the blacksmith's forge on the Kentish marshes, through his education as a 'gentleman' and his life as an idle *flâneur* in London, to his eleven-year period of hard-working self-exile with the 'Eastern Branch' of Clarriker and Company and, finally, his return to England as a modestly successful businessman: 'we were not in a grand way of business, but we had a good name, and worked for our profits, and did very well' (3: 19, 475). In this respect, as Robert Stange observed in his very lucid essay on this novel (first published in 1954), Pip's story is 'the classic legend of the nineteenth century': 'the young man of talents, who progresses from the country to the city, ascends in the social hierarchy, and moves from innocence to experience'.[7] This 'fable of cultural emergence'[8] and self-improvement is embedded in numerous nine-teenth-century novels and in self-help texts, from George Lillie Craik's *The Pursuit of Knowledge under Difficulties* (1829), to Samuel Smiles's *Self-Help* (1859). In *Great Expectations,* however, this fable intersects with, or emerges from, other kinds of story or fable, which are just as central to nineteenth-century culture as the self-help narrative, most notably the romance and the tale of lost illusions. *Great Expectations* offers a sardonic commentary on one of the dominant plot paradigms of nineteenth-century fiction – the romance plot in which an unexpected inheritance, or the actions of a secret or acknowledged benefactor providentially shape the life of the fictional hero or heroine, resolving earlier difficulties and smoothing the way to the happy-ever-after of married prosperity. For much of the novel Pip is represented as misreading the plot of both his social and personal relationships and believing that he is a character in precisely this kind of story. One of the important rev-elations of the plot of *Great Expectations* is that the reality of Pip's story is that his benefactor is not the grotesque fairy godmother, Miss Havisham, but the transported criminal Magwitch, and that he has not been brought up to inherit Miss Havisham's ward Estella, but that he is Magwitch's 'brought-up London gentleman' (2: 20, 317), a point to which I return below.

Great Expectations is a disenchanted romance – even with the supposedly 'happy' ending, substituted on the advice of Bulwer Lytton, in which Pip (seeing 'the shadow of no parting from her') walks hand-in-hand with Estella from the grounds of the ruined Satis House, which is awaiting redevelopment. In one sense this ending represents the fulfilment of Pip's ambitions: having become a modestly wealthy businessman he seems set (at least in his own mind) to marry the girl of his dreams. Except that this projected ending might also be a figment of his imagination, a consolatory fantasy, yet another fragment he shores against the ruins of his lost illusions. For, at one level, what looks like the classic nineteenth-century self-help story is an interrogation of that story. This classic tale of social mobility and self-improvement also dramatizes and explores the social and psychological consequences and costs of these processes. As Robin Gilmour observed, *Great Epectations* 'spoke to a generation which was acutely conscious of having made advances in the civilisation of everyday life',[9] and, as numerous late twentieth-century critics pointed out, it did so in a way which anticipated later nineteenth-century investigations of the discontents of civilization. Whereas much of Dickens's earlier fiction had been concerned to demonstrate and deplore the ways in which the freedom and happiness of individuals is threatened by outmoded and barbaric 'wrong systems, wrong institutions, bad habits, bad values',[10] this novel reveals a world in which individual human freedom and fulfilment is frustrated by what are usually promulgated as society's 'great expectations', and those values usually associated with progress, civilization and modernity.

As earlier chapters have indicated, much recent Dickens criticism (like much work on the nineteenth-century novel in general) focuses on Dickens's fiction as the site of the construction of the modern bourgeois subject, the product of urban capitalism. *Great Expectations* is, indeed, a crucial site in this process. The novel begins with its hero-narrator's childish speculations on identity, in which he identifies himself in relation to the graves of his dead father, mother (*'Wife of the Above'*) and siblings, and also in relation to the 'marsh country' which has been the medium of his existence hitherto. It goes on to chart the unmaking and remaking of Pip's identity as he is taken out of the forge and 'forged' as modern urban subject. This process involves both the making (by metaphorically hammering and twisting) and imitation, (with its associations of fraud and duplicity) which are implied in the meanings of the verb 'to forge'. It is also a process that involves self-division and self-alienation, as is demonstrated in Pip's tortuous and tortured apprehension of his personal history as the history of a 'self-swindler' (2: 9, 223), and in his nightmare visions of his multiple objectified and alienated selves (in the illness following Magwitch's death), when he 'confounded impossible existences with my own identity', imagining that he was 'a brick in the house-wall ... entreating to be released from the giddy place where the builders had set me', or that he was 'a steel beam of a vast engine ... implor[ing] in my own person to have the engine stopped' (3: 18, 457). Pip's self-division and self-alienation is also represented in a series of doubles: Trabbs's boy, who reminds him of his origins; his dark double, Orlick (Uriah Heep to Pip's David Copperfield), who acts as his tormentor, but also acts out his suppressed fantasies of revenge against his sister, who, having brought up Pip 'by hand', is subsequently felled by the deadly hand of Orlick; Bentley Drummle who acts out his repressed feelings of violence towards Estella, and even Estella on to whom is projected

Pip's feminized self-identification with 'the victimized, battered, self-emasculated male'.[11]

Pip's self-division and self-alienation is also mirrored and explored in numerous other characters – for example, in the representation of the obsessive compulsive behaviour of Jaggers, whose repeated handwashing signals his desire to cleanse the taint of, and thus dissociate himself from, his criminal clients. Modern self-division is, perhaps, most striking in the comic-grotesque representation of Wemmick, who is shown as having self-consciously formalized the opposition of domestic and commercial values which had become endemic in Victorian society by 1861, by adopting entirely different personae and value systems for home and office, and by constructing his Walworth castle – a Heath Robinson parody of the Englishman's home – as the ultimate self-created private space: it is a domestic fortress, buttressed against the incursions of the public world. Wemmick is a lower-class and more benign anticipation of Jekyll and Hyde: he changes from upright citizen and expansively affectionate son not as a result of drinking a mysterious potion of his own making, but (as it were) from breathing the air of commodification and corruption as he nears Jaggers's office in Little Britain. However, as we are constantly reminded – through the interconnectedness of the stories of Magwitch and Pip, and through Dickens's representation of Jaggers's criminal clients – there is no escape from the fact that Walworth sentiments and Walworth comfort are financed indirectly (and in some cases directly) by underhand or criminal activity. Like Wilkie Collins's sensation novels of the 1860s (alongside one of which – *The Woman in White* – this novel was reviewed), *Great Expectations* exposes the darker side of Victorian society, raising questions about the origins of the wealth on which Victorian domesticity and Victorian civilization is based.

Class, commodification and criminality – and the interconnections between them – are at the centre of *Great Expectations*. Wemmick and the petty criminals of Little Britain put their faith (in their various ways) in 'portable property' (2: 5, 199). In the greater Britain beyond its confines the trade is in people as well as goods: Australian landowners and Jaggers alike acquire convicted criminals to labour for them; Magwitch invests in Pip as his brought-up (and bought-up) London gentleman, and Miss Havisham speculates in (and with) the future of Estella her b(r)ought-up lady. The roles of 'lady' and 'gentleman' are thus exposed as forms of both manufacture and masquerade, and in these two cases they are attached specifically to perverted social aspirations, class hatred, 'gender trouble', and colonialism. To take the case of the 'bought-up London gentleman' first. In the extraordinary scene of recognition and reversal in Chapter 20 of Book 2, Pip's prosperity, culture, and civility (however superficial we might feel them to be) are revealed as having been paid for by money acquired by hard labour in one of Britain's colonies by a convicted and transported criminal. The dramatic focus of the scene is on Pip's horror and disgust at the animal-like physical presence of the man who claims to be his second father, and on his shocked recognition that the story he has been telling about his 'expectations' is false. However, Magwitch's revelations have far wider implications. They link Pip's prosperity to his own criminality (the stealing of the file and the pork pie), to the ressentiment of a former criminal who can repay his debt to British society but who can never (legally) return to it, and who can acquire the wealth of a 'gentleman' by work (a crucial component of the self-improvement ideology) but who is unable to acquire the social or cultural status of a gentleman. Magwitch's revelations also link Pip's prosperity and culture, like the prosperity and culture of Britain itself, to a colonial origin. This link to the colonies has been foregrounded in recent post-colonial readings of the novel, which locate *Great Expectations* in the history of 'the development of Britain's cultural identity, as that identity imagines itself in a geographically conceived world'.[12] In this case, Edward Said has argued, the penal colony of Australia, the space of Britain's social residue, is opposed to the Orient, in this case Egypt, where Pip forges his new life, the space of 'normality' and enterprise.

Magwitch's purchase and (proxy) moulding of Pip is portrayed as being motivated by feelings of resentment and revenge against those metropolitan gentlemen who have consigned him to the colonies and against the British colonists who keep him in a subaltern position:

> The blood horses of them colonists might fling up the dust over me as I was walking; what do I say? I says to myself, 'I'm making a better gentleman nor ever *you*'ll be!' When one of 'em says to another, 'He was a convict a few year ago, and is a ignorant common fellow now, for all he's lucky,' what do I say? I says to myself, 'If I ain't a gentleman, nor yet ain't got no learning, I'm the owner of such ...' (2: 20, 317)

Miss Havisham's purchase and moulding of Estella is similarly represented as being produced by feelings of resentment and revenge against gentlemen in general – as a consequence of having been jilted by Compeyson, who, in Magwitch's words, 'set up fur a gentleman ... and had been to a public boarding-school and had learning' (3: 3, 343). There is, then, a symmetry between the stories of Estella and Pip, but what kinds of story does the novel and its narrator tell of Estella, and what is the relationship between her story and Pip's? Some recent feminist-influenced readings of *Great Expectations* have drawn our attention to the difference of view that results from attempts to retrieve Estella's story from Pip's narrative. Estella is an elusive character, apparently lacking autonomy. She certainly lacks an independent voice in the novel. Because *Great Expectations* is a first-person narrative, Estella is always spoken of and spoken for by Pip. Estella is thus doubly the product of masculine discourse; that of the author and that of the narrator. Carolyn Brown reads the discursive construction of Estella as a reflection of what she describes as '"normal" masculine narcissism'; in other words Estella represents the femininity that is contained or excluded in the construction of modern masculinity.[13] However, Estella is constructing as well as constructed. Pip's narrative (and perhaps Dickens's) also assigns to Estella an important role on the production of Pip's classed as well as his gendered identity; it is, of course, Estella's remarks on his coarse hands and boots, and his propensity to call knaves Jacks which first make Pip conscious of his lack of gentlemanly refinement. In pursuing this haughty and elusive object of desire Pip combines both romantic desire and class anxiety, with the promise of happiness and economic success – all (as Hilary Schor points out) 'conveniently presented in the one figure ... of the heroine of romance, who will become the contested site of "value" in the novel'.[14] In one of the boldest re-readings of *Great Expectations*, as 'Estella's novel – with its bitter realism and its own change of heart', Schor suggests that Pip's story, like Dickensian art more generally, 'writes itself through (the fear of) the woman's story'.[15] Estella thus becomes the most important of a series of 'shadowy women' (Pip's dead mother, Mrs Joe, Miss Havisham), who haunt Pip's narrative (and the novel), but whom Pip can neither see nor hear clearly. Throughout the novel Pip constantly misinterprets what Estella says. Even in the final chapter, when Estella takes her farewell of Pip by affirming her hope that they 'will continue friends apart',

Pip reports his response thus: 'I saw no shadow of another parting from her' (3: 20, 479). Whose words should the reader privilege here, and how is he or she to construe them? If we listen to Estella, as Hilary Schor invites us to do, we may read back from those words the story of *her* progress; 'I have been bent and broken, but – I hope – into better shape' (3: 20, 478). When it is retrieved from Pip's story of his own victimization and suffering, Estella's story is also one of victimization and suffering. It is a story of male (physical) violence against women, and of the psychological and social violence done to women by the shapes into which they have to be bent in order to produce and underwrite the modern masculine subject.

To read for the plot of Estella and her expectations is to resist the dominant story of *Great Expectations* – the story of the confessional male subject, Pip. As in *David Copperfield*, so, too, in *Great Expectations*, Dickens's handling of the autobiographical form raises questions about authorship and authority: Pip is the author (writer) of the narrative, but not the sole author (creator) of the *story* or *plot* that he narrates. The Pip who narrates is the product of other people's dreams and fantasies and a character in other people's stories. The story that he tells is, in part, the story of how he learns that this is the case. It is the story of how he is brought to the recognition that – in ways that he does not fully comprehend – his great expectations are not his own, and that he is the vehicle or instrument of the desires and expectations of others. As in *David Copperfield*, so, too, in this later novel, the confessional form of autobiography is represented as a form of self-policing. Pip's history is a history of both specific and generalized guilt and oppression. It is a form of self-repression as much as (or, perhaps, even more than) it is a form of self-expression.

This is, of course, to stray back into the 'disciplinary' readings to which I referred in my discussions of *David Copperfield* and *Bleak House*. However, one does not have to have recourse to Foucauldian theory to read *Great Expectations* as a novel about discipline and punishment, about imprisonment and surveillance. All of these things are foregrounded in Pip's narrative of how he was bought up by hand, experienced generalized feelings of guilt for the crime of being alive, as well as specific feelings of guilt for the 'crimes' he does commit (from stealing pork pies under duress to betraying Joe and the life of the forge). Crime and criminality are at the centre of *Great Expectations* as they are of so many of

Dickens's novels. Here, in this late novel, Dickens is concerned with a pervasive criminality, and with the social, psychological, and even physiological determinants of crime – the novel's descriptions of Estella's murderous mother, for example, anticipate Cesare Lombroso's photographs of criminal types. Moreover, like *Little Dorrit*, *Great Expectations* is full of both places and states of imprisonment, from the prison ships off the Kentish coast, the penal colony of Australia, and Newgate itself, through the domestic prison of Satis House, to imprisoning social and gender roles. *Great Expectations* has often been read as the story of Pip's journey away from the shades of the prison-house through moral growth, or through a process of redemption and rebirth, marked by his changing attitude to Magwitch and his purging illness. (Interestingly, Pip's most altruistic acts almost always involve him in 'criminal' behaviour, as when he seeks to help Magwitch escape.) But this novel can also be read as a story of repetition and (re)containment, rather than as one of liberation; it can be read as the story of Pip's journey from one state of imprisonment to another; for example, from the imprisonment of his childhood under his sister's rule at the forge to the 'prison' of bourgeois masculinity, and the role of imperial subject. Certainly, it has become increasingly difficult to see Pip's story as one which has a happy ending. Whichever of Dickens's endings one privileges, it would seem that the consolations of heterosexual romance and the conventional fictional closure of marriage, parenthood and prosperity are (at least for Pip) only possible in the 'pre-modern' world of the forge.

IV   The ways we live now: *Our Mutual Friend*

If *Great Expectations* had looked back to the past of Dickens's childhood, *Our Mutual Friend* (published in monthly parts between May 1864 and November 1865) returned to 'the way we live now' (to borrow, once more, the title of Trollope's novel of 1874–5). Like *Bleak House*, Dickens's last completed novel is an anatomy of 'these times of ours' (*OMF*, 1: 1, 13). What are the characteristics of these times, as they are represented in *Our Mutual Friend*? The novel's opening chapter, which introduces the 'half savage' Gaffer Hexam pursuing his own form of fishing in the 'slime and ooze' of the Thames at Southwark, suggests that they are dark, dirty and disreputable times. As the scene moves westward across London, the times appear to be bright, glittering and disreputable times. They are times which are characterized by rapid (and for the bemused Twemlow, confusing) social change and mobility, as personified in the Veneerings – 'bran-new people in a bran-new house in a bran-new quarter of London' (1: 2, 17). These times of ours are also times of social aspiration and self-improvement, as represented in a benign comic-parodic form in the changing fortunes of Noddy Boffin and his wife, and more complexly and darkly in the rise and fall of Charley Hexam and (especially) Bradley Headstone, who seek to raise themselves through education, but who apparently only succeed in forcing out both *joie de vivre* and moral sense as they cram their minds with rote learning. Viewed from another angle, 'these times of ours' are times of stasis and stolidity, as personified in that self-satisfied son of Empire, Mr Podsnap, and in the graceless and unimaginative physical and mental furniture of Podsnappery (1: 11, 131ff.). As many of the novel's sub-plots suggest, 'these times of ours' are self-interested times, in which a 'friendly move' is often decidedly unfriendly in its aim to rob, deceive or defraud. In short they are times in which the concept of 'mutuality' upon which civil society depends has become troublingly destabilized.

In all its aspects, this anatomy of modern times is articulated in terms of figures of decline, descent and transformation. The first – decline – is derived in part from Gibbon, whose 'Decline and Fall of the Rooshan Empire' (or, as Gibbon had it, the Roman Empire) is mangled for Boffin's delectation by Silas Wegg, the 'literary man with the wooden leg' (1: 5, 58) and one of the novel's many sharp and calculating economists. It also derives, as does the second figure – descent – from Darwin, whose *Origin of Species* (1859), and the debate it generated in the early 1860s, underlies so much of the novel's concern with evolution, adaptation and degeneration. *Our Mutual Friend* is a novel peopled by 'birds of prey' (1: 13, 161), inhabitants of the 'Dismal Swamp' (1: 17, 208), and insect-like creatures who swarm and multiply on the dust heaps of London. It is a novel which dramatizes the contemporary fear that in the struggle for survival in a world whose philosophy might be summed up (adapting Boffin's words) as 'scrunch or be scrunched' (3: 5, 459), the fittest (in the sense of the most adaptive to the prevailing environment) may not necessarily be the best in the human and moral sense. The final figure – that of transformation – comes mainly from the Bible and fairy stories.

Our Mutual Friend is also a novel about economics and about economies – social, psychological, sexual and moral. The book begins with two lessons in economics from Gaffer Hexam, who instructs Rogue Riderhood on the use-value of money and the philosophical impossibility of robbing a dead man: 'Has a dead man any use for money? Is it possible for a dead man to have money? What world does a dead man belong to? 'Tother world. What world does money belong to? This world. How can money be a corpse's?' (1: 1, 16). Gaffer also offers his daughter Lizzie a lesson about circulation and conversion. This is an urban form of subsistence economics in which death and waste are converted into life, and the detritus of the river (the surplus value of the city of London) is Lizzie's 'living', her 'meat and drink' (1: 1, 15). Recycling, and the conversion of waste into money and, ultimately, 'living' are at the heart of this novel – from Gaffer's gloomy trade, to Venus's recycling of human body parts and other paraphernalia, to the dust mounds from which old John Harmon made the money with which he sought to endow Bella Wilfer (on the grounds that he admired her mercenary nature), and which is put to various good ('living') uses by Mr and Mrs Boffin and John Harmon the younger. If the conversion process involved in some of these forms of recycling has something of the aspect of a mysterious or magical transformation (as in the last example), *Our Mutual Friend* constantly reminds us that this kind of wealth creation has a material base, unlike the entirely speculative modern economy of Shares, which is the circulation of an abstraction. Shares, which are part of the 'bran-new world' of the Veneerings and Lammles, are the subject of an intensely hortatory economics lesson from the narrator. It is a satirical lecture on the way we live now:

> As is well known to the wise in their generation, traffic in Shares is the one thing to have to do with in this world. Have no antecedents, no established character, no cultivation, no ideas, no manners; have Shares. Have Shares enough to be on Boards of Direction in capital letters, oscillate on mysterious business between London and Paris, and be great. Where does he come from? Shares. Where is he going to? Shares. What are his tastes? Shares. Has he any principles? Shares. What squeezes him into Parliament? Shares. ... O mighty Shares! To set those blaring images so high, *and to* cause us smaller vermin, as under the influence of henbane or opium, to cry out night and day, 'Relieve us of our money, scatter it

for us, buy us and sell us, ruin us, only we beseech ye take rank among the powers of the Earth and fatten on us!' (1: 10, 118)

This passage would seem to be a fairly direct commentary on the speculation mania of the 1850s and 1860s, which was the subject of numerous books, pamphlets, articles in periodicals (including Dickens's *All the Year Round*) and novels (including *Little Dorrit* and *A Tale of Two Cities*). As I noted in the previous section, Dickens's fiction in the 1860s also explored the ways in which human beings became objects of speculation, for example in the speculation in human futures made by Miss Havisham and Magwitch. Such speculation is rife in *Our Mutual Friend*: Old John Harmon speculates in the future of Bella Wilfer, and there is also a futures market for spouses, in which Alfred and Sophronia Lammle make a very bad speculation. When the Boffins seek an orphan to take the place of John Harmon, we are informed that there is a market for this particular commodity, and that 'the suddenness of an orphan's rise in the market was not to be paralleled by the maddest records of the Stock Exchange' (1: 16, 195).

This multi-plotted novel teaches its own – often contradictory – lessons in economics. It attacks cupidity and greed, and (like the other novels discussed in this chapter) demonstrates the psychological and social alienation of a system in which, as Thomas Carlyle put it, the cash nexus had become the sole relation between man and man. At the same time, however, it seeks to provide a human face for capitalism. At the centre of *Our Mutual Friend*, as Mary Poovey has pointed out,[16] is a narrative about the conversion of material wealth into metaphoric wealth and human value, which is a moralized version of the economics lesson that Gaffer Hexam gives to Lizzie in the opening chapter. In this narrative the Boffins and the young John Harmon are shown as practising a kind of moral alchemy by transforming or converting the meanings and uses of the money that has been produced by Old Harmon's dust heaps, and ultimately by making the dust heaps disappear altogether. As a result of this virtuous alchemy, human ordure (one of the contents of the dust heaps) is transformed into a newly humanized order: Harmony Jail is transformed into Boffin's Bower, and ultimately into John and Bella Harmon's West End dream-home, via a short period in 'the charm – ingest of doll's houses' (4: 5, 663) in Blackheath. This narrative also involves the replacement of one form of speculation or gambling in the human futures market for another. Whereas Old John Harmon had invested his capital in a speculation on the marriage of his son to the mercenary Bella Wilfer, Noddy Boffin takes a gamble on his instinct that Bella can be redeemed from her mercenary preoccupations and, together with John Rokesmith (Harmon), he invests his time and labour in a masquerade of miserliness that is designed to show her the error of her ways.

The story of Bella's conversion from false, mercenary values via a plot which is used to convert monetary wealth into human value is one of the central conversion narratives of the novel. It is also a bourgeois romance in which wealth is moralized and recuperated. Thus, towards the end of the novel, Mrs Boffin gazes on the image of madonna (Bella) and child (the inexhaustible infant) seated in the nursery of their new home on the day of the great revelations, and observes: 'It looks as if the old man's spirit has found rest at last. … And as if his money had turned bright again, after long rust in the dark, and was at last beginning to sparkle in the sunlight' (4: 13, 757). The role of the newly domesticated woman in this process of recuperation of wealth is extremely interesting. Bella has first to accept her role as the contented wife of someone 'in a China House' (4: 5, 665), and to train herself in the values of domesticity and motherhood in her doll's house, before she can occupy her role as the wife of a man of independent means in a fine West End mansion: in other words, the plot permits her to have the object of her original desire at such a time as she no longer desires it. This conversion narrative (as Mary Poovey has noted) tells a fascinating story about male power in the domestic sphere, where 'men are able to exercise precisely the kind of control that is not available in the unpredictable world of financial speculation'. The Harmon/Boffin plot reveals that in the domestic sphere

> the return on a man's investment of intelligence and love satisfies all of his desires. Through his calculated deceit, Harmon turns Bella into the wife he wants, so that when he realizes her wishes at the end of the novel, he actually realizes his own.[17]

If the transformation of Bella into a model of middle-class domestic femininity is central to her own conversion narrative and to John Harmon's conversion of his father's plot to his own ends, then the domesticity of another woman, Lizzie Hexam, is central to the conversion of Eugene Wrayburn in another narrative that frustrates the wishes of the father. Lizzie is in many ways Bella's opposite: she is domestic, hard-working and self-sacrificing from the outset. However, like Bella, she is at the centre of a complex narrative about class and gender. In her role as what Lady Tippins describes as a 'female waterman' (4: 17, 793), Lizzie is a masculin-ized woman, physically strong and more skilled in boating than most of the male characters. She is also a working-class 'lady', who inspirits her father's mean riverside dwelling with the values and virtues of the middle-class home. If, at the beginning of the novel, Bella is one stereotypical candidate for the role of fallen women, through her desire for wealth and luxury, then Lizzie is the other, through her economic vulnerability and her lack of adequate famil-ial protection. This opposition was integral to the mid-nineteenth century discourse on prostitution with which Dickens would have been very familiar, not least through his work with Angela Burdett Coutts in rescuing 'unfortunates'. Lizzie is (as it were) inoculated against falling partly as a consequence of her apparently innate, middle-class femininity. She is also saved from the role of fallen woman by her capacity for hard work, as demonstrated in her arduous toil at her river trade, her subsequent role in assisting Jenny Wren in the making of doll's dresses, and, finally, when she moves out of London to work at the Paper Mill.

This working-class version of the Angel in the House is also the focus of male needs and demands. As Eve Kosofsky Sedgwick has argued, Lizzie is placed in a series of 'Girardian triangles' which enact the way in which relations between men and within patri-archy are conducted through women but never end in them. These triangles, which as Sedgwick points out reach 'from the lowest class to the professional class',[18] become a way of mapping both class and gender, and the ways in which each is defined in terms of the other. In the first of these triangular relationships Lizzie pro-tects her father from the abyss, and her brother Charley from their father's resentment at his desire for self-improvement, until such time as Charley is able to make his escape from the river. The second triangle is formed by Lizzie, Charley and his schoolmaster Bradley Headstone. At first Headstone seeks to exclude Lizzie for fear that the illiterate boatwoman will drag her brother down, and frustrate his designs for Charley, but he subsequently develops a passionate attachment to her, and becomes part of a third triangle with Eugene Wrayburn, who is also in love with Lizzie.

The intricate interconnections between class and gender in this last triangle are particularly complex. Both Eugene's and Bradley's feelings for Lizzie are mediated through their sense of her social inferiority, and each man regards the other with feelings of class disdain (Eugene) or resentment (Bradley). The dilettante Eugene occupies a liminal social and gender position. As a barrister without a vocation (or, indeed, employment of any kind), who is living on his expectations of inherited wealth with his schoolfriend Mortimer Lightwood, Eugene is both improperly masculinized and inadequately socialized at the beginning of the novel. Despite (or perhaps because of) this, Eugene is a focus for Bradley's class resentment. His feline ease and grace, together with his air of disdainful superiority, are a constant provocation to the schoolteacher's sense of self-worth and his dogged pursuit of self-betterment and respectability. Wrayburn and Headstone are alike in that they both seek to distance themselves from their upbringing and their socially ordained lot in life. But whereas the upper-class Wrayburn is alternately bored and amused by his antecedents, Headstone is 'proud, moody and sullen' about his pauper origins and desires that they should be forgotten.

Headstone is one of Dickens's most powerful studies in repression. As the following passage indicates, this character is a dramatic exploration of the discontents of civilization, as well as part of the novel's continuation of the savage critique of the instrumental education offered to the poor seen earlier in *Hard Times,* and in the schooling of the Toodles's son Rob the Grinder in *Dombey and Son*:

> Bradley Headstone in his decent black waistcoat, and decent white shirt ... looked a thoroughly decent young man of six-and-twenty. He was never seen in any other dress, and yet there was a certain stiffness in his manner of wearing this ... recalling some mechanics in their holiday clothes. He had acquired mechanically a great store of teacher's knowledge. He could ... sing at sight mechanically ... even play the great church organ mechanically. From his early childhood up, his mind had been a place of mechanical stowage. The arrangement of his wholesale warehouse, so that it might always be ready to meet the demands of retail dealers – history here, geography there ... had imparted to his countenance a look of care; while the habit of questioning and being questioned had given him a suspicious manner, or a manner that would be better described as one of lying in wait ...
>
> Suppression of so much to make room for so much, had given him a constrained manner. ... Yet there was enough of what was

animal, and of what was fiery (though smouldering), still visible in him ...   (2: 1, 218)

'Self-government', the restraint of 'what was animal, and ... fiery', is the key to Bradley's rise in the social scale, as it is to the Smilesian self-help narrative in general. The costs of such self-government are suggested in the tormented scene in which Bradley confesses his love for Lizzie and at the same time reveals his fixation with Wrayburn:

> 'You are the ruin – the ruin – the ruin – of me. I have no resources in myself. I have no confidence in myself. I have no government of myself when you are near me or in my thoughts ... .
> 'You draw me to you. If I were shut up in a strong prison you would draw me out ...
> ... 'With Mr Eugene Wrayburn in my mind, I went on. With Mr Eugene Wrayburn in my mind, I spoke to you just now ... .
> ... 'I had to wrestle with my self-respect when I submitted to be drawn to you in spite of Mr Eugene Wrayburn.'   (2: 15, 388)

Similarly, when Lizzie flees London, Wrayburn replaces his stalking of her with a cat-and-mouse game in which he lures Headstone into stalking him around the streets of the metropolis, in a passionate pursuit which Eve Sedgwick has read as homoerotic. Headstone is Wrayburn's dark double, and the violence that the schoolteacher plots and ultimately enacts against the lawyer equates to the violence that Wrayburn would perpetrate against Lizzie in seducing and abandoning her; this is the old story that he plots for her.

In the old story that Dickens's novel plots, the upper-class male is governed and redeemed by suffering and the patient love of a good woman, while the failure of the lower-class man to govern himself ends in self-destruction. Like Pip in *Great Expectations*, Eugene emerges from a period of unconsciousness and semiconscious hallucinations into a new life. The Wrayburn–Lizzie–Headstone narrative is, in part, the story of a rite of passage, by means of which Wrayburn emerges from the liminal state of post-adolescence and becomes a fully socialized middle-class male. This rite of passage story, like that of John Harmon, involves the testing and/or making of a domestic woman. Both stories also involve a move into a different narrative register – that of the romance or fairy tale in which the Cinderella figure (Lizzie) or the petulant princess (Bella) is united with her prince.

Like most of Dickens's novels, *Our Mutual Friend* makes frequent allusions to the characters and patterns of romance and fairy tales: Cinderella, Little Red Riding-Hood, Sleeping Beauty, Beauty and the Beast, all stories of endangered women, rescued by love and the intervention of good spirits. Jenny Wren – the crippled doll's dressmaker – and Riah – the good Jew – are two such good spirits, and both perform a guardian angel and fairy-godmother role. These two fantastical characters also figure in the novel's biblical allusions and in its use of Christian symbolism. Riah may have an Old Testament appearance, but he is associated with the New Testament values of resurrection and redemption suggested by Jenny Wren's curious fancy to go up on his roof, high over the streets of London and 'be dead'. This state is described by Jenny as one of complete tranquillity and peace, in which '"you hear the people who are still alive, crying, and working, and calling to one another down in the close dark streets, and you seem to pity them so! And such a chain has fallen from you, and such a strange good sorrowful happiness comes upon you!"' (2: 5, 279). This momentary dying into life is repeated in the Christian imagery that characterizes the depiction of the death of Betty Higden, the latest vehicle for Dickens's career-long attack on the Poor Law (as he emphasizes in his Postscript to the novel). This Christian imagery also recurs in the watery 'death' (or baptism) and 'resurrection' of Eugene Wrayburn. If 'being dead' is a state of forgetfulness or transcendence of the painful world of work and the 'close dark streets', it is also found in the enchanted domestic space to which Bella and Harmon finally repair to resume their regenerated lives. This apparently incongruous connection is one of the many incongruities that serve to remind us that this is a novel that plays with stories, recycling and renewing them, exposing them for the consolatory fictions that they are, but also redeploying their sustaining (or possibly self-deluding) power.

V The sense of unending: *The Mystery of Edwin Drood*[19]

Like many of Dickens's novels, *Our Mutual Friend* is, among many other things, a detective story: it has a violent death, a missing person, and Mr Inspector (among others) trying to solve the novel's many mysteries. For many readers *The Mystery of Edwin Drood* is *simply* a detective story. As G. K. Chesterton put it in his introduction to the 1915 Everyman edition of the novel: 'It is as a detective story first and last that we have to consider *The Mystery of Edwin Drood*... . Here alone among the Dickens novels it is necessary to speak of the plot and the plot alone.'[20] Of course, *Edwin Drood* is doubly a detective story, doubly a mystery, because of the peculiar circumstances of its 'ending'. It was cut short by Dickens's death on Thursday 9 June 1870 when only three of the projected twelve monthly parts had appeared and just six numbers had been written – the last 'underwritten by two pages' (*Life,* II: 365). This abrupt curtailment of the novel has made successive generations of readers into detectives, compelled to speculate on Dickens's intentions for the denouement of his plot, scrutinizing the text for clues as to how this story of the disappearance of Edwin Drood was to develop. Was Edwin murdered? Was his killer the hot-headed Neville Landless with whom he had quarrelled, or his mysterious uncle, John Jasper, who is obsessed with Rosa Bud, the woman to whom Edwin has been pledged since childhood? Who is the mysterious and implausibly coiffured Dick Datchery, and what is his interest in Jasper?

Edwin Drood has an unusual (perhaps unique) critical history in that most twentieth-century studies of this novel have concentrated on solving its mystery rather than on analysing, interpreting or evaluating it. Among those critics who have concentrated their critical attentions on the fragment, rather than seeking to write beyond Dickens's ending, some of the most interesting have focused on its representation of dualism and self-division, its exploration of social and psychological alienation, and its engagement with issues of class, race, gender and sexuality. Some of the most interesting late-twentieth-century analyses read the novel as a peculiarly modern form of Gothic: a form of urban Gothic in which John Jasper signifies 'the shadow side of a society in paralysis',[21] or of paranoid Gothic which plots the political and psychological contradictions that underlie male homophobia.[22]

What place does *The Mystery of Edwin Drood* occupy in Dickens's work as a whole? Wilkie Collins described it as 'Dickens's last laboured effort, the melancholy work of a worn-out brain' (*CH,* 588). On the other hand, just over fifty years after Collins's judgement appeared in *The Pall Mall Gazette,* Edmund Wilson read the fragment as quintessential Dickens: a study of a tormented and murderous self-division by a novelist who was himself divided between a fascination (and sometimes identification) with the antisocial energies of the criminal and the rebel, and a commitment (however ambivalent) to the religious and domestic pieties of bourgeois life. Many commentators have noted that Dickens experienced more than his usual difficulty in writing *Edwin Drood*, pointing to evidence that he had lost his knack of writing exactly the right number of sheets for a number, and that he was using up his plot (as inferred from his number plans) rather too quickly. Wilson interpreted these difficulties as signifying an aesthetic and psychological inability to complete the novel, a problem resolved by Dickens's death, which left him literally unable to complete it. For Wilson this incompletion was the source of the novel's power. Noting that 'the last chapters were to be written in the condemned cell, to which [the murderous uncle's] wickedness, all elaborately elicited from him as if told of another, had brought him' (*Life*, II: 366), Wilson writes:

> In this last condemned cell of Dickens, one of the halves of the divided John Jasper was to have confronted the other half. But this continuation – 'difficult to work,' as Dickens told Forster – was never, as it turned out, to take place. Dickens in his moral confusion was never to dramatize himself completely, was never in this last phase of his art to succeed in coming quite clear.[23]

In *The Mystery of Edwin Drood*, Wilson argued, Dickens's habitual 'protest against the age has turned into a protest against the self'.[24] More recent readings of the novel, however, have claimed that this unfinished narrative is less a protest against the self than an exploration of the social formation of selfhood or subjectivity. Despite its apparent retreat to the Trollopian pastures of Cloisterham and the period of its author's childhood, Dickens's last novel focuses on mid- and late-nineteenth century concerns of gender instability, sexuality, race and Empire.

Some readers have been puzzled by the novel's setting. Angus Wilson, for example, remarked that 'the oddest aspect' of the fragment is 'the degree to which England has shrunk to a cathedral town and its classes to the upper-middle, professional class'.[25] This class shrinkage is, perhaps, odd if one looks back to the great social panoramas of Dickens's other late novels, but not if one looks forward to the deliberately restricted social world of, say, Robert Louis Stevenson's *The Strange Case of Dr Jekyll and Mr Hyde* (1886). Like Stevenson, writing some sixteen years after the strange case of the termination of *Edwin Drood*, Dickens, in his last novel, was less concerned with exploring the relations between classes (and, as was his wont, insisting on the inter-connections of classes) than with anatomizing a particular class, its constitutive elements, and its anxieties. In *Edwin Drood* (as in *Jekyll and Hyde*) middle-class male professionals represent the nation at large. Like the London of Stevenson's novella, Cloisterham is a world of bachelors: Jasper, Drood, Neville Landless, the Reverend Septimus Crisparkle and Tartar (his former school fag) are all young unmarried men, and, in Staples Inn, the lawyer Grewgious is a 'poor old Angular bachelor' (*ED*, 20, 180).

What kind of men are Dickens's young bachelors? Drood is a self-confessedly 'shallow, surface kind of fellow', who is on the brink of reluctantly embracing his parentally decreed destiny of joining the family firm, carrying 'Pussy' (Rosa Bud) off from school as Mrs Edwin Drood, and going 'engineering in the East' (2: 11), where the 'triumphs' of his engineering skill 'are to change the whole condition of an undeveloped country' (3: 19), and he is to 'wake up Egypt a little' (8: 54). Crisparkle, a 'minor canon' is a model of muscular Christianity and public school athleticism, who lives innocently with his mother and starts the day with cold dips and boxing. This crisp and sparkling model of manly Englishness resolutely stands by the 'dark' Neville Landless when the latter is accused of Drood's murder: 'Good fellow! Manly fellow! ... He was simply and staunchly true to his duty alike in the large case and in the small' (17: 152). John Jasper, on the other hand, lives an outwardly respectable bachelor existence, but in his 'ambition, aspiration, restlessness, dissatisfaction' (2: 11), in his double life and his self-division, he represents the dis-contents of bourgeois civilization:

> ' ... what a quiet life mine is. No whirl and uproar around me, no distracting commerce or calculation, no risk, no change of place, myself devoted to the art I pursue, my business, my pleasure.' ...
> 'I hate it. The cramped monotony of my existence grinds me away by the grain.' (2: 10)

Another of the male professionals, Thomas Sapsea, the Auctioneer, is a widower. Sapsea, 'the purest Jackass in Cloisterham' (4: 24), is this novel's Podsnap. Self-important and socially aspiring, Sapsea '"dresses at" the Dean' and affects an ecclesiastical intonation. He is profoundly insular and boasts, 'If I have not gone to foreign countries ... foreign countries have come to me ... in the way of business' (4: 26). Subsequently Mayor of Cloisterham, he shares the town's propensity (as glossed by the narrator) to regard 'Natives' as

> nomadic persons, encamping now in Asia, now in Africa, now in the West Indies, and now at the North Pole. ... [A]lways black, always of great virtue, always calling themselves Me, and everybody else Massa or Missie ... and always reading tracts of the obscurest meaning in broken English, but always accurately understanding them in the purest mother tongue. (16: 146)

Sapsea has two major categories for understanding the world – English and Un-English. He classifies Neville Landless's dark complexion as 'Un-English', and when once he has once declared anything to be Un-English, he considers that thing everlastingly sunk in the bottomless pit (15: 135–6).

The relationship between the 'English' and the 'Un-English' is central to the novel's preoccupation with foreignness, exoticism and orientalism. The novel opens in what social commentators of Dickens's day were wont to describe as 'darkest England' – a London opium den, the scene of Jasper's opium dream which transforms the 'ancient English Cathedral tower' of Cloisterham into an hallucinatory Turkish spectacle in which 'Ten thousand scimitars flash in the sunlight, and thrice ten thousand dancing-girls strew flowers' (1: 1). Jasper surfaces from his dream to the sight of foreigners – 'a Chinaman, a Lascar, and a haggard woman' who has 'opium-smoked herself into a strange likeness of the Chinaman' (1: 2). If the Princess Puffer is orientalized and masculinized by her inhaling of foreign substances, John Jasper is feminized by his passivity and orientalized by his opium smoking and by his own dark, brooding appearance. The novel's other examples of exotic foreignness include the Landless twins, who have been brought up in Ceylon. Both brother and sister are represented as dark, and 'untamed', and Helena is described by the narrator as being 'of almost the gypsy type' (6: 42). In many respects the representation of the Landless twins embodies Imperial fears about going native. For example, several of the characters in the novel see Neville as 'tigerish', a quality that he himself attributes to his colonial upbringing:

> I have been brought up among abject and servile dependents, of an inferior race, and I may have easily contracted some affinity with them ... it may be a drop of what is tigerish in their blood. (7: 47)

If this native taint has made Neville an animal, it has masculinized his sister, as is seen in her 'manly' daring and in her habit of cross-dressing on their escape bids from their guardians in Ceylon. Even the behaviour of the novel's models of English masculinity is labelled as Un-English, when Crisparkle and Tartar greet each other with a prolonged handshake and, even more remarkably, engage in a form of greeting that looks suspiciously like an embrace.

Foreignness and orientalism thus complicate and destabilize gender boundaries, and problematize sexuality: for example, in Jasper's 'womanish' (13: 119) devotion to his adoring nephew. Together with Rosa Bud, Jasper and Drood form one of those 'erotic triangles' discussed in the last section. Eve Kosofsky Sedgwick has suggested that this particular erotic triangle is 'a recasting' of the triangle of Headstone, Wrayburn and Lizzie Hexam. In each case 'the first-mentioned of the male rivals murderously attacks the second; probably each himself is killed before the end of the novel; and each of the women perceives instinctively that, far from loving her as *he* imagines he does, the violent rival is really intent on using her as a counter in an intimate struggle of male will that is irrelevant and inimical to her'.[26] In *Edwin Drood* this triangulation of desire is mapped onto a more overt representation of race (rather than class) and a more complex investigation of the relationship between England and Empire than is the case in *Our Mutual Friend*. It is also complicated by the fact that, whereas in *Our Mutual Friend* Headstone is Wrayburn's dark double, in *Edwin Drood* the self-divided John Jasper is his own dark double, his own monstrous other. Jasper is a Jekyll and Hyde figure, whose 'imperious desire to hold [his] head high, and wear a more than commonly grave countenance before the public' commits him 'to a profound duplicity of life'.[27] As I have already indicated, Dickens apparently intended to end his novel with a curiously displaced 'confessional' narrative in which the murderer, as Henry Jekyll was to do a decade and a half later, was to give a 'Full Statement of the Case'. In Forster's account, in his life of Dickens, the 'originality' of the story 'was to consist in the review of his career by the murderer himself at the close, when its temptations were to be dwelt upon as if, not he the culprit, but some other man, were the tempted' (*Life*, II: 366). In other words, it would appear that Dickens's design was to represent as a pathological state that condition of dissociation which Stevenson's Henry

Jekyll was later to articulate in the concluding section of *The Strange Case of Dr Jekyll and Mr Hyde*, when he writes:

> It was on the moral side, and in my own person, that I learned to recognise the thorough and primitive duality of man: I saw that, of the two natures that contended in the field of my consciousness, even if I could rightly be said to be either, it was only because I was radically both: and from an early date ... I had learned to dwell with pleasure, as a beloved daydream, on the thought of separation of these elements. If each, I told myself, could be housed in separate identities, life would be relieved of all that was unbearable.[28]

The separation of the 'polar Twins' of his being that Jekyll produces by an act of conscious design through the ingestion of a chemical compound of his own creation, Jasper produces through the recreational ingestion of opium. The literary effects of these representations of the chemical production of an *alter ego* are remarkably similar. In both cases late nineteenth-century fears about the nature of civilization and modernity are evoked. On the one hand, the brutal acts of Hyde and the presumed violent act of Jasper speak to and for the fear that (Western) civilization is only skin deep and that a primitive savage lurks beneath the skin of the son of Empire. On the other hand, the self-division of those eminently respectable English men of the professions, Jasper and Jekyll, speaks to a widespread *fin de siècle* fear that the price of civilization is the dangerous suppression of energies and desires which are either 'dark' in themselves, or take on dark forms when suppressed.

The Mystery of Edwin Drood anticipates another *fin de siècle* motif in its representation of Jasper's hypnotic power over Rosa Bud. Jasper, like Svengali, the hypnotic mentor of the heroine of George Du Maurier's 1894 novel *Trilby*, and like Count Dracula in Bram Stoker's 1897 novel, colonizes a young woman's mind and holds imperial sway over her, with terrifying consequences for the colonized subject:

> 'He terrifies me. He haunts my thoughts, like a dreadful ghost. I feel that I am never safe from him. I feel as if he could pass in through the wall when he is spoken of.' ...
> 'He has made me a slave with his looks.' (*ED*, 7: 53)

In this case, however, the would-be colonizer is also colonized, and the would-be enslaver is also enslaved. The man who desires to hold imperial sway over Rosa is himself 'colonized' by his desire and by his oriental habit of opium smoking, and the would-be enslaver is himself 'made a slave' to the altered consciousness of the opium dream. Eve Kosofsky Sedgwick has linked the novel's representation of the 'split between opium-consciousness and hypnosis consciousness' in Jasper to its representation of the construction of heterosexuality. The split, she has suggested, seems to correspond, on the one hand, to 'a divorce in Jasper's mind of homosocial from heterosexual desire', and, on the other, to 'a compartmentalization of passivity from an active mobilization of the will'. This double process of splitting and compartmentalizing is the means by which Jasper (and perhaps 'Cloisterham man' more generally) establishes and preserves 'an illusion of psychic equilibrium'.[29] To paraphrase Sedgwick, Jasper needs to feel that his feelings about men and women are essentially different – that the hypnotic power he seeks to exercise over Rosa is love not hatred, and that the dreams about Edwin that he indulges in his opium trance are indeed hatred and not love. Jasper's self-splitting is thus not a mere incidental by-product of the cramped and grinding life of the bourgeois male, but it is the very grounds of his (and perhaps, by extension, modern) subjectivity.

It is the modernity, or even post-modernity, of *The Mystery of Edwin Drood* which has preoccupied many recent commentators on the novel. Its incompleteness, although in one sense entirely accidental, has appealed to the 'postmodernist temper' of the late twentieth century, 'which congratulate[d] itself on having grown out of the infantile craving for the consolations of narrative closure, preferring devices and figures of deferral, suspension, [and] openness'.[30] After Dickens's untimely death, *Drood* became the most writerly of texts, a text of which every reading was also a writing beyond the author's (non-)ending. It would appear that the literal death of this author has enabled generations of readers to anticipate the readerly liberation afforded by Barthes' and Foucault's proclamations of the death of the Author. Numerous continuations or completions of *Drood* have resulted in its taking on the qualities of a fictional hypertext in which the reader can choose different endings, and different routes to particular endings. Of course, the apparently endless desire to end *Drood* may also be read as an indication of the uneven development of post-modernism, in so far as it suggests the persistence of a residual desire for narrative closure, and a belief that one can mine a text for clues to the author's intentions about its ultimate direction. Mining this particular text might lead us to the conclusion that it is pregnant with an uncanny foreknowledge of its own failure to end, as Steven Connor has persuasively argued. In its presentation of the uneasy relationship between the past and present in the cathedral town of Cloisterham (echoing the Uncommercial Traveller's recollection of time past and time present in 'Dullborough Town'), in its tendency to portray characters as interrupting themselves or each other at significant points, in Edwin's 'unfinished picture of a blooming schoolgirl' (Rosa), in the suspension of the engagement between Edwin and Rosa, and in the prematurely broken-off opium dreams of Jasper, *The Mystery of Edwin Drood* does indeed seem to have a pervasive fascination with 'the unfinished, the deferred and the broken'.[31] The Dickens reader will look for – and may find – intimations of resolution, resurrection and regeneration in *Drood*, but in this novel-without-an-ending they will remain no more than hints. In this endless novel there is no *envoi* in which the narrator takes his leave of his characters and readers, reconciling them to the world and its imperfections or moving them to contemplate the necessity for and the possibility of change. Dickens, who played such a major role in developing the form of the nineteenth-century serial novel, forged a career out of making his readers want more. It is fitting that he should have left the readers of his last novel not only wanting but also needing more.

Notes

CHAPTER 1: INTRODUCTION: THE DICKENS PHENOMENON AND THE DICKENS INDUSTRY

1. *Daily News,* 10 June 1870 (the day after Dickens's death), included in *CH,* p. 504.

2. [Charles Eliot Norton] 'Charles Dickens', *North American Review,* 106 (1868), p. 671.

3. Virginia Woolf, *'David Copperfield', The Nation,* 2 August 1925.

4. John Middleton Murry, *Pencillings: Little Essays on Literature* (London: Collins, 1923), pp. 40–1.

5. See John Bowen, *Other Dickens: Pickwick to Chuzzlewit* (Oxford: Oxford University Press, 2000).

6. Alexander Welsh, *From Copyright to Copperfield* (Cambridge, Mass.: Harvard University Press, 1987), p. 7.

7. Edward Fitzgerald, *Letters of Edward Fitzgerald,* ed. J. M. Cohen (London: Centaur Press, 1960), p. 232.

8. F. R. Leavis and Q. D. Leavis, *Dickens the Novelist* (Harmondsworth: Penguin, 1972 [1970]), p. 2.

9. Wilkie Collins, *Rambles beyond Railways* (London: Richard Bentley, 1851), included in *CH,* p. 16.

10. *Daily News,* 10 June 1870, included in *CH,* p. 504.

11. See Steven Connor (ed.), *Charles Dickens* (London: Longman, 1996), p. 30. See also Michael Slater, '1920–1940: "Superior Folk" and Scandalmongers', *The Dickensian,* 66 (1970), 121–42.

12. See Philip Collins, '1940–1960: Enter the Professionals', *The Dickensian ,* 66 (1970), 143–82.

13. *Blackwood's Edinburgh Magazine,* 77 (1855), 451–66, p. 451.

14. Hippolyte Taine, *History of English Literature,* trans. H. V. Laun, 2 vols (London: Chatto and Windus, 1871), vol. II, p. 343.

15. 'Sensation Novels', *Blackwood's Edinburgh Magazine,* 91 (1862), 464–84, p. 574.

16. 'John Ruskin's *Modern Painters,* vol. III', *Westminster Review,* April 1856, reprinted in *George Eliot: Selected Critical Writings,* ed. Rosemary Ashton (Oxford: World's Classics, 1992), p. 248.

17. 'The Natural History of German Life', *Westminster Review,* July 1856, included in Ashton, *George Eliot: Selected Critical Writings,* pp. 264–5.

18. 'The movement of Mr Dickens's fancy in [*Our Mutual Friend*] ... is, to our mind, a movement lifeless, forced, mechanical'; reprinted in *The House of Fiction: Essays on the Novel by Henry James,* ed. Leon Edel (London: Rupert Hart-Davis, 1957), p. 254.

19. See 'The Work of Art in an Age of Mechanical Reproduction', in Walter Benjamin, *Illuminations,* trans. Harry Zohn (London: Jonathan Cape, 1970).

20. Dorothy Van Ghent, *The English Novel: Form and Function* (New York: Rhinehart and Winston, 1953), p. 128.

21. 'Charles Dickens', *National Review,* October 1858, 458–86, at p. 459 (not included in the extract reprinted in *CH*).

22. Leslie Stephen, *Dictionary of National Biography* (London: Smith, Elder, 1883).

23. *London Quarterly Review,* January 1871, quoted by K. J. Fielding in '1870–1900: Forster and Reaction', *The Dickensian,* 66 (1970) 85–100, p. 88.

24. In his *Letters in Criticism,* ed. John Tasker (London: Chatto and Windus, 1974), p. 96.

25. F. R. Leavis, *The Great Tradition* (London: Chatto and Windus, 1948), p. 29.

26. *The English Novel from Dickens to Lawrence* (London: Hogarth Press, 1970), p. 29. Subsequent references are given in the text.

27. Leavis, *The Great Tradition,* pp. 29–30.

28. Edmund Wilson, 'Dickens: the Two Scrooges', *The Wound and the Bow: Seven Studies in Literature* (London: Methuen, 1961 [1941]), p. 45.

29. Ibid., p. 31.

30. See Steven Connor, *Charles Dickens* (Oxford: Blackwell, 1985), pp. 7–55.

31. Barbara Johnson, *The Critical Difference: Essays in the Contemporary Rhetoric of Reading* (Baltimore, Md: Johns Hopkins University Press, 1980), p. 5.

32. J. Hillis Miller, 'Introduction' to *Bleak House,* ed. Norman Page (Harmondsworth: Penguin, 1971), p. 30.

33. Mikhail Bakhtin, 'Discourse in the Novel', in *The Dialogic Imagination*, trans. Carl Emerson and Michael Holquist (Austin: University of Texas Press, 1981), p. 291.

34. Bakhtin *The Dialogic Imagination*, p. 308.

35. Raymond Williams, *Writing in Society* (London: Verso, 1983), p. 203.

36. Terry Eagleton, *Criticism and Ideology: A Study in Marxist Literary Theory* (London: Verso, 1976), p. 103.

37. Jeremy Tambling, 'Prison-Bound: Dickens and Foucault', *Essays in Criticism*, 36 (1986), 11–3; also included in Tambling's *Dickens, Violence and the Modern State: Dreams of the Scaffold* (Basingstoke: Macmillan – now Palgrave, 1995).

38. D. A. Miller, *The Novel and the Police* (Berkeley, Los Angeles and London: University of California Press), pp. 2, ix and viii.

39. Mary Poovey, *Making a Social Body: British Cultural Formation, 1830–1864* (Chicago and London: University of Chicago Press, 1995), pp. 4ff. Subsequent references are given in the text.

40. Eve Kosofsky Sedgwick, *Between Men: English Literature and Male Homosocial Desire* (New York: Columbia University Press, 1985), p. 177.

41 Nancy Armstrong, *Desire and Domestic Fiction* (New York: Oxford University Press, 1987), p. 10. Subsequent references are given in the text.

42. Edward Said, *Culture and Imperialism* (London: Chatto and Windus, 1993), pp. 87–8.

43. Deirdre David, *Rule Britannia: Women, Empire and Victorian Writing* (Ithaca, N.Y.: Cornell University Press, 1995), p. xiii. See also Benedict Anderson, *Imagined Communities* (London: Verso, 1983), and Homi Bhabha (ed.), *Nation and Narration* (London: Routledge, 1990).

44. Bakhtin, *The Dialogic Imagination*, p. 33.

45. Charles Baudelaire, *The Painter of Modern Life and other Essays*, trans. and ed. Jonathan Mayne (London: Phaidon, 1964), p. 9. Baudelaire's essay was written in 1859–60 and published in French in 1863.

CHAPTER 2: THE MAKING OF THE NOVELIST AND THE SHAPING OF THE NOVEL, 1835–41

1. Abraham Hayward, *Quarterly Review*, 59 (1837), included in *CH*, 62.

2. Richard Sennett, *The Fall of Public Man* (Cambridge: Cambridge University Press, 1977), p. 195.

3. Raymond Williams, *The English Novel from Dickens to Lawrence* (London: Hogarth Press, 1970), p. 32.

4. Deborah Epstein Nord, *Walking the Victorian Streets: Women, Representation and the City* (Ithaca, NY: Cornell University Press, 1995).

5. Charles Baudelaire, *The Painter of Modern Life and other Essays*, trans. and ed. Jonathan Mayne (London: Phaidon Press, 1964), p. 9.

6. Walter Benjamin, *Charles Baudelaire: A Lyric Poet in the Era of High Capitalism*, trans. Harry Zohn (London: Verso, 1997), p. 36.

7. See Dana Brand, *The Spectator and the City in Nineteenth-Century American Literature* (Cambridge: Cambridge University Press, 1991).

8. See Richard D. Altick, *The Shows of London* (Cambridge, Mass.: Belknap Press of Harvard University Press, 1978).

9. Quoted in John Butt and Kathleen Tillotson, *Dickens at Work* (London: Methuen, 1957), p. 44.

10. Georg Simmel, 'The Metropolis and Mental Life', in *The Sociology of Georg Simmel*, trans. and ed. by Kurt H. Wolff (New York: The Free Press, 1964), pp. 409–24.

11. Walter Benjamin, *Charles Baudelaire*, p. 38.

12. Reprinted in *Charles Dickens: A Critical Anthology*, ed. Stephen Wall (Harmondsworth: Penguin, 1970), p. 82.

13. G. K. Chesterton, *Charles Dickens* (London: Methuen, 1906), p. 79.

14. John Lucas, *The Melancholy Man: A Study of Dickens's Novels* (Brighton: Harvester Press, 1980 [1970]), pp. 1 and 3.

15. David Musslewhite, *Partings Welded Together: Politics and Desire in the Nineteenth-Century English Novel* (London: Methuen, 1987), p. 182.

16. Grahame Smith, *The Novel and Society: Defoe to George Eliot* (London: Batsford, 1984), p. 179.

17. John Hillis Miller, *Charles Dickens: The World of His Novels* (Cambridge, Mass.: Harvard University Press, 1958), p. 5.

18. John Kucich, *Excess and Restraint in the Novels of Charles Dickens* (Athens, Ga.: University of Georgia Press, 1981), p. 209.

19. Hillis Miller, *Charles Dickens*, p. 58.

20. Musslewhite, *Partings Welded Together*, p. 184.

21. Richard Dellamora, 'Pure Oliver: or Representation without Agency', in John Schad (ed.), *Dickens Refigured: Bodies, Desires and other*

Histories (Manchester: Manchester University Press, 1996), pp. 55–79, p. 77.

22. Nancy Armstrong, *Desire and Domestic Fiction* (New York: Oxford University Press, 1987), pp. 185, and 186.

23. Hillis Miller, *Charles Dickens*, p. 92.

24. Steven Marcus, *Dickens: From Pickwick to Dombey* (London: Chatto and Windus, 1965), pp. 100–10.

25. Tobias Smollet, *Roderick Random* (London: J. Osborn, 1748), ch. 56.

26. See Leonore Davidoff and Catherine Hall, *Family Fortunes: Men and Women of the English Middle-class, 1780–1850* (London: Hutchinson, 1987).

27. Armstrong, *Desire and Domestic Fiction*, p. 48.

28. Elizabeth Barrett Browning on learning that Tennyson was working on *The Princess*. See *The Letters of Robert Browning to Elizabeth Barrett Browning, 1845–6*, ed. Elvan Klintner (Cambridge, Mass.: The Belknap Press of Harvard University Press, 1969), vol. 2, p. 427.

29. National Edition of the Works of Charles Dickens, ed. W. B. Matz (London: Chapman and Hall, 1906–8), vol. XXXIII, pp. 342–4.

30. Marcus, *Dickens: From Pickwick to Dombey*, p. 129.

31. Lucas, *The Melancholy Man*, p. 73.

32. Sue Zemka, 'From the Punchmen to Pugin's Gothics: the Broad Road to a Sentimental Death in *The Old Curiosity Shop*', *Nineteenth-Century Literature*, 48 (1993), 291–309, at pp.291 and 292.

33. 1841 Preface to *Oliver Twist* (*OT*), liii.

34. Deirdre David, *Rule Britannia: Women, Empire, and Victorian Writing* (Ithaca, NY: Cornell University Press, 1995), p. 58.

35. A. C. Swinburne, 'Charles Dickens', *Quarterly Review*, 196 (1902), 20–39, at p. 22; Oscar Wilde, quoted in Hesketh Pearson, *Oscar Wilde* (London: Methuen, 1946), p. 208.

36. See William Wordsworth, 'She Dwelt among the Untrodden Ways', and 'The Old Cumberland Beggar'.

37. See F. S. Schwarzbach, *Dickens and the City* (London: Athlone Press, 1979).

38. David, *Rule Britannia*, pp. 44 and 58.

39. Paul Schlicke (ed.), 'Dickens and his Critics', *OCS*, 623.

40. John Carey, *The Violent Effigy: A Study of Dickens's Imagination* (London: Faber, 1973), p. 64.

41. David, *Rule Britannia*, p. 64.

42. Ibid., p. 60.

43. Lucas, *The Melancholy Man*, p. 92.

44. Marcus, *Dickens: From Pickwick to Dombey*, p. 172.

45. Steven Connor, 'Space, Place and the Body of Riot in *Barnaby Rudge*', in Connor (ed.), *Charles Dickens* (London: Longman, 1996), pp. 211–29.

46. Andrew Sanders, *The Victorian Historical Novel* (Basingstoke: Macmillan, – now Palgrave, 1978), p. 70.

47. William Lovett, *The Life and Struggles of William Lovett* (New York: Garland, 1984 [1876]), p. 209.

48. Thomas Carlyle, 'The Condition of England Question', in *Chartism* (1840), *Thomas Carlyle: Selected Writings*, ed. Alan Shelston (Harmondsworth: Penguin, 1971), p. 151.

49. Carlyle, *Selected Writings*, p. 151.

50. Connor, in *Charles Dickens,* p. 277.

CHAPTER 3: TRAVAILS IN HYPER-REALITY, 1842–8

1. See Robert L. Patten, *Charles Dickens and his Publishers* (Oxford: Oxford University Press, 1978).

2. John Bowen, *Other Dickens: Pickwick to Chuzzlewit* (Oxford: Oxford University Press, 2000), p. 183.

3. Steven Marcus, *Dickens: From Pickwick to Dombey* (London: Chatto and Windus, 1965), p. 213.

4. Margaret Cardwell, Introduction to *MC*, p. x.

5. Alexander Welsh, *From Copyright to Copperfield: the Identity of Dickens* (Cambridge, Mass.: Harvard University Press, 1987), p. 12.

6. Bowen, *Other Dickens*, p. 184.

7. Quoted in John Lucas, *The Melancholy Man: A Study of Dickens's Novels* (Sussex: Harvester Press, 1970), p. 135.

8. Lucas, *The Melancholy Man*, pp. 113, 125 and 116.

9. Cardwell, Introduction to *MC*, p. iii.

10. Thomas Carlyle, *Chartism*, in *Selected Writings*, ed. Alan Shelston (Harmondsworth: Penguin, 1991), p. 193.

11. See Hippolyte Taine, 'Charles Dickens, son talent et ses oeuvres', *Revue des Deux Mondes*, February 1856.

12. Michael Slater, *Dickens and Women* (London: Dent, 1983), p. 224.

13. G. K. Chesterton, *Charles Dickens* (London: Methuen, 1906), p. 101; Bowen, *Other Dickens*, p. 218.

14. Wilkie Collins, *Armadale* [1864–6], ed. Catherine Peters (Oxford: Oxford World's Classics, 1989), p. 506.

15. Walter Benjamin, *Charles Baudelaire: A Lyric Poet in the Era of High Capitalism*, trans. Harry Zohn (London: Verso, 1997), p. 43.

16. Ellen Winter and Granville Hicks (eds), *The Letters of Lincoln Steffens* (New York: Harcourt Brace and Co., 1938), I: 463.

17. T. A. Jackson, *Charles Dickens: The Progress of a Radical* (London: Lawrence and Wishart, 1937), p. 172.

18. See J. Hillis Miller, 'The Genres of *A Christmas Carol*', *The Dickensian*, 89 (1993), 193–206.

19. Kathleen Tillotson, 'A Background for *A Christmas Carol*', *The Dickensian*, 89 (1993), 165–9, at p. 166.

20. Miller, 'The Genres of *A Christmas Carol*', p. 203.

21. Audrey Jaffe, 'Specular Sympathy: Visuality and Ideology in Dickens's *A Christmas Carol*', *PMLA*, 109 (1994), 254–65, at p. 257.

22. Ibid., p. 259.

23. *The Morning Chronicle*, 24 December 1846.

24. Cited by Ruth Glancy in her introduction to the World's Classics Edition of *Christmas Books* (Oxford: Oxford University Press, 1988), pp. xvi, xvii.

CHAPTER 4: MID-VICTORIAN SELF-FASHIONINGS, 1846–50

1. See R. L. Patten, *Dickens and His Publishers* (Oxford: Oxford University Press, 1978).

2. Quoted in Malcolm Elwin, *Thackeray: A Personality* (London: Jonathan Cape, 1932), p. 188.

3. Kathleen Tillotson, *Novels of the Eighteen-Forties* (Oxford: Oxford University Press, 1954), p. 157.

4. Humphrey House, *The Dickens World* (London: Oxford University Press, 1941), p. 136.

5. Gabriel Pearson, 'Towards a Reading of *Dombey and Son*', in J. Gross and G. Pearson (eds), *Dickens in the Twentieth Century* (London: Routledge & Kegan Paul, 1962) p. 57.

6. David Musslewhite, *Partings Welded Together: Politics and Desire in the Nineteenth-Century English Novel* (London: Methuen, 1987), p. 208.

7. John Ruskin, letter to Charles Eliot Norton, 19 June 1970, in *CH*, 443.

8. The planning of *Dombey* coincided with Dickens's collaboration with Angela Burdett-Coutts in her scheme to found a 'Home' or 'Asylum' for 'fallen women'.

9. Andrew Elfenbein, 'Managing the House in *Dombey and Son*: Dickens and the Uses of Analogy', *Studies in Philology*, 92 (1995), 361–82, at p. 361.

10. See Louise Yelin, 'Strategies for Survival: Florence and Edith in *Dombey and Son*', *Victorian Studies*, 22 (1979), 297–319, at p. 297.

11. Deborah Epstein Nord, *Walking the Victorian Streets: Women, Representation, and the City* (Ithaca, NY: Cornell University Press, 1995), pp. 95 and 96.

12. Helen Moglen, 'Theorizing Fiction/Fictionalizing Theory: the Case of *Dombey and Son*', *Victorian Studies*, 35 (1992), 159–84, at p. 159.

13. Ibid., pp. 160 and 169.

14. Robert Clark, 'Riddling the Family Firm: the Sexual Economy of *Dombey and Son*', *English Literary History*, 51 (1984), 69–84, at pp. 69, 73 and 82.

15. Suvendrini Perera, 'Wholesale, Retail and for Exportation: Empire and the Family Business in *Dombey and Son*', *Victorian Studies*, 33 (1990), 603–20, at p. 605.

16. Deirdre David, *Rule Britannia: Women, Empire, and Victorian Writing* (Ithaca, NY: Cornell University Press, 1995), p. 164.

17. Simon Edwards, 'David Copperfield: the Decomposing Self', *The Centennial Review*, 29 (1985), 328–52, at p. 335.

18. Alexander Welsh, *From Copyright to Copperfield: the Identity of Dickens* (Cambridge, Mass., 1987), p. 171.

19. Gwendolyn Needham, 'The Undisciplined Heart of *David Copperfield*', *Nineteenth-Century Fiction*, 9 (1954), 81–107.

20. John Peck (ed.), *David Copperfield and Hard Times: Contemporary Critical Essays* (Basingstoke: Macmillan – now Palgrave, 1995), p. 11.

21. Leaflet advertising The *Christmas Books, DL*, V: 699.

22. Mary Poovey, *Uneven Developments: The Ideological Work of Gender in Mid-Victorian England* (Chicago: Chicago University Press, 1988), p. 101.

23. Margaret Myers, 'The Lost Self: Gender in *David Copperfield*', in *Gender Studies: New Directions in Feminist Criticism*, ed. Judith Spector (Bowling Green, Oh.: Bowling Green State University Press, 1986), p. 128.

24. Hilary Schor, *Dickens and the Daughter of the House* (Cambridge: Cambridge University Press, 1999), p. 12.

25. Myers, 'The Lost Self', p. 122.

26. Poovey, *Uneven Developments*, p. 90.

27. Charles Dickens, 'Preliminary Word' to *Household Words*, 30 March 1850, *DJ*, I: 177.

CHAPTER 5: THE NOVELIST AS JOURNALIST IN HARD TIMES, 1850–57

1. Ann Lohrli, *Household Words Conducted by Charles Dickens: Table of Contents, List of Contributors and Their Contributions* (Toronto: University of Toronto Press, 1973), p. 3. This section is particularly indebted to Lohrli's work.

2. See Audrey Jaffe, *Vanishing Points: Dickens, Narrative and the Subject of Omniscience* (Berkeley, Cal.: University of California Press, 1991), p. 23.

3. Lohrli, *Household Words*, p. 4.

4. Elizabeth Gaskell, *The Letters of Mrs Gaskell*, ed. J. A. V. Chapple and Arthur Pollard (Manchester: Manchester University Press, 1966), letter no. 418.

5. Quoted in Lohrli, *Household Words*, p. 9.

6. John Butt and Kathleen Tillotson, *Dickens at Work* (London: Methuen, 1957) p. 179.

7. Elizabeth Gaskell, Preface to *Mary Barton* (London: Chapman and Hall, 1848).

8. Thomas Carlyle, *Past and Present* (London: Oxford University Press, World's Classics, 1932 [1843]), 3: 3, p. 155.

9. Thomas Carlyle, 'Chartism', in *Thomas Carlyle: Selected Writings*, ed. Alan Shelston (Harmondsworth: Penguin, 1971), p. 151.

10. Carlyle, *Past and Present*, 3: 2, p. 151.

11. Charlotte Brontë, 11 March 1852, quoted in Robert Newsom, '*Villette* and *Bleak House*: Authorizing Women', *Nineteenth-Century Literature*, 46 (1991–2), 54–81, at p. 55.

12. Virginia Blain, 'Double Vision and the Double Standard in *Bleak House*: A Feminist Perspective', *Literature and History*, 11 (1985), 31–46, at p. 31.

13. Raymond Williams, *Politics and Letters: Interviews with 'New Left Review'* (London: New Left Books, 1979), p. 247.

14. See J. Hillis Miller, Introduction to *Bleak House*, ed. Norman Page (Harmondsworth: Penguin, 1971).

15. Walter Benjamin, *Charles Baudelaire: A Lyric Poet in the Era of High Capitalism* (London: Verso, 1997), pp. 38 and 40.

16. Tzvetan Todorov, 'The Typology of Detective Fiction', in *The Poetics of Prose*, trans. Richard Howard (Oxford: Blackwell, 1977), pp. 45–52.

17. D. A. Miller, *The Novel and the Police* (Berkeley and London: University of California Press, 1988), pp. 89 and 84.

18. Allon White, 'Bakhtin, Sociolinguistics, Deconstruction', in his *Carnival, Hysteria and Writing: Collected Essays and an Autobiography* (Oxford: Oxford University Press, 1994), p. 136.

19. Mikhail Bakhtin, 'Discourse in the Novel', in *The Dialogic Imagination: Four Essays,* trans. Carl Emerson and Michael Holquist, ed. Michael Holquist (Austin: University of Texas Press, 1981), p. 300.

20. Pam Morris, *Bleak House* (Buckingham: Open University Press, 1991), p. 56.

21. John Lucas, *The Melancholy Man: a Study of Dickens's Novels* (Sussex: Harvester Press, 1970), p. 254.

22. F. R. Leavis, *Dickens the Novelist* (Harmondsworth: Penguin, 1970), p. 251.

23. Catherine Gallagher, *The Industrial Reformation of English Fiction: Discourse and Narrative Form* (Berkeley, Cal.: University of California Press, 1985), p. 183.

24. See Harry Stone, *Dickens' Working Notes for His Novels* (Chicago: University of Chicago Press, 1987), p. 273.

25. George Gissing, *Charles Dickens: A Critical Study* (London: Blackie and Sons, 1926 [1898]), p. 58.

26. George Bernard Shaw, Foreword to *Great Expectations* (Edinburgh: R. and R. Clark, 1937), p. ix.

27. T. A. Jackson, *Charles Dickens: The Progress of a Radical* (London: Lawrence and Wishart, 1937), p. 169.

28. Edmund Wilson, *The Wound and the Bow* (London: Methuen, 1961 [1941]), pp. 52 and 61.

29. Jackson, *Charles Dickens*, p. 165.

30. Bakhtin, *The Dialogic Imagination*, p. 302 (the emphasis is Bakhtin's).

31. Hilary M. Schor, *Dickens and the Daughter of the House* (Cambridge: Cambridge University Press, 1999), pp. 133–4.

32. Ibid., p. 132.

33. Patricia Ingham, *Invisible Writing: Readings in Language and Ideology* (Manchester: Manchester University Press, 2000), p. 161.

CHAPTER 6: THESE TIMES OF OURS, 1858–70

1. *All the Year Round*, 26 November 1859.

2. See, for example, essays by Chris Vanden Bossche, Catherine Gallagher, Elliot Gilbert and Michael Timko in *Dickens Studies Annual*, 12 (1983); J. M Rignall, 'Dickens and the Catastrophic Continuum of History in *A Tale of Two Cities*', *English Literary History*, 51 (1984), 575–87; Cates Baldridge, 'Alternatives to Bourgeois Individualism in *A Tale of Two Cities*', *Studies in English Literature*, 30 (1990), 633–54. My own discussion of the novel is particularly indebted to these last two essays.

3. See Catherine Gallagher, 'The Duplicity of Doubling in *A Tale of Two Cities*', *Dickens Studies Annual*, 12 (1983), 125–45.

4. Rignall, 'Dickens and the Catastrophic Continuum of History in *A Tale of Two Cities*', pp. 580 and 575.

5. Ibid., p. 575.

6. Baldridge, 'Alternatives to Bourgeois Individualism in *A Tale of Two Cities*', p. 634 (both quotations).

7. G. Robert Stange, 'Expectations Well Lost: Dickens' Fable for his Time', *College English*, 16 (1954), 9–17, at p. 10.

8. Robin Gilmour, *The Idea of the Gentleman in the Victorian Novel* (London: Arnold, 1981), at p. 135.

9. Ibid., p. 123.

10. Robert Garis, *The Dickens Theatre: a Reassessment of the Novels* (Oxford: Clarendon Press, 1965), p. 201.

11. Hilary Schor, *Dickens and the Daughter of the House* (Cambridge: Cambridge University Press, 1999), p. 159.

12. Edward Said, *Culture and Imperialism* (London: Chatto and Windus, 1993), p. 52.

13. Carolyn Brown, '*Great Expectations*: Masculinity and Modernity', *Essays and Studies*, 40 (1987), 60–74, p. 71.

14. Schor, *Dickens and the Daughter of the House*, p. 156.

15. Ibid., p. 154.

16. Mary Poovey, 'Speculation and Virtue in *Our Mutual Friend*', in *Making a Social Body: British Cultural Formation, 1830–1864* (Chicago: University of Chicago Press, 1995), pp. 154–81.

17. Ibid., p. 166.

18. Eve Kosofsky Sedgwick, *Between Men: English Literature and Male Homosocial Desire* (New York: Columbia University Press, 1985), p. 165.

19. My title for this section is borrowed from Steven Connor's 'Dead? Or Alive? *Edwin Drood* and the Work of Mourning', *The Dickensian*, 89 (1993), 85–102, p. 101.

20. G. K. Chesterton (ed.), *Edwin Drood* (London: Dent, 1915), pp. vii–viii.

21. Laurence Frank, *Charles Dickens and the Romantic Self* (Lincoln, Nebr.: University of Nebraska Press, 1984), p. 236.

22. See Sedgwick, *Between Men,* especially chapters 6, 9 and 10.

23. Edmund Wilson, 'Dickens: the Two Scrooges', in *The Wound and the Bow: Seven Studies in Literature* (London: Methuen, 1961 [1941]), p. 104.

24. Ibid., p. 102.

25. Angus Wilson, *The World of Charles Dickens* (London: Secker and Warburg, 1970), p. 291.

26. Sedgwick, *Between Men*, p. 181.

27. Robert Louis Stevenson, 'Henry Jekyll's Full Statement of the Case', 'The Strange Case of Dr Jekyll and Mr Hyde', in *Dr Jekyll and*

Mr. Hyde and Other Stories, ed. Jenni Calder (Harmondsworth: Penguin, 1979), at p. 81.

28. Stevenson, *Jekyll and Hyde*, p. 82.

29. Sedgwick, *Between Men*, all quotations at p. 189.

30. Connor, 'Dead? Or Alive? *Edwin Drood* and the Work of Mourning' (1993), p. 87.

31. Ibid., p. 95.